Cairo printing office

Sudan penal code

Cairo printing office

Sudan penal code

ISBN/EAN: 9783742875402

Manufactured in Europe, USA, Canada, Australia, Japa

Cover: Foto ©Suzi / pixelio.de

Manufactured and distributed by brebook publishing software
(www.brebook.com)

Cairo printing office

Sudan penal code

Cairo printing office

Sudan penal code

THE

SUDAN PENAL CODE

1899.

CAIRO :
NATIONAL PRINTING OFFICE.
1899.

CONTENTS.

ARRANGEMENT OF SECTIONS.

CHAPTER I.

INTRODUCTION.

CHAPTER II.

GENERAL EXPLANATIONS.

5

Sudan Penal Code.

CHAPTER III.

Of Punishments.

CHAPTER IV.

General Exceptions.

6

Sudan Penal Code.

CHAPTER V.

OF JOINT ACTS.

CHAPTER VI.

OF ABETMENT.

7

CHAPTER VII.

OF ATTEMPTS TO COMMIT OFFENCES.

CAAPTER VIII.

OF OFFENCES AGAINST THE STATE.

Sudan Penal Code.

Sudan Penal Code.

CHAPTER XII.

OF CONTEMPTS OF THE LAWFUL AUTHORITY OF PUBLIC SERVANTS.

Sudan Penal Code.

CHAPTER XIII.

OF FALSE EVIDENCE AND OFFENCES AGAINST PUBLIC JUSTICE.

Of False Evidence.

Of the Screening of Offenders, etc.

Of Resistance to Apprehension.

11

Sudan Penal Code.

Of Fraudulent dealings with Property.

CHAPTER XIV.

OF OFFENCES RELATING TO COIN.

CHAPTER XV.

OF OFFENCES RELATING TO REVENUE STAMPS.

12

Sudan Penal Code.

CHAPTER XVI.

OF OFFENCES RELATING TO WEIGHTS AND MEASURES.

CHAPTER XVII.

OF OFFENCES AFFECTING THE PUBLIC HEALTH, SAFETY, CONVENIENCE, DECENCY AND MORALS.

CHAPTER XVIII.

OF OFFENCES RELATING TO RELIGION.

CHAPTER XIX.

OF OFFENCES AFFECTING THE HUMAN BODY.

Of Offences affecting Life.

Of the causing of Miscarriage, of Injuries to unborn Children, of the Exposure of Infants, and of the Concealment of Births.

Of Hurt.

Sudan Penal Code.

15

Sudan Penal Code.

16

Sudan Penal Code.

SECTIONS.

302. Extortion by putting a person in fear of death or grievous hurt.
303. Putting person in fear of death, or of grievous hurt, in order to commit extortion.
304. Extortion by threat of accusation of an offence punishable with death, etc.
305. Putting person in fear of accusation of offence in order to commit extortion.

Of Robbery and Brigandage.

306. Robbery.
    When theft is robbery.
    When extortion is robbery.
307. Brigandage.
308. Punishment for robbery.
309. Attempt to commit robbery.
310 Voluntarily causing hurt in committing robbery.
311. Punishment for bringandage.
312. Brigandage with murder.
313. Robbery or brigandage, with attempt to cause death or grievous hurt.
314. Making preparation to commit brigandage.
315. Punishment for belonging to gang of brigands.
316. Punishment for belonging to gang of thieves.
317. Assembling for purpose of committing brigandage.

Of Criminal Misappropriation of Property.

318. Dishonest misappropriation of property.
319. Dishonest misappropriation of property possessed by deceased person at the time of his death.

Of Criminal Breach of Trust.

320. Criminal breach of trust.
321. Punishment for criminal breach of trust.
322. Criminal breach of trust by carrier, etc.
323. Criminal breach of trust by clerk or servant.
324. Criminal breach of trust by public servant, or by banker, merchant or agent.

Of the Receiving of Stolen Property.

325. Stolen property.
326. Dishonestly receiving stolen property.
327. Dishonestly receiving property stolen in the commission of brigandage.
328. Habitually dealing in stolen property.
329. Assisting in concealment of stolen property.

Of Cheating.

330. Cheating.

B

17

Sudan Penal Code.

Sudan Penal Code.

CHAPTER XXI.

OF OFFENCES RELATING TO DOCUMENTS AND TO PROPERTY OR OTHER MARKS.

Of Property and other Marks.

19

Sudan Penal Code.

CHAPTER XXII.

OF THE CRIMINAL BREACH OF CONTRACTS OF SERVICE.

CHAPTER XXIII.

OF OFFENCES RELATING TO MARRIAGE.

CHAPTER XXIV.

OF DEFAMATION.

CHAPTER XXV.

OF CRIMINAL INTIMIDATION, INSULT AND ANNOYANCE.

THE SUDAN PENAL CODE.

CHAPTER I.

INTRODUCTION.

IT is hereby enacted as follows :—

1. This Ordinance shall be called the Sudan Penal *Title and extent of operation of the Code.* Code, and shall take effect in such parts of the Sudan as the Governor General may, from time to time, by notice in the "Sudan Gazette" order.

2. Every person shall, subject to the exigencies of *Punishment of offences committed within any part of the Sudan where Code is in force.* martial law wherever the same shall for the time being be in force, be liable to punishment under this Code and not otherwise for every act or omission contrary to the provisions thereof, of which he shall be guilty within any part of the Sudan in which this Code is in force.

3. Every act which, if done in a part of the Sudan in *Punishment of offences committed elsewhere.* which this Code is in force, would constitute an offence under this Code, may be punished as if it had been done in a part of the Sudan in which this Code is in force

(i) if such act is done in any part of the Sudan by a public servant or by a person ordinarily resident in a part of the Sudan in which this Code is in force ; or

(ii) if such act is done, whether within the Sudan or elsewhere, by a subject of the Khedive of Egypt domiciled in a part of the Sudan in which this Code is in force.

4. Nothing in this Code is intended to vary, suspend, *Certain laws not to be affected by this Code.* or affect any of the provisions of any law for punishing mutiny, desertion, or other military offences of officers, soldiers, or sailors serving in the Sudan.

23

CHAPTER II.

GENERAL EXPLANATIONS.

Sense of expression once explained. **5.** Every expression which is explained in any part of this Code, is used in every part of this Code in conformity with the explanation, unless the context otherwise requires.

Gender. **6.** The pronoun "he" and its derivatives are used of any person, whether male or female.

Number. **7.** Unless the contrary appears from the context, words importing the singular number include the plural number, and words importing the plural number include the singular number.

"Man." "Woman." **8.** The word "man" denotes a male human being of any age: the word "woman" denotes a female human being of any age.

"Person." **9.** The word "person" includes any Company or Association or body of persons, whether incorporated or not.

"Public." **10.** The word "public" includes any class of the public or any community.

"Magistrate." **11.** The word "Magistrate" denotes not only every person who is officially designated as a Magistrate, but also every person who is empowered by law to give, in any legal proceeding, civil or criminal, a definitive judgment, or a judgment which, if not appealed against, would be definitive, or a judgment which, if confirmed by some other authority, would be definitive, or

who is one of a body of persons, which body of persons is empowered by law to give such a judgment.

"Court of Justice." **12.** The words "Court of Justice" denote a Magistrate who is empowered by law to act judicially alone, or a body of Magistrates which is empowered by law to act judicially as a body, when such Magistrate or body of Magistrates is acting judicially.

"Public servant." **13.** The words "public servant" denote a person falling under any of the descriptions hereinafter following, namely—

First.—Every person exercising executive or administrative functions in the Government of the Sudan or of any part thereof;

24

Second.—Every Commissioned Officer in the Military or Naval Forces of the Khedive of Egypt or of the Sovereign of Great Britain while serving in the Sudan;

Third.—Every Magistrate;

Fourth.—Every officer of a Court of Justice whose duty it is, as such officer, to investigate or report on any matter of law or fact, or to make, authenticate, or keep any document, or to take charge or dispose of any property, or to execute any judicial process, or to administer any oath, or to interpret, or to preserve order, in the Court; and every person specially authorized by a Court of Justice to perform any of such duties;

Fifth.—Every assessor, or other person assisting a Court of Justice or a public servant exercising judicial or quasi-judicial functions;

Sixth.— Every arbitrator or other person to whom any cause or matter has been referred for decision or report by any Court of Justice, or by any other competent public authority:

Seventh.—Every person who holds any office by virtue of which he is empowered to place or keep any person in confinement;

Eighth.—Every officer of Government whose duty it is, as such officer, to prevent offences, to give information of offences, to bring offenders to justice, or to protect the public health, safety, or convenience;

Ninth.—Every officer whose duty it is, as such officer, to take, receive, keep, or expend any property on behalf of Government, or to make any survey, assessment, or contract, on behalf of Government, or to execute any revenue-process, or to investigate or to report on any matter affecting the pecuniary interests of Government, or to make, authenticate, or keep any document relating to the pecuniary interests of Government, or to prevent the infraction of any law for the protection of the pecuniary interests of Government, and every officer in the service or pay of Government or remunerated by fees or commission for the performance of any public duty;

Tenth.—Every officer whose duty it is, as such officer, to take, receive, keep, or expend any property, to make any survey or assessment or to levy any rate or tax for

25

any secular common purpose of any village, town or district, or to make, authenticate, or keep any document for the ascertaining of the rights of the people of any village, town or district.

Explanation 1.—Persons falling under any of the above descriptions are public servants, whether appointed by the Government or not.

Explanation 2.—Wherever the words "public servant" occur, they shall be understood of every person who is in actual possession of the situation of a public servant, whatever legal defect there may be in his right to hold that situation.

"Movable property." **14.** The words "movable property" are intended to include corporeal property of every description, except land and things attached to the earth or permanently fastened to anything which is attached to the earth.

"Wrongful gain." **15.** "Wrongful gain" is gain by unlawful means of property to which the person gaining is not legally entitled.

"Wrongful loss." "Wrongful loss" is the loss by unlawful means of property to which the person losing it is legally entitled.

Gaining wrongfully.
Losing wrongfully. A person is said to gain wrongfully when such person retains wrongfully, as well as when such person acquires wrongfully. A person is said to lose wrongfully when such person is wrongfully kept out of any property, as well as when such person is wrongfully deprived of property.

"Dishonestly." **16.** Whoever does anything with the intention of causing wrongful gain to one person or wrongful loss to another person, is said to do that thing "dishonestly."

"Fraudulently." **17.** A person is said to do a thing fraudulently if he does that thing with intent to defraud but not otherwise.

"Reason to believe." **18.** A person is said to have "reason to believe" a thing if he has sufficient cause to believe that thing but not otherwise.

Property in possession of wife, clerk or servant. **19.** When property is in the possession of a person's wife, clerk, or servant, on account of that person, it is in that person's possession within the meaning of this Code.

Explanation.—A person employed temporarily or on a particular occasion in the capacity of a clerk or servant, is a clerk or servant within the meaning of this section.

20. A person is said to "counterfeit," who causes one *"Counterfeit."* thing to resemble another thing, intending by means of that resemblance to practice deception, or knowing it to be likely that deception will thereby be practised.

Explanation 1.—It is not essential to counterfeiting that the imitation should be exact.

Explanation 2.—When a person causes one thing to resemble another thing, and the resemblance is such that a person might be deceived thereby, it shall be presumed, until the contrary is proved, that the person so causing the one thing to resemble the other thing intended by means of that resemblance to practise deception or knew it to be likely that deception would thereby be practised.

21. The word "document" denotes any matter ex- *"Document."* pressed or described upon any substance by means of letters, figures, or marks, or by more than one of those means, intended to be used, or which may be used, as evidence of that matter.

Explanation 1.—It is immaterial by what means or upon what substance the letters, figures, or marks are formed, or whether the evidence is intended for, or may be used in, a Court of Justice, or not.

Illustrations.

A writing expressing the terms of a contract, which may be used as evidence of the contract, is a document.

A cheque upon a banker is a document.

A power-of-attorney is a document.

A map or plan which is intended to be used or which may be used as evidence, is a document.

A writing containing directions or instructions is a document.

Explanation 2.—Whatever is expressed by means of letters, figures, or marks as explained by mercantile or other usage, shall be deemed to be expressed by such letters, figures or marks within the meaning of this section, although the same may not be actually expressed.

22. The words "valuable security" denote a document *"Valuable security."* which is, or purports to be, a document whereby any legal right is created, extended, transferred, restricted, extinguished, or released, or whereby any person acknowledges that he lies under legal liability, or has not a certain legal right.

23. The words "a will" denote any testamentary *"A will."* document.

27

Words referring to acts include illegal omissions.   **24.** In every part of this Code, except where a contrary intention appears from the context, words which refer to acts done extend also to illegal omissions.

"Act." **"Omission."**   **25.** The word "act" denotes as well a series of acts as a single act: the word "omission" denotes as well a series of omissions as a single omission.

Effect caused partly by act and partly by omission.   **26.** Wherever the causing of a certain effect, or an attempt to cause that effect, by an act or by an omission, is an offence, it is to be understood that the causing of that effect partly by an act and partly by an omission is the same offence.

"Voluntarily."   **27.** A person is said to cause an effect "voluntarily," when he causes it by means whereby he intended to cause it, or by means which, at the time of employing those means, he knew or had reason to believe to be likely to cause it.

Illustration.

A sets fire, by night, to an inhabited house in a large town, for the purpose of facilitating a robbery, and thus causes the death of a person. Here, A may not have intended to cause death, and may even be sorry that death has been caused by his act: yet, if he knew that he was likely to cause death, he has caused death voluntarily.

"Offence."   **28.** Except where otherwise appears from the context, the word "offence" includes an offence under any law for the time being in force.

"Illegal."   **29.** The word "illegal" is applicable to everything which is an offence, or which is prohibited by law, or which furnishes ground for a civil action: and a person **"Legally bound to do."** is said to be "legally bound to do" whatever it is illegal in him to omit.

"Injury."   **30.** The word "injury" denotes any harm whatever illegally caused to any person, in body, mind, reputation, or property.

"Life."   **31.** The word "life" denotes the life of a human being, unless the contrary appears from the context.

"Death.   **32.** The word "death" denotes the death of a human being, unless the contrary appears from the context.

'Animal."   **33.** The word "animal" does not include a human being.

"Vessel."   **34.** The word "vessel" denotes anything made for the conveyance by water of human beings, or of property.

35. Wherever the word "year" or the word "month" "Year." "Month."
is used, it is to be understood that the year or the month
is to be reckoned according to the Gregorian calendar.

36. The word "oath" includes a solemn affirmation "oath."
substituted by law for an oath, and any declaration
required or authorized by law to be made before a public
servant or to be used for. the purpose of proof, whether
in a Court of Justice or not.

37. Nothing is said to be done or believed in good "Good faith."
faith which is done or believed without due care and
attention.

38. Such grave and sudden provocation as, under any "Provocation."
section of this Code, modifies the nature of an offence or
mitigates the penalty which may be inflicted shall not be
deemed to include

(i) provocation sought or voluntarily provoked by the
offender as an excuse for committing an offence ;

(ii) provocation given by anything done in obedience
to the law, or by a public servant in the lawful exercise
of the powers of such public servant ; or

(iii) provocation given by anything done in the lawful
exercise of the right of private defence.

Illustrations.

(a) A is lawfully arrested by Z. a police-officer. A, excited to
sudden and violent passion by the arrest, kills Z. A is not protected
by section 228 (*1*).

(b) A appears as a witness before Z, a Magistrate. Z says that he
does not believe a word of A's deposition. A, provoked thereby,
causes hurt to Z. He is punishable under section 252, and not under
section 250.

(c) A attempts to pull Z's nose. Z, in self-defence, lays hold
of A. A, provoked thereby, attacks Z and causes him grievous hurt.
A is punishable under section 253, and not under section 251.

39. A consent is not such a consent as is intended by Consent known
any section of this Code, if the consent is given by a to be given under
person under fear of injury, or under a misconception of fear or miscon-
fact, and if the person doing the act knows, or has reason ception.
to believe, that the consent was given in consequence of
such fear or misconception ; or

if the consent is given by a person who, from unsound- Consent of insane
ness of mind, or intoxication, is unable to understand the or intoxicated
person.

29

nature and consequence of that to which he gives his consent; or

Consent of child. if the consent is given by a person who is under twelve years of age.

"Harbour." **40.** A person is said to "harbour" another person who has committed or intends to commit an offence or who is seeking to evade apprehension, when he supplies that other with shelter, food, drink, money, clothes, arms, ammunition, or means of conveyance, or assists that other in any way to evade apprehension.

CHAPTER III.

OF PUNISHMENTS.

"Punishments." **41.** The punishments to which offenders are liable under the provisions of this Code are—

First,—Death;

Secondly,—Forfeiture of property;

Thirdly,—Imprisonment;

Fourthly,—Fine;

Fifthly,—Flogging;

Sixthly,—Whipping.

Commutation of sentence of death. **42.** In every case in which sentence of death shall have been passed, the Governor General may, without the consent of the offender, commute the punishment for any other punishment provided by this Code.

Fractions of terms of punishment. **43.** In calculating fractions of terms of punishment, imprisonment for life shall be reckoned as equivalent to imprisonment for twenty years.

Forfeiture of property, in respect of offences punishable with imprisonment. **44.** Whenever any person is sentenced to imprisonment for a term of seven years or upwards, the Court may adjudge that the rents and profits of all his movable and immovable estate during the period of his imprisonment shall be forfeited to Government, subject to such provision for his family and dependants as the Government may think fit to allow during such period.

Amount of fine. **45.** Where no sum is expressed to which a fine may extend, the amount of fine to which the offender is liable is unlimited, but shall not be excessive.

46. Whenever an offender is sentenced to a fine, Sentence of imprisonment for non-payment whether with or without imprisonment, and whether of fine. under this Code or under any other law for the time being in force, it shall be competent to the Court which sentences such offender to direct by the sentence that, in default of payment of the fine, the offender shall suffer imprisonment for a certain term, which imprisonment shall be in excess of any other imprisonment to which he may have been sentenced or to which he may be liable under a commutation of a sentence.

47. The term for which the Court directs the offender Limit to im- to be imprisoned in default of payment of a fine, shall non-payment of not exceed one-fourth of the term of imprisonment which fine, when im- is the maximum fixed for the offence, if the offence be fine awardable. punishable with imprisonment as well as fine.

48. If the offence be punishable with fine only, the Imprisonment for non-payment term for which the Court directs the offender to be impris- offence punish- oned in default of payment of fine, shall not exceed the able with fine following scale, that is to say, for any term not exceeding two months when the amount of the fine shall not exceed P.T. 300, and for any term not exceeding four months when the amount shall not exceed P.T. 600, and for any term not exceeding six months in any other case.

49. The imprisonment which is imposed in default of Imprisonment to terminate on payment of a fine shall terminate whenever the fine or a paymentoffineor of a proportional proportion of the fine exceeding the proportion which part of fine. the unexpired term of imprisonment bears to the whole term is either paid or levied by process of law.

Illustration.

A is sentenced to a fine of P.T. 600 and to four months' imprison- ment in default of payment. If P.T. 300 of the fine be paid or levied before the expiration of two months of the imprisonment, A will be discharged as soon as the two months are completed. If P.T. 300 be paid or levied at the time of the expiration of those two months, or at any later time while A continues in imprisonment, A will be imme- diately discharged.

50. Where a fine or any part thereof remains unpaid, Death not to dis- charge property the death of the offender does not discharge from liability from liability for for payment thereof any property which would, after his payment of fine. death, be legally liable for his debts.

51. Where anything is an offence falling within two Limit of punish- ment of offence or more separate definitions of any law in force for made up of several offences.

the time being by which offences are defined or punished, or

where an offence consists of a series of acts each of which, or any one or more of which, constitutes the same or some other offence,

the offender shall not, unless it be otherwise expressly provided, be punished with a more severe punishment than the Court which tries him could award for any one of such offences.

Illustrations.

(*a*) A gives Z fifty strokes with a stick. Here A can be punished for one beating only, although each blow may by itself constitute an offence.

(*b*) But if, while A is beating Z, Y interferes, and A intentionally strikes Y, here, as the blow given to Y is no part of the act whereby A voluntarily causes hurt to Z, A is liable to one punishment for voluntarily causing hurt to Z, and to another for the blow given to Y.

Punishment of person guilty of one of several offences, the judgment stating that it is doubtful of which. 52. In all cases in which judgment is given that a person is guilty of one of several offences specified in the judgment, but that it is doubtful of which of these offences he is guilty, the offender shall be punished for the offence for which the lowest punishment is provided, if the same punishment is not provided for all.

Flogging. 53. A sentence of flogging, not exceeding twenty-five lashes, may be passed, by the Court of a Magistrate of the first or second class sitting as a Summary Court, on an adult male offender, in lieu of any term of imprisonment to which he might be sentenced under this Code.

Whipping. 54. A sentence of whipping, not exceeding twenty-five strokes, may be passed, by the Court of a Magistrate of the first or second class sitting as a Summary Court, on any male offender who, in the opinion of the Court, is less than sixteen years of age, in lieu of any other punishment to which he might be sentenced for any offence not punishable with death.

CHAPTER IV.

GENERAL EXCEPTIONS.

Definitions in the Code to be understood subject to exceptions. 55. Throughout this Code, every definition of an offence and every penal provision shall be understood subject to the exceptions contained in this Chapter, though

32

these exceptions are not repeated in such definition or penal provision.

56. Nothing is an offence which is done by a person who is, or who in good faith believes himself to be, bound by law to do it or justified by law in doing it. Act done by a person bound or justified or believing himself bound or justified by law.

Illustrations.

(a) A, a soldier, fires on a mob by the order of his superior officer, in conformity with the commands of the law. A has committed no offence.

(b) A, an officer of a Court of Justice, being ordered by that Court to arrest Y, and, after due enquiry, believing Z to be Y, arrests Z. A has committed no offence.

(c) A sees Z commit what appears to A to be a murder. A, in the exercise, to the best of his judgment, exerted in good faith, of the power which the law gives to all persons of apprehending murderers in the fact, seizes Z, in order to bring Z before the proper authorities. A has committed no offence, though it may turn out that Z was acting in self-defence.

57. Nothing is an offence which is done by a Magistrate when acting judicially in the exercise of any power which is, or which in good faith he believes to be, given to him by law. Act of Magistrate when acting judicially.

58. Nothing which is done in pursuance of, or which is warranted by, the judgment or order of a Court of Justice, if done whilst such judgment or order remains in force, is an offence, notwithstanding the Court may have had no jurisdiction to pass such judgment or order, provided the person doing the act in good faith believes that the Court had such jurisdiction. Act done pursuant to the judgment or order of Court.

59. Nothing is an offence which is done by accident or misfortune, and without any criminal intention or knowledge, in the doing of a lawful act in a lawful manner by lawful means and with proper care and caution. Accident in doing a lawful act.

Illustration.

A is at a work with a hatchet; the head flies off and kills a man who is standing by. Here, if there was no want of proper caution on the part of A, his act is excusable and not an offence.

60. Nothing is an offence by reason of any harm which it may cause or be intended by the doer to cause, or be known by the doer to be likely to cause, if it be done without any criminal intention to cause harm, and in good faith for the purpose of preventing or avoiding Act likely to cause harm, but done without criminal intent, and to prevent other harm or to benefit person harmed.

other harm to person or property, or of benefitting the person to whom harm is or may be caused;

provided

(i) that, having regard to all the circumstances of the case, the doing of the thing was reasonable : and

(ii) that, where the circumstances so require, the thing is done with reasonable care and skill.

Provided, also

(i) that this exception does not extend to the intentional causing of death, or to the attempting to cause death, in order to prevent or avoid harm to property only ; and

(ii) that the death of a person shall, under no circumstances, be deemed to be for the benefit of that person; and

(iii) that mere pecuniary benefit is not benefit within the meaning of this section.

Illustrations.

(a) A passenger train travelling at a high speed is approaching a stationary passenger train upon the same line of rails. A railway employé, as the only means of preventing a collision which would probably involve the lives of many passengers, switches the moving train into a siding. The employé is not guilty of an offence if under all the circumstances his act was reasonable, although a fatal though less serious accident will probably result, and a fatal accident in fact occurs.

(b) A in a great fire pulls down houses in order to prevent the conflagration from spreading. He does this with the intention in good faith of saving human life or property. Here, if it is found that under the circumstances A's act was reasonable, A is not guilty of an offence.

(c) A, a surgeon, knowing that a particular operation is likely to cause the death of Z, who suffers under a painful complaint, but not intending to cause Z's death, and intending in good faith Z's benefit, performs that operation. Z dies in consequence of the operation. If the operation is one which, under all the circumstances, it was reasonable for A to perform and it is performed with reasonable care and skill, A has committed no offence.

If, through drunkenness, the operation is performed unskilfully, A is not protected by this section.

Whether Z (or some competent person on his behalf) has consented to the operation, or not, is a material circumstance in judging whether it was reasonable to perform the operation.

(d) Z is seized by a crocodile. A fires at the crocodile, knowing it to be likely that the shot may kill Z, but not intending to kill Z, and in good faith intending Z's benefit. In fact, A kills Z. A has committed no offence.

61. Nothing is an offence which is done by a child under seven years of age. *Act of a child under seven years of age.*

62. Nothing is an offence which is done by a child above seven years of age and under twelve, who has not attained sufficient maturity of understanding to judge of the nature and consequence of his conduct on that occasion. *Act of a child above seven and under twelve of immature understanding.*

63. Nothing is an offence which is done by a person who, at the time of doing it, by reason of unsoundness of mind, is incapable of knowing the nature of the act, or that he is doing what is either wrong or contrary to law. *Act of a person of unsound mind.*

64. Nothing is an offence which is done by a person who, at the time of doing it, is, by reason of intoxication, incapable of knowing the nature of the act, or that he is doing what is either wrong, or contrary to law ; provided that the thing which intoxicated him was administered to him without his knowledge or against his will. *Act of a person incapable of judgment by reason of intoxication caused against his will.*

65. In cases where an act which is not an offence unless done with a particular knowledge or intent is done by a person in a state of intoxication, the fact of intoxication shall be taken into account in determining the knowledge or intent with which the act was done. *Offence requiring a particular intent or knowledge committed by one who is intoxicated.*

66. Nothing which is not intended to cause death or grievous hurt, and which is not known by the doer to be likely to cause death or grievous hurt, is an offence by reason of any harm which it may cause, or be intended by the doer to cause, to any person above eighteen years of age, who has given consent, whether express or implied, to suffer that harm ; or by reason of any harm which it may be known by the doer to be likely to cause to any such person who has consented to take the risk of that harm. *Act not intended and not known to be likely to cause death or grievous hurt done by consent.*

Explanation.—The exception contained in this clause does not extend to acts which are offences independently of any harm which they may cause or be intended or likely to cause to the consenting person.

Illustration.

A and Z agree to fence with each other for amusement. This agreement implies the consent of each to suffer any harm which, in the course of such fencing, may be caused without foul play ; and if A, while playing fairly, hurts Z, A commits no offence.

Communication made in good faith. **67.** No communication made in good faith is an offence by reason of any harm to the person to whom it is made, if it is made for the benefit of that person.

Illustration.

A, a surgeon, in good faith, communicates to a patient his opinion that he cannot live. The patient dies in consequence of the shock. A has committed no offence, though he knew it to be likely that the communication might cause the patient's death.

Act to which a person is compelled by threats. **68.** Except murder, and offences against the State punishable with death, nothing is an offence which is done by a person who is compelled to do it by threats which, at the time of doing it, reasonably cause the apprehension that instant death to that person will otherwise be the consequence: provided that the person doing the act did not of his own accord, or from a reasonable apprehension of harm to himself short of instant death, place himself in the situation by which he became subject to such constraint.

Act causing slight harm. **69.** Nothing is an offence by reason that it causes, or that it is intended to cause, or that it is known to be likely to cause, any harm, if that harm is so slight that no person of ordinary sense and temper would complain of such harm.

Of the Right of Private Defence.

Things done in private defence. **70.** Nothing is an offence which is done in the exercise of the right of private defence.

Right of private defence of the body and of property. **71.** Every person has a right, subject to the restrictions contained in sections 73 and 74, to defend—

First.—His own body, and the body of any other person, against any offence affecting the human body;

Secondly.—The property, whether movable or immovable, of himself or of any other person, against any act which is an offence falling under the definition of theft, robbery, mischief, or criminal trespass, or which is an attempt to commit theft, robbery, mischief, or criminal trespass.

Right of private defence against act of a person of unsound mind, etc. **72.** When an act, which would otherwise be a certain offence is not that offence, by reason of the youth, the want of maturity of understanding, the unsoundness of

36

mind or the intoxication of the person doing that act, or
by reason of any misconception on the part of that person,
every person has the same right of private defence against
that act which he would have if the act were that
offence.

Illustrations.

(*a*) Z. under the influence of madness, attempts to kill A; Z is
guilty of no offence. But A has the same right of private defence
which he would have if Z were sane.

(*b*) A enters by night a house which he is legally entitled to enter.
Z, in good faith, taking A for a house-breaker, attacks A   Here Z, by
attacking A under this misconception, commits no offence.   But A has
the same right of private defence against Z, which he would have if Z
were not acting under that misconception.

73. There is no right of private defence against an act
which does not reasonably cause the apprehension of death
or of grievous hurt, if done, or attempted to be done, by
a public servant acting in good faith under colour of his
office, though that act may not be strictly justifiable
by law.

There is no right of private defence against an act
which does not reasonably cause the apprehension of death
or of grievous hurt, if done, or attempted to be done, by
the direction of a public servant acting in good faith under
colour of his office, though that direction may not be
strictly justifiable by law.

There is no right of private defence in cases in which
there is time to have recourse to the protection of the
public authorities.

Explanation 1.—A person is not deprived of the right
of private defence against an act done, or attempted to be
done, by a public servant, as such, unless he knows, or
has reason to believe, that the person doing the act is
such public servant.

Explanation 2.—A person is not deprived of the right
of private defence against an act done, or attempted to
be done, by the direction of a public servant, unless he
knows, or has reason to believe, that the person doing
the act is acting by such direction, or unless such person
states the authority under which he acts, or, if he has
authority in writing, unless he produces such authority,
if demanded.

*Acts against
which there is
no right of pri-
vate defence.*

Extent to which
the right may be
exercised.

74. The right of private defence in no case extends to the inflicting of more harm than it is necessary to inflict for the purpose of defence.

Right of private
defence against
deadly assault
when there is
risk of harm to
innocent person.

75. If, in the exercise of the right of private defence against an assault which reasonably causes the apprehension of death, the defender be so situated that he cannot effectually exercise that right without risk of harm to an innocent person, his right of private defence extends to the running of that risk.

Illustration.

A is attacked by a mob who attempt to murder him. He cannot effectually exercise his right of private defence without firing on the mob, and he cannot fire without risk of harming young children who are mingled with the mob. A commits no offence if by so firing he harms any of the children.

CHAPTER V.

OF JOINT ACTS.

Acts done by
several persons
in furtherance
of common inten-
tion.

76. When a criminal act is done by several persons, in furtherance of the common intention of all, each of such persons is liable for that act in the same manner as if it were done by him alone.

When such an
act is criminal
by reason of its
being done
with a criminal
knowledge or
intention.

77. Whenever an act, which is criminal only by reason of its being done with a criminal knowledge or intention, is done by several persons, each of such persons who joins in the act with such knowledge or intention is liable for the act in the same manner as if the act were done by him alone with that knowledge or intention.

Co-operation by
doing one of
several acts
constituting an
offence.

78. When an offence is committed by means of several acts, whoever intentionally co-operates in the commission of that offence by doing any one of those acts, either singly or jointly with any other person, commits that offence.

Illustrations.

(*a*) A and B agree to murder Z by severally and at different times giving him small doses of poison. A and B administer the poison according to the agreement, with intent to murder Z. Z dies from the effects of the several doses of poison so administered to him. Here A and B intentionally co-operate in the commission of murder, and as each of them does an act by which the death is caused, they are both guilty of the offence, though their acts are separate.

(*b*) A and B are joint jailors, and as such, have the charge of Z, a prisoner, alternately for six hours at a time. A and B, intending to cause Z's death, knowingly co-operate in causing that effect by illegally omitting, each during the time of his attendance, to furnish Z with food supplied to them for that pupose. Z dies of hunger. Both A and B are guilty of the murder of Z.

(*c*) A, a jailor, has the charge of Z, a prisoner. A, intending to cause Z's death, illegally omits to supply Z with food; in consequence of which Z is much reduced in strength, but the starvation is not sufficient to cause his death. A is dismissed from his office, and B succeeds him. B, without collusion or co-operation with A, illegally omits to supply Z with food, knowing that he is likely thereby to cause Z's death. Z dies of hunger. B is guilty of murder; but as A did not co-operate with B, A is guilty only of an attempt to commit murder.

79. Where several persons are engaged or concerned in the commission of a criminal act, they may be guilty of different offences by means of that act.

Persons concerned in criminal act may be guilty of different offences.

Illustration.

A attacks Z under such circumstances of grave provocation that his killing of Z would be only culpable homicide not amounting to murder. B, having ill-will towards Z and intending to kill him, and not having been subject to the provocation, assists A in killing Z. Here, though A and B are both engaged in causing Z's death, B is guilty of murder, and A is guilty only of culpable homicide.

CHAPTER VI.

OF ABETMENT.

80. A person abets the doing of a thing, who—

Abetment of a thing.

First.—Instigates any person to do that thing; or,

Secondly.—Engages with one or more other person or persons in conspiracy for the doing of that thing, if an act or illegal omission takes place in pursuance of that conspiracy, and in order to the doing of that thing; or,

Thirdly.—Intentionally aids or facilitates, by any act or illegal omission, the doing of that thing.

Explanation.—A person who, by wilful mis-representation, or by wilful concealment of a material fact which he is bound to disclose, voluntarily causes or procures, or attempts to cause or procure, a thing to be done, is said to instigate the doing of that thing.

Illustrations.

(a) A, a public officer, is authorized by a warrant from a Court of Justice to apprehend Z. B, knowing that fact and also that C is not Z, wilfully represents to A that C is Z, and thereby intentionally causes A to apprehend C. Here B abets by instigation the apprehension of C.

(b) A, a police officer, bound as such officer to give information of all designs to commit robbery and knowing that Z intends to commit a robbery, illegally omits to give information of Z's intention, knowing that the commission of the robbery is likely to be thereby facilitated. Here A has abetted the robbery.

Abettor.

81. A person abets an offence who abets either the commission of an offence, or the commission of an act which would be an offence, if committed by a person capable by law of committing an offence with the same intention or knowledge as that of the abettor.

Explanation 1.—The abetment of the illegal omission of an act may amount to an offence although the abettor may not himself be bound to do that act.

Explanation 2.—To constitute the offence of abetment, it is not necessary that the act abetted should be committed, or that the effect requisite to constitute the offence should be caused.

Illustrations.

(a) A instigates B to murder C. B refuses to do so, A is guilty of abetting B to commit murder.

(b) A instigates B to murder D. B in pursuance of the instigation stabs D. D recovers from the wound; A is guilty of instigating B to commit murder.

Explanation 3.—It is not necessary that the person abetted should be capable by law of committing an offence, or that he should have the same guilty intention or knowledge as that of the abettor, or any guilty intention or knowledge.

Illustrations.

(a) A, with a guilty intention, abets a child or a lunatic to commit an act which would be an offence, if committed by a person capable by law of committing an offence and having the same intention as A. Here A, whether the act be committed or not, is guilty of abetting an offence.

(b) A, intending to cause a theft to be committed, instigates B to take property belonging to Z out of Z's possession. A induces B to believe that the property belongs to A. B takes the property out of Z's possession, in good faith, believing it to be A's property. B, acting under this misconception, does not take dishonestly, and therefore does not commit theft. But A is guilty of abetting theft, and is liable to the same punishment as if B had committed theft.

Explanation 4.—The abetment of an offence being an offence, the abetment of such an abetment is also an offence.　　-

Illustration.

A instigates B to instigate C to murder Z. B accordingly instigates C to murder Z, and C commits that offence in consequence of B's instigation. B is liable to be punished for his offence with the punishment for murder; and as A instigated B to commit the offence, A is also liable to the same punishment.

Explanation 5.—It is not necessary to the commission of the offence of abetment by conspiracy that the abettor should concert the offence with the person who commits it. It is sufficient if he engage in the conspiracy in pursuance of which the offence is committed.

Illustration.

A concerts with B a plan for poisoning Z. It is agreed that A shall administer the poison. B then explains the plan to C, mentioning that a third person is to administer the poison, but without mentioning A's name. C agrees to procure the poison, and procures and delivers it to B for the purpose of its being used in the manner explained. A administers the poison; Z dies in consequence. Here, though A and C have not conspired together, yet C has been engaged in the conspiracy in pursuance of which Z has been murdered. C has therefore committed the offence defined in this section, and is liable to the punishment for murder.

82. Whoever abets any offence, shall, if the act abetted is committed in consequence of the abetment, and no express provision is made by this Code or by any other law for the time being in force for the punishment of such abetment, be punished with the punishment provided for the offence.

Punishment of abetment if the act abetted is committed in consequence and where no express provision is made for its punishment.

Explanation.—An act or offence is said to be committed in consequence of abetment, when it is committed in consequence of the instigation, or in pursuance of the conspiracy, or with the aid which constitutes the abetment.

Illustrations.

(*a*) A offers a bribe to B, a public servant, as a reward for showing A some favour in the exercise of B's official functions. B accepts the bribe. A has abetted the offence defined in section 123.

(*b*) A instigates B to give false evidence. B, in consequence of the instigation, commits that offence. A is guilty of abetting that offence, and is liable to the same punishment as B.

(*c*) A and B conspire to poison Z. A, in pursuance of the conspiracy, procures the poison and delivers it to B in order that he may administer it to Z.. B, in pursuance of the conspiracy, administers the poison to Z in A's absence and thereby causes Z's death   Here B is guilty of murder. A is guilty of abetting that offence by conspiracy, and is liable to the punishment for murder.

Punishment of abetment if person abetted does act with different intention from that of abettor.

83. Whoever abets the commission of an offence shall, if the person abetted does the act with a different intention or knowledge from that of the abettor, be punished with the punishment provided for the offence which would have been committed if the act had been done with the intention or knowledge of the abettor and with no other.

Liability of abettor when one act abetted and different act done.

Proviso.

84. When an act is abetted and a different act is done, the abettor is liable for the act done, in the same manner and to the same extent as if he had directly abetted it:

provided the act done was a probable consequence of the abetment, and was committed under the influence of the instigation, or with the aid or in pursuance of the conspiracy which constituted the abetment.

Illustrations.

(*a*) A instigates a child to put poison into the food of Z and gives him poison for that purpose. The child, in consequence of the instigation, by mistake puts the poison into the food of Y, which ·is by the side of that of Z. Here, if the child was acting under the influence of A's instigation, and the act done was under the circumstances a probable consequence of the abetment, A is liable in the same manner and to the same extent as if he had instigated the child to put the poison into the food of Y.

(*b*) A instigates B and C to break into an inhabited house at midnight for the purpose of robbery, and provides them with arms for that purpose. B and C·break into the house and, being resisted by Z, one of the inmates, murder Z. Here, if that murder was the probable consequence of the abetment, A is liable to the punishment provided for murder.

Abettor when liable to cumulative punishment for act abetted and for act done.

85. If the act for which the abettor is liable under the last preceding section is committed in addition to the act abetted, and constitutes a distinct offence, the abettor is liable to punishment for each of the offences.

Liability of abettor for an effect caused by the act abetted

86. When an act is abetted with the intention on the part of the abettor of causing a particular effect, and an act for which the abettor is liable in consequence of the abetment causes a different effect from that intended by the abettor, the abettor is liable for the effect caused, in the same manner and to the same extent as if he had abetted the act with the intention of causing that effect, provided he knew that the act abetted was likely to cause that effect. — *different from that intended by the abettor.*

Exception.—The abettor shall not be liable under this section to the punishment for murder, unless he knew that death would be the probable effect of the act abetted. (Cf. section 227.)

Illustration.

A instigates B to cause grievous hurt to Z. B, in consequence of the instigation, causes grievous hurt to Z. Z dies in consequence. Here, if A knew that the grievous hurt abetted was likely to cause death, A is liable to be punished with the punishment provided for culpable homicide or for murder, as the case may be.

87. Whenever any person who if absent would be liable to be punished as an abettor is present when the act or offence for which he would be punishable in consequence of the abetment is committed, he shall be deemed to have committed such act or offence. — *Abettor present when offence is committed.*

88. Whoever abets the commission of an offence punishable with death or imprisonment for life, shall, if that offence be not committed in consequence of the abetment, and no express provision is made by this Code or by any other law for the time being in force for the punishment of such abetment, be punished with imprisonment for a term which may extend to seven years, and shall also be liable to fine; — *Abetment of offence punishable with death for life—if offence not committed;*

and, if the abettor is a public servant whose duty it is to prevent the commission of such offence, he shall be liable to imprisonment for a term which may extend to ten years, and shall also be liable to fine. — *if abettor be a public servant whose duty it is to prevent offence.*

Illustration.

A instigates B to murder Z. The offence is not committed. If B had murdered Z, he would have been subject to the punishment of death. Therefore A is liable to imprisonment for a term which may extend to seven years, or if he is a public servant whose duty it is to prevent the murder, to ten years, and also in any event to a fine.

89. Whoever abets an offence punishable with imprisonment shall, if that offence be not committed in consequence of the abetment, and no express provision is made by this Code or by any other law for the time being in force — *Abetment of offence punishable with imprisonment—if offence be not committed;*

for the punishment of such abetment, be punished with imprisonment for a term which may extend to one-fourth part of the longest term provided for that offence, or with such fine as is provided for that offence or with both;

if abettor be a public servant whose duty it is to prevent offence.

and, if the abettor is a public servant whose duty it is to prevent the commission of such offence, he shall be punished with imprisonment for a term which may extend to one-half of the longest term provided for that offence, or with such fine as is provided for the offence, or with both.

Illustrations.

(*a*) A offers a bribe to B, a public servant, as a reward for showing A some favour in the exercise of B's official functions. B refuses to accept the bribe. A is punishable under this section.

(*b*) A, a police officer, whose duty it is to prevent robbery, abets the commission of robbery. Here, though the robbery be not committed, A is liable to one-half of the longest term of imprisonment provided for that offence and also to fine.

Abetting commission of offence by the public, or by more than ten persons.

90. Whoever abets the commission of an offence by the public generally or by any number or class of persons exceeding ten, shall be punished with imprisonment for a term which may extend to three years, or with fine, or with both.

Illustration.

A affixes in a public place a placard instigating a sect consisting of more than ten members to meet at a certain time and place, for the purpose of attacking the members of an adverse sect, while engaged in a procession. A has committed the offence defined in this section.

Abetment of thing done or intended to be done in a place where this Code is not in force.

91. Whoever, being in a part of the Sudan in which this Code is in force, abets the doing of a thing elsewhere than in such a part of the Sudan, shall, if the doing of the thing is an offence under any law in force in the place where the thing is done or intended to be done and also under this Code, be punished as if the thing had been done or it had been intended that the thing should be done in a part of the Sudan in which this Code is in force.

CHAPTER VII.

OF ATTEMPTS TO COMMIT OFFENCES.

Punishment for attempting to commit offences punishable with imprisonment.

92. Whoever attempts to commit an offence punishable with imprisonment, or to cause such an offence to be committed, and in such attempt does any act towards the

44

commission of the offence, shall, where no express provision is made by this Code or any other law for the time being in force for the punishment of such attempt, be punished with imprisonment for a term which may extend to one-half of the longest term provided for that offence, or with such fine as is provided for the offence, or with both.

Illustrations.

(*a*) A makes an attempt to steal some jewels by breaking open a box, and finds after so opening the box that there is no jewel in it. He has done an act towards the commission of theft, and therefore is guilty under this section.

(*b*) A makes an attempt to pick the pocket of Z by thrusting his hand into Z's pocket. A fails in the attempt in consequence of Z's having nothing in his pocket. A is guilty under this section.

CHAPTER VIII.

Of Offences against the State.

93. Whoever wages war against the Government of the Sudan or the Khedive of Egypt, or attempts to wage such war, or abets the waging of such war, shall be punished with death, or imprisonment for life, and shall forfeit all his property.

Waging or attempting to wage war, or abetting waging of war, against the Government or the Khedive.

Illustrations.

(*a*) A joins an insurrection against the Government. A has committed the offence defined in this section.

(*b*) A, being resident in a part of the Sudan in which this Code is in force, supplies arms to tribes in an unsettled district which are at war with the Government. A is guilty of abetting the waging of war against the Government.

94. Whoever conspires to commit any of the offences punishable by section 93, or conspires to overawe the Government by means of criminal force or the show of criminal force, shall be punished with imprisonment which may extend to fourteen years.

Conspiracy to commit offences punishable by section 93.

Explanation.—To constitute a conspiracy under this section, it is not necessary that any act or illegal omission shall take place in pursuance thereof.

45

Collecting arms, etc., with intention of waging war against the Government or the Khedive.

95. Whoever collects men, arms or ammunition or otherwise prepares to wage war, with the intention of either waging or being prepared to wage war against the Government of the Sudan or the Khedive of Egypt, shall be punished with imprisonment for a term not exceeding fourteen years, and shall forfeit all his property.

Exciting disaffection.

96. Whoever by words, either spoken or intended to be read, or by signs, or by visible representation, or otherwise, excites or attempts to excite feelings of disaffection to the Government established by law in the Sudan, shall be punished with imprisonment for a term which may extend to three years, or with fine, or with both.

Public servant voluntarily allowing prisoner of State or war to escape.

97. Whoever, being a public servant and having the custody of any State prisoner or prisoner of war, voluntarily allows such prisoner to escape from any place in which such prisoner is confined, shall be punished with imprisonment for a term which may extend to fourteen years, and shall also be liable to fine.

Public servant negligently suffering such prisoner to escape.

98. Whoever, being a public servant and having the custody of any State prisoner or prisoner of war, negligently suffers such prisoner to escape from any place of confinement in which such prisoner is confined, shall be punished with imprisonment for a term which may extend to three years, and shall also be liable to fine.

Aiding escape of, rescuing, or harbouring such prisoner.

99. Whoever knowingly aids or assists any State prisoner or prisoner of war in escaping from lawful custody, or rescues or attempts to rescue any such prisoner, or harbours or conceals any such prisoner who has escaped from lawful custody, or offers or attempts to offer any resistance to the recapture of such prisoner, shall be punished with imprisonment for a term which may extend to fourteen years, and shall also be liable to fine.

Explanation.—A State prisoner or prisoner of war, who is permitted to be at large on his parole within certain limits in the Sudan, is said to escape from lawful custody if he goes beyond the limits within which he is allowed to be at large.

Breach of official trust.

100. Any person who, by reason or by means of his employment as a public servant, or of his holding any contract with the Government of the Sudan or of Egypt or of Great Britain or with any Department of any of such Governments, or by reason or by means of his em-

46

ployment by any person holding any such contract, lawfully or unlawfully acquires any information in respect of which he is under an obligation of secrecy, and at any time communicates or attempts to communicate such information to any person to whom the same ought not, in the interests of any of such Governments, or otherwise in the public interest, to be communicated at that time, is said to "commit a breach of official trust."

101. Whoever commits a breach of official trust shall

(i) if the communication is made or attempted to be made to the agent of a foreign Government, be punished with imprisonment for a term which may extend to fourteen years, and shall also be liable to fine; and

(ii) in any other case, shall be punished with imprisonment for a term which may extend to one year, or with fine, or with both.

Punishment for breach of official trust.

102. Whoever, being in possession of information as to the military or naval defences of the Sudan, or as to the military or naval affairs of the Government of the Sudan or of Egypt or of Great Britain, in whatever manner such information has been obtained, at any time wilfully communicates the same to any person to whom he knows that it ought not, in the interest of any of such Governments, to be communicated at that time, shall

(i) if the communication is made to the agent of a foreign Government, be punished with imprisonment for a term which may extend to fourteen years, and shall also be liable to fine; and

(ii) in any other case, shall be punished with imprisonment for a term which may extend to one year, or with fine, or with both.

Disclosure of military information.

Explanation.—If the communication is made to the agent of a Government at war with Egypt the offender will be punishable under section 93.

CHAPTER IX.

Of Offences relating to the Army and Navy.

103. Whoever abets the committing of mutiny by an officer, soldier, or sailor in any military or naval forces serving in the Sudan, or attempts to seduce any such

Abetting mutiny, or attempting to seduce a soldier or sailor from his duty.

officer, soldier, or sailor from his allegiance or his duty, shall be punished with imprisonment for a term which may extend to fourteen years, and shall also be liable to fine.

Abetment of mutiny, if mutiny is committed in consequence thereof.

104. Whoever abets the committing of mutiny by any officer, soldier, or sailor in any military or naval forces serving in the Sudan, shall, if mutiny be committed in consequence of that abetment, be punished with death, or with imprisonment for a term which may extend to fourteen years, and shall also be liable to fine.

Abetment of assault by soldier or sailor on his superior officer, when in execution of his office.

105. Whoever abets an assault by an officer, soldier, or sailor in any military or naval forces serving in the Sudan, on any superior officer being in the execution of his office,

(i) if such assault be committed in consequence of that abetment, shall be punished with imprisonment for a term which may extend to seven years, and shall also be liable to fine; and

(ii) if such assault be not committed in consequence of that abetment, shall be punished with imprisonment for a term which may extend to three years, and shall also be liable to fine.

Abetment of desertion of soldier or sailor.

106. Whoever abets the desertion of any officer, soldier, or sailor in any military or naval forces serving in the Sudan, shall be punished with imprisonment for a term which may extend to two years, or with fine, or with both.

Harbouring deserter.

107. Whoever, except as hereinafter excepted, knowing or having reason to believe that an officer, soldier, or sailor in any military or naval forces serving in the Sudan, has deserted, harbours such officer, soldier, or sailor, shall be punished with imprisonment for a term which may extend to two years, or with fine, or with both.

Exception.—This provision does not extend to the case in which the harbour is given by a wife to her husband.

Abetment of act of insubordination by soldier or sailor.

108. Whoever abets what he knows to be an act of insubordination by an officer, soldier, or sailor in any military or naval forces serving in the Sudan, shall, if such act of insubordination be committed in consequence of that abetment, be punished with imprisonment for a term which may extend to six months, or with fine, or with both.

109. Whoever, not being a soldier in the Military or Naval service of the Khedive of Egypt or of the Sovereign of Great Britain, wears any garb or carries any token resembling any garb or token used by such a soldier, with the intention that it may be believed that he is such a soldier, shall be punished with imprisonment for a term which may extend to three months, or with fine which may extend to L.E. 5, or with both. *Wearing garb or carrying token used by soldier.*

CHAPTER X.

OF OFFENCES AGAINST THE PUBLIC TRANQUILITY.

110. An assembly of five or more persons is designated an "unlawful assembly," if the common object of the persons composing that assembly, is— *Unlawful assembly.*

First.—To overawe by criminal force, or show of criminal force, the Executive Government of the Sudan or of any part of the Sudan, or any public servant in the exercise of his lawful power; or

Second.—To resist the execution of any law, or of any legal process; or

Third.—To commit any mischief or criminal trespass, or other offence; or

Fourth.—By means of criminal force, or show of criminal force, to enforce any right or supposed right; or

Fifth.—By means of criminal force, or show of criminal force, to compel any person to do what he is not legally bound to·do, or to omit to do what he is legally entitled to do.

Explanation.—An assembly which was not unlawful when it assembled, may subsequently become an unlawful assembly.

111. Whoever, being aware of facts which render any assembly an unlawful assembly, intentionally joins that assembly, or continues in it, is said to be a member of an unlawful assembly. *Being member of unlawful assembly.*

112. Whoever is a member of an unlawful assembly, shall be punished with imprisonment for a term which may extend to six months, or with fine, or with both. *Punishment*

D   49

113. Whoever, being armed with any deadly weapon, or with anything which, used as a weapon of offence, is likely to cause death, is a member of an unlawful assembly, shall be punished with imprisonment for a term which may extend to two years, or with fine, or with both.

Joining unlawful assembly, armed with deadly weapon.

114. Whoever joins or continues in an unlawful assembly, knowing that such unlawful assembly has been commanded in the manner prescribed by law to disperse, shall be punished with imprisonment for a term which may extend to two years, or with fine, or with both.

Joining or continuing in unlawful assembly, knowing it has been commanded to disperse.

115. Whenever force or violence is used by an unlawful assembly, or by any member thereof, in prosecution of the common object of such assembly, every member of such assembly is guilty of the offence of rioting.

Rioting.

116. Whoever is guilty of rioting, shall be punished with imprisonment for a term which may extend to two years, or with fine, or with both.

Punishment for rioting.

117. Whoever is guilty of rioting, being armed with a deadly weapon, or with anything which, used as a weapon of offence, is likely to cause death, shall be punished with imprisonment for a term which may extend to three years, or with fine, or with both.

Rioting, armed with deadly weapon.

118. If an offence is committed by any member of an unlawful assembly in prosecution of the common object of that assembly, every person who, at the time of the committing of that offence, is a member of the assembly, is guilty of that offence.

Every member of unlawful assembly guilty of offence committed in prosecution of common object.

119. Whoever promotes, or does any act with intent to assist the promotion of an unlawful assembly, shall be punishable as a member of such unlawful assembly, and for any offence which may be committed by any member thereof, in the same manner as if he had himself been a member of such unlawful assembly.

Promoter of an unlawful assembly liable as a member.

120. Whoever knowingly joins or continues in any assembly of five or more persons likely to cause a disturbance of the public peace, after such assembly has been lawfully commanded to disperse, shall be punished with imprisonment for a term which may extend to six months, or with fine, or with both.

Knowingly joining or continuing in assembly of five or more persons after it has been commanded to disperse.

Explanation.—If the assembly is an unlawful assembly within the meaning of section 110, the offender will be punishable under section 114.

121. Whoever assaults or threatens to assault, or ob- Assaulting or obstructing public servant when suppressing riot, etc. structs or attempts to obstruct, any public servant in the discharge of his duty as such public servant, in endeavouring to disperse an unlawful assembly, or to suppress a riot or affray, or uses, or threatens, or attempts to use criminal force to such public servant, shall be punished with imprisonment for a term which may extend to three years, or with fine, or with both.

122. When two or more persons, by fighting, in a Affray. public place, disturb the public peace, each of such persons is said "to commit an affray," and shall be punished with imprisonment for a term which may extend to one month, or with fine which may extend to L.E. 2, or with both.

CHAPTER XI.

Of Offences by or relating to Public Servants.

123. Whoever, being or expecting to be a public servant, Public servant taking gratification other than legal remuneration in respect of an official act. accepts or obtains, or agrees to accept, or attempts to obtain, from any person, for himself or for any other person, any gratification whatever, whether pecuniary or otherwise, other than legal remuneration, as a motive or reward for doing or forbearing to do any official act, or for showing or forbearing to show, in the exercise of his official functions, favour or disfavour to any person, or for rendering or attempting to render any service or disservice to any person, with any Department of the Government or with any public servant, as such, shall be punished with imprisonment for a term which may extend to three years, or with fine, or with both.

Explanations.—"Expecting to be a public servant." If a person not expecting to be in office obtains a gratification by deceiving others into a belief that he is about to be in office, and that he will then serve them, he may be guilty of cheating, but he is not guilty of the offence defined in this section.

"A motive or reward for doing." A person who receives a gratification as a motive for doing what he does not intend to do, or as a reward for doing what he has not done, comes within these words.

Illustrations.

(*a*) A, a Mamur, obtains from Z, a merchant, a situation in Z's office for A's brother, as a reward to A for deciding a cause in favour of Z. A has committed the offence defined in this section.

(*b*) A, a Mudir, accepts a sum of money from a large land-owner. It does not appear that A accepted this sum as a motive or reward for doing or forbearing to do any particular official act, or for rendering or attempting to render any particular service to the land-owner. But it does appear that A accepted the sum as a motive or reward for generally showing favour in the exercise of his official functions to the land-owner. A has committed the offence defined in this section.

(*c*) A, a public servant, induces Z erroneously to believe that A's influence with the Government has obtained for Z the position of Sheikh, and thus induces Z to give A money as a reward for this service. A has committed the offence defined in this section.

Taking gratification, in order to influence public servant. **124.** Whoever accepts, or obtains, or agrees to accept, or attempts to obtain, from any person, for himself or for any other person, any gratification whatever as a motive or reward for inducing any public servant to do or to forbear to do any official act, or in the exercise of the official functions of such public servant to show favour or disfavour to any person, or to render or attempt to render any service or disservice to any person with any Department of the Government or with any public servant, as such, shall be punished with imprisonment for a term which may extend to three years, or with fine, or with both.

Punishment for abetment by public servant of offence defined in section 124. **125.** Whoever, being a public servant, in respect of whom an offence under section 124 is committed, abets the offence, shall be punished with imprisonment for a term which may extend to three years, or with fine, or with both.

Public servant obtaining valuable thing without consideration from person concerned in proceeding or business transacted by such public servant. **126.** Whoever, being a public servant accepts or obtains, or agrees to accept or attempts to obtain, for himself, or for any other person, any valuable thing, without consideration, or for a consideration which he knows to be inadequate,

from any person whom he knows to have been, or to be, or to be likely to be, concerned in any proceeding or business transacted or about to be transacted by such public servant, or having any connection with the official functions of himself or of any public servant to whom he is subordinate,

or from any person whom he knows to be interested in or related to the person so concerned,.

shall be punished with imprisonment for a term which may extend to two years, or with fine, or with both.

Illustrations.

(*a*) A, an Inspector, hires a house of Z, who has a boundary case pending before him. It is agreed that A shall pay L.E.2 a month, the house being such that, if the bargain were made in good faith, A would be required to pay L.E. 5 a month. A has obtained a valuable thing from Z without adequate consideration.

(*b*) Z's brother is apprehended and taken before A, a Magistrate, on a charge of perjury. A sells to Z shares in a company at a premium, when they are selling in the market at a discount. Z pays A for the shares accordingly. The money so obtained by A is a valuable thing obtained by him without adequate consideration.

127. Whoever, being a public servant, knowingly disobeys any direction of the law as to the way in which he is to conduct himself as such public servant, intending to cause or knowing that he is likely thereby to cause injury to any person, or intending thereby to save, or knowing it to be likely that he will thereby save, any person from legal punishment, or subject him to a less punishment than that to which he is liable, or with intent to save, or knowing that he is likely thereby to save, any property from forfeiture or any charge to which it is liable by law, shall be punished with imprisonment for a term which may extend to two years, or with fine, or with both.

Public servant disobeying direction of law with intent to cause injury or to save person from punishment or property from forfeiture.

128. Whoever, being a public servant, and being, as such public servant, charged with the preparation of any record or other writing, or with the translation of any document, frames that record or writing or translates that document in a manner which he knows or believes to be incorrect, with intent to cause, or knowing it to be likely that he will thereby cause, loss or injury to the public or to any person, or with intent thereby to save, or knowing it to be likely that he will thereby save, any person from legal punishment, or with intent to save, or knowing that he is likely thereby to save any property from forfeiture or other charge to which it is liable by law, shall be punished with imprisonment for a term which may extend to three years, or with fine, or with both.

Public servant framing incorrect record or writing or mistranslating document with intent to cause injury or to save person from punishment or property from forfeiture.

129. Whoever, being a public servant, corruptly or maliciously makes or pronounces in any stage of a judicial

Public servant in judicial proceeding corruptly

making report, etc., contrary to law.	proceeding, any report, order, verdict, or decision which he knows to be contrary to law, shall be punished with imprisonment for a term which may extend to seven years, or with fine, or with both.
Commitment for trial or confinement by person having authority who knows that he is acting contrary to law.	**130.** Whoever, being in any office which gives him legal authority to commit persons for trial or to confinement, or to keep persons in confinement, corruptly or maliciously commits any person for trial or to confinement, or keeps any person in confinement, in the exercise of that authority, knowing that in so doing he is acting contrary to law, shall be punished with imprisonment for a term which may extend to seven years, or with fine, or with both.
Public servant intentionally omitting to apprehend, or permitting or aiding escape from confinement or custody.	**131.** Whoever, being a public servant, legally bound as such public servant to apprehend any person or to keep any person in confinement or custody, intentionally omits to apprehend such person, or intentionally suffers such person to escape, or intentionally aids such person in escaping or attempting to escape from such confinement or custody, shall be punished as follows, that is to say;

with imprisonment for a term which may extend to fourteen years, with or without fine, if such person is under sentence of death; or

with imprisonment for a term which may extend to seven years, with or without fine, if such person is subject by a sentence of a Court of Justice, or by virtue of a commutation of such sentence to imprisonment for a term of ten years or upwards, or is charged with or liable to be apprehended for an offence punishable with death; or

with imprisonment for a term which may extend to three years, or with fine, or with both, if such person is subject by a sentence of a Court of Justice to imprisonment for a term not extending to ten years, or is charged with or liable to be apprehended for an offence punishable with imprisonment for a term which may extend to ten years; or

with imprisonment for a term which may extend to two years, or with fine, or with both, in any case not above specified.

Public servant negligently omitting to apprehend or permitting to escape from con-	**132.** Whoever, being a public servant legally bound as such public servant to apprehend any person, or to keep any person in confinement or custody, negligently omits

to apprehend that person or negligently suffers that per- finement or custody.
son to escape from confinement or custody, shall be
punished with imprisonment for a term which may extend
to two years, or with fine, or with both.

133. Whoever, being a public servant, and being Public servant unlawfully
legally bound as such public servant not to engage in trade, engaging in trade.
engages in trade, shall be punished with imprisonment
for a term which may extend to one year, or with fine,
or with both.

134. Whoever, being a public servant, and being Public servant unlawfully
legally bound as such public servant, not to purchase or buying or bidding for property.
bid for certain property, purchases or bids for that pro-
perty, either in his own name or in the name of another,
or jointly or in shares with others, shall be punished with
imprisonment for a term which may extend to two years,
or with fine, or with both; and the property, if purchased,
shall be confiscated.

135. Whoever pretends to hold any particular office Personating a public servant.
as a public servant, knowing that he does not hold such
office, or falsely personates any other person holding such
office, and in such assumed character does or attempts to
do any act under color of such office, shall be punished
with imprisonment for a term which may extend to two
years, or with fine, or with both.

136. Whoever, not belonging to a certain class of Wearing garb or carrying token
public servants, wears any garb or carries any token re- used by public servant with
sembling any garb or token used by that class of public fraudulent intent.
servants, with the intention that it may be believed, or
with the knowledge that it is likely to be believed,
that he belongs to that class of public servants, shall be
punished with imprisonment for a term which may extend
to three months, or with fine which may extend to L.E. 5,
or with both.

CHAPTER XII.

Of Contempts of the Lawful Authority of Public Servants.

137. Whoever absconds in order to avoid being served Absconding to avoid service of
with a summons, notice, or order proceeding from any summons or
public servant legally competent, as such public servant, other proceeding.

to issue such summons, notice or order, shall be punished
with imprisonment for a term which may extend to one
month, or with fine which may extend to L.E. 10, or
with both;

or, if the summons or notice or order is to attend in
person or by agent, or to produce a document in a Court
of Justice, with imprisonment for a term which may extend to six months, or with fine which may extend to
L.E. 20, or with both.

Preventing service of summons or other proceeding, or preventing publication thereof.   **138.** Whoever in any manner intentionally prevents
the serving on himself, or on any other person, of any
summons, notice, or order proceeding from any public
servant legally competent, as such public servant, to issue
such summons, notice, or order,

or intentionally prevents the lawful affixing to any
place of any such summons, notice, or order,

or intentionally removes any such summons, notice, or
order from any place to which it is lawfully affixed,

or intentionally prevents the lawful making of any
proclamation, under the authority of any public servant
legally competent, as such public servant, to direct such
proclamation to be made,

shall be punished with imprisonment for a term which
may extend to one month, or with fine which may extend
to L.E. 10, or with both;

or, if the summons, notice, order, or proclamation is to
attend in person or by agent, or to produce a document
in a Court of Justice, with imprisonment for a term which
may extend to six months, or with fine which may extend to L.E. 20, or with both.

Non-attendance in obedience to an order from public servant.   **139.** Whoever, being legally bound to attend in per-
sor n oby an agent at a certain place and time in obedience
to a summons, notice, order, or proclamation proceeding
from any public servant legally competent, as such public
servant, to issue the same,

intentionally omits to attend at that place or time, or
departs from the place where he is bound to attend before
the time at which it is lawful for him to depart,

shall be punished with imprisonment for a term which
may extend to one month, or with fine which may extend
to L.E. 10, or with both;

or if the summons, notice, order, or proclamation is to
attend in person or by agent in a Court of Justice, with

imprisonment for a term which may extend to six months, or with fine which may extend to L.E. 20, or with both.

140. Whoever, being legally bound to produce or deliver up any document to any public servant, as such, intentionally omits so to produce or deliver up the same, shall be punished with imprisonment for a term which may extend to one month, or with fine which may extend to L.E. 10, or with both; *Omission to produce document to public servant by person legally bound to produce it.*

or, if the document is to be produced or delivered up to a Court of Justice, with imprisonment for a term which may extend to six months, or with fine which may extend to L.E. 20, or with both.

141. Whoever, being legally bound to give any notice or to furnish information on any subject to any public servant, as such, intentionally omits to give such notice or to furnish such information in the manner and at the time required by law, shall be punished with imprisonment for a term which may extend to one month, or with fine which may extend to L.E. 10, or with both; *Omission to give notice or information to public servant by person legally bound to give it.*

or, if the notice or information required to be given respects the commission of an offence, or is required for the purpose of preventing the commission of an offence, or in order to the apprehension of an offender, with imprisonment for a term which may extend to six months, or with fine which may extend to L.E. 20, or with both.

142. Whoever, being legally bound to furnish information on any subject to any public servant, as such, furnishes, as true, information on the subject which he knows or has reason to believe to be false, shall be punished with imprisonment for a term which may extend to six months, or with fine which may extend to L.E. 20, or with both; *Furnishing false information.*

or, if the information which he is legally bound to give respects the commission of an offence, or is required for the purpose of preventing the commission of an offence, or in order to the apprehension of an offender, with imprisonment for a term which may extend to two years, or with fine, or with both.

Explanation.—In section 141 and in this section the word "offence" includes an offence against any law in force in the place where such offence is committed, although the offence is committed elsewhere than in a part of the Sudan in which this Code is in force.

143. Whoever gives to any public servant any information which he knows or believes to be false, intending thereby to cause, or knowing it to be likely that he will thereby cause, such public servant—

(a) to do or omit anything which such public servant ought not to do or omit if the true state of facts respecting which such information is given were known by him, or

(b) to use the lawful power of such public servant to the injury or annoyance of any person,

shall be punished with imprisonment for a term which may extend to six months or with fine which may extend to L.E. 20, or with both.

Illustrations.

(a) A informs a Magistrate that Z, a police-officer, subordinate to such Magistrate, has been guilty of neglect of duty or misconduct, knowing such information to be false, and knowing it to be likely that the information will cause the Magistrate to dismiss Z. A has committed the offence defined in this section.

(b) A falsely informs a public servant that Z has contraband salt in a secret place, knowing such information to be false, and knowing that it is likely that the consequence of the information will be a search of Z's premises, attended with annoyance to Z. A has committed the offence defined in this section.

(c) A falsely informs a policeman that he has been assaulted and robbed in the neighbourhood of a particular village. He does not mention the name of any person as one of his assailants, but knows it to be likely that in consequence of this information the police will make enquiries and institute searches in the village to the annoyance of the villagers or some of them. A has committed an offence under this section.

144. Whoever refuses to bind himself by an oath or affirmation to state the truth, when required so to bind himself by a public servant legally competent to require that he shall so bind himself, shall be punished with imprisonment for a term which may extend to six months, or with fine which may extend to L.E. 20, or with both.

145. Whoever, being legally bound to state the truth on any subject to any public servant, refuses to answer any question demanded of him touching that subject by such public servant in the exercise of the legal powers of such public servant, shall be punished with imprisonment for a term which may extend to six months, or with fine which may extend to L.E. 20, or with both.

146. Whoever refuses to sign any statement made by him, when required to sign that statement by a public servant legally competent to require that he shall sign that statement, shall be punished with imprisonment for a term which may extend to three months, or with fine which may extend to L. E. 10, or with both. Refusing to sign statement.

147. Whoever offers any resistance to the taking of any property by the lawful authority of any public servant, knowing or having reason to believe that he is such public servant, shall be punished with imprisonment for a term which may extend to six months, or with fine which may extend to L.E. 20, or with both. Resistance to taking of property by lawful authority of public servant.

148. Whoever intentionally obstructs any sale of property offered for sale by the lawful authority of any public servant, as such, shall be punished with imprisonment for a term which may extend to one month, or with fine which may extend to L.E. 10, or with both. Obstructing sale of property offered for sale by authority of public servant.

149. Whoever, at any sale of property held by the lawful authority of a public servant as such, purchases or bids for any property on account of any person, whether himself or any other, whom he knows to be under a legal incapacity to purchase that property at that sale, or bids for such property not intending to perform the obligations under which he lays himself by such bidding, shall be punished with imprisonment for a term which may extend to one month, or with fine which may extend to L.E. 10, or with both. Illegal purchase or bid for property offered for sale by authority of public servant.

150. Whoever voluntarily obstructs any public servant in the discharge of his public functions, shall be punished with imprisonment for a term which may extend to three months, or with fine which may extend to L.E. 10, or with both. Obstructing public servant in discharge of public functions.

151. Whoever, being bound by law to render or furnish assistance to any public servant in the execution of his public duty, intentionally omits to give such assistance, shall be punished with imprisonment for a term which may extend to six months, or with fine which may extend to L.E. 10, or with both. Omission to assist public servant when bound by law to give assistance.

152. Whoever, knowing that, by an order promulgated by a public servant lawfully empowered to promulgate such order, he is directed to abstain from a certain act, Disobedience to order duly promulgated by public servant.

or to take certain order with certain property in his possession or under his management, disobeys such direction,

shall, if such disobedience causes or tends to cause obstruction, annoyance, or injury, or risk of obstruction, annoyance, or injury, to any person lawfully employed, be punished with imprisonment for a term which may extend to one month, or with fine which may extend to L.E. 5, or with both;

and if such disobedience causes or tends to cause danger to human life, health, or safety, or causes or tends to cause a riot or affray, shall be punished with imprisonment for a term which may extend to six months, or with fine which may extend to L.E. 20, or with both.

153. Whoever holds out any threat of injury to any public servant, or to any person in whom he believes that public servant to be interested, for the purpose of inducing that public servant to do any act, or to forbear or delay to do any act, connected with the exercise of the public functions of such public servant, shall be punished with imprisonment for a term which may extend to two years, or with fine, or with both.

Threat of injury to public servant.

154. Whoever holds out any threat of injury to any person for the purpose of inducing that person to refrain or desist from making a legal application for protection against any injury to any public servant legally empowered as such to give such protection, or to cause such protection to be given, shall be punished with imprisonment for a term which may extend to one year, or with fine, or with both.

Threat of injury to induce person to refrain from applying for protection to public servant

---

CHAPTER XIII.

OF FALSE EVIDENCE AND OFFENCES AGAINST PUBLIC JUSTICE.

Of False Evidence.

155. Whoever being legally bound by an oath or by any express provision of law to state the truth, or being bound by law to make a declaration upon any subject, makes any statement which is false, and which he either

Giving false evidence.

knows or believes to be false, or does not believe to be true, is said to give false evidence.

Explanation 1.—A statement is within the meaning of this section, whether it is made verbally or otherwise.

Explanation 2.—A false statement as to the belief of the person attesting is within the meaning of this section, and a person may be guilty of giving false evidence by stating that he believes a thing which he does not believe, as well as by stating that he knows a thing which he does not know.

Illustrations.

(*a*) A, in support, of a just claim which B has against Z for L.E. 10, falsely swears on a trial that he heard Z admit the justice of B's claim. A has given false evidence.

(*b*) A, being bound by an oath to state the truth, states that he believes a certain signature to be the handwriting of Z, when he does not believe it to be the handwriting of Z. Here A states that which he knows to be false, and therefore gives false evidence.

(*c*) A, knowing the general character of Z's handwriting, states that he believes a certain signature to be the handwriting of Z; A in good faith believing it to be so. Here A's statement is merely as to his belief, and is true as to his belief, and therefore, although the signature may not be the handwriting of Z, A has not given false evidence.

(*d*) A, being bound by an oath to state the truth, states that he knows that Z was at a particular place on a particular day, not knowing anything upon the subject. A gives false evidence whether Z was at that place on the day named or not.

(*e*) A, an interpreter or translator, gives or certifies as a true interpretation or translation of a statement or document, which he is bound by oath to interpret or translate truly, that which is not and which he does not believe to be a true interpretation or translation. A has given false evidence

156. Whoever causes any circumstance to exist, or makes any false entry in any book or record, or makes any document containing a false statement, intending that such circumstance, false entry, or false statement may appear in evidence in a judicial proceeding, or in a proceeding taken by law before a public servant as such, or before an arbitrator, and that such circumstance, false entry, or false statement, so appearing in evidence, may cause any person who in such proceeding is to form an opinion upon the evidence, to entertain an erroneous opinion touching any point material to the result of such proceeding, is said "to fabricate false evidence." _{Fabricating false evidence.}

61

Illustrations.

(a) A puts jewels into a box belonging to Z, with the intention that they may be found in that box, and that this circumstance may cause Z to be convicted of theft. A has fabricated false evidence.

(b) A makes a false entry in his shop-book for the purpose of using it as corroborative evidence in a Court of Justice. A has fabricated false evidence.

(c) A, with the intention of causing Z to be convicted of a criminal conspiracy, writes a letter in imitation of Z's handwriting, purporting to be addressed to an accomplice in such criminal conspiracy, and puts the letter in a place which he knows that the officers of the police are likely to search. A has fabricated false evidence.

157. Whoever intentionally gives false evidence in any stage of a judicial proceeding, or fabricates false evidence for the purpose of being used in any stage of a judicial proceeding, shall be punished with imprisonment for a term which may extend to seven years, and shall also be liable to fine;

and whoever intentionally gives or fabricates false evidence in any other case, shall be punished with imprisonment for a term which may extend to three years, and shall also be liable to fine.

Explanation 1.—A trial before a Court-Martial is a judicial proceeding.

Explanation 2.—An investigation directed by law preliminary to a proceeding before a Court of Justice, is a stage of a judicial proceeding, though that investigation may not take place before a Court of Justice.

Illustration.

A, in an enquiry before a Magistrate for the purpose of ascertaining whether Z ought to be committed for trial, makes on oath a statement which he knows to be false. As this enquiry is a stage of a judicial proceeding, A has given false evidence.

Explanation 3.—An investigation directed by a Court of Justice according to law, and conducted under the authority of a Court of Justice, is a stage of a judicial proceeding, though that investigation may not take place before a Court of Justice.

Illustration.

A, in an enquiry before an officer deputed by a Court of Justice to ascertain on the spot the boundaries of land, makes on oath a statement which he knows to be false. As this enquiry is a stage of a judicial proceeding, A has given false evidence.

Marginal note: Punishment for false evidence.

158. Whoever gives or fabricates false evidence, intending thereby to cause, or knowing it to be likely that he will thereby cause, any person to be convicted of an offence which is capital under this Code or under any other law to which such person is amenable, shall be punished with imprisonment for a term which may extend to fourteen years, and shall also be liable to fine; *Giving or fabricating false evidence with intent to procure conviction of capital offence;*

and if an innocent person be convicted and executed in consequence of such false evidence, the person who gives such false evidence shall be punished either with death or with imprisonment for life or for any less term, and shall also be liable to fine. *if innocent person be thereby convicted and executed.*

159. Whoever gives or fabricates false evidence, intending thereby to cause, or knowing it to be likely that he will thereby cause any person to be convicted of an offence which, under this Code or under any other law to which such person is amenable, is not capital but is punishable with imprisonment for a term of seven years or upwards, shall be punished as a person convicted of that offence would be liable to be punished. *Giving or fabricating false evidence with intent to procure conviction of offence punishable with imprisonment.*

160. Whoever corruptly uses or attempts to use, as true or genuine evidence, any evidence which he knows to be false or fabricated, shall be punished in the same manner as if he gave or fabricated false evidence. *Using evidence known to be false.*

161. Whoever issues or signs any certificate required by law to be given or signed, or relating to any fact of which such certificate is by law admissible in evidence, knowing or believing that such certificate is false in any material point, shall be punished in the same manner as if he gave false evidence. *Issuing or signing false certificate.*

162. Whoever corruptly uses or attempts to use any such certificate as a true certificate, knowing the same to be false in any material point, shall be punished in the same manner as if he gave false evidence. *Using as true a certificate known to be false.*

163. Whoever, in any declaration made or subscribed by him, which declaration any Court of Justice, or any public servant or other person, is bound or authorised by law to receive as evidence of any fact, makes any statement which is false, and which he either knows or believes to be false or does not believe to be true, touching any point material to the object for which the declaration is made or used, shall be punished in the same manner as if he gave false evidence. *False statement made in declaration which is by law receivable as evidence.*

164. Whoever corruptly uses or attempts to use as true any such declaration, knowing the same to be false in any material point, shall be punished in the same manner as if he gave false evidence.

Explanation.—A declaration which is inadmissible merely upon the ground of some informality, is a declaration within the meaning of sections 163 and 164.

Of the Screening of Offenders, &c.

165. Whoever, knowing or having reason to believe that an offence has been committed, causes any evidence of the commission of that offence to disappear, with the intention of screening the offender from legal punishment, or with the intention of screening the offender from legal punishment or of preventing his apprehension gives any information respecting the offence which he knows or believes to be false, or harbours or conceals a person whom he knows or has reason to believe to be the offender,

shall, if the offence which he knows or believes to have been committed is punishable with death, be punished with imprisonment for a term which may extend to five years, and shall also be liable to fine;

and if the offence is punishable with imprisonment which may extend to ten years, shall be punished with imprisonment for a term which may extend to three years, and shall also be liable to fine;

and if the offence is punishable with imprisonment for any term not extending to ten years, shall be punished with imprisonment for a term which may extend to one-fourth part of the longest term of the imprisonment provided for the offence, or with fine, or with both.

Exception.—The provisions of this section shall not extend to the case of the harbouring or concealment of an offender by the husband or wife of the offender.

Illustration.

A, knowing that B has murdered Z, assists B to hide the body with the intention of screening B from punishment. A is liable to imprisonment for five years, and also to fine.

166. Whoever accepts or attempts to obtain, or agrees to accept, any gratification for himself or any other person, or any restitution of property to himself or any other

(marginal notes)
Using as true such declaration knowing it to be false.

Screening or harbouring offender;

if a capital offence;

if punishable with ten years' imprisonment;

if punishable with less than ten years' imprisonment.

Taking gift, etc., to screen an offender from punishment, or person, in consideration of his concealing an offence or of his screening any person from legal punishment for any offence, or of his not proceeding against any person for the purpose of bringing him to legal punishment,

or gives or causes, or offers or agrees to give or cause any gratification to any other person, or to restore or cause the restoration of any property to any other person, in consideration of that other person's concealing an offence, or of his screening any person from legal punishment for any offence, or of his not proceeding against any person for the purpose of bringing him to legal punishment,

offering gift or restoration of property in consideration of screening offender—

shall, if the offence is punishable with death, be punished with imprisonment for a term which may extend to five years, and shall also be liable to fine;

if a capital offence;

and if the offence is punishable with imprisonment which may extend to ten years, shall be punished with imprisonment for a term which may extend to three years, and shall also be liable to fine;

if punishable with imprisonment.

and if the offence is punishable with imprisonment not extending to ten years, shall be punished with imprisonment for a term which may extend to one-fourth part of the longest term of imprisonment provided for the offence, or with fine, or with both.

Exception.—The provisions of this section do not extend to any case in which the offence may lawfully be compounded.

Explanation.—In section 165 and in this section the word "offence" includes any act done elsewhere than in a part of the Sudan in which this Code is in force for which the offender could be arrested in such part of the Sudan: and for the purposes of such sections the punishment for the offence shall be deemed to be the same as the punishment would be if the act were done in such part of the Sudan.

167. Whoever, knowing or having reason to believe that any persons are about to commit or have recently committed robbery or brigandage, harbours them or any of them, with the intention of facilitating the commission of such robbery or brigandage or of screening them or any of them from punishment, shall be punished with imprisonment for a term which may extend to seven years, and shall also be liable to fine.

Penalty for harbouring robbers or brigands.

E

Explanation.—For the purposes of this section it is immaterial whether the robbery or brigandage is intended to be committed, or has been committed, within a part of the Sudan in which this Code is in force or elsewhere.

Exception.—This provision does not extend to the case in which the harbour is by the husband or wife of the offender.

Resistance or obstruction to lawful apprehension of another person.

168. Whoever intentionally offers any resistance or illegal obstruction to the lawful apprehension of any other person, or rescues or attempts to rescue any other person from any confinement or custody in which that person is lawfully detained, shall be punished with imprisonment for a term which may extend to two years, or with fine, or with both;

or, if such other person is charged with or liable to be apprehended for an offence punishable with imprisonment for a term which may extend to ten years, shall be punished with imprisonment for a term which may extend to three years, and shall also be liable to fine;

or, if such other person is charged with, or liable to be apprehended for an offence punishable with death, or, is subject, under the sentence of a Court of Justice, or by virtue of a commutation of such a sentence, to imprison-. ment for a term of ten years or upwards, shall be punished with imprisonment for a term which may extend to seven years, and shall also be liable to fine;

or, if such other person is under sentence of death, shall be punished with imprisonment for a term not exceeding ten years, and shall also be liable to fine.

Of Resistance to Apprehension.

Resistance or obstruction by a person to his lawful apprehension.

169. Whoever intentionally offers any resistance or illegal obstruction to the lawful apprehension of himself for any offence with which he is charged or of which he has been convicted, or escapes or attempts to escape from any custody in which he is lawfully detained for any such offence, shall be punished with imprisonment for a term which may extend to two years, or with fine, or with both.

Explanation.—The punishment in this section is in addition to the punishment for which the person to be apprehended or detained in custody, is or may be liable

for any offence with which he is or may be charged, or of
which he has been convicted.

170. Whoever, in any case not provided for in section 169, intentionally offers any resistance or illegal
obstruction to the lawful apprehension of himself, or
escapes or attempts to escape from any custody in which
he is lawfully detained, shall be punished with imprisonment for a term which may extend to six months, or with
fine, or with both.

Resistance or obstruction to lawful apprehension, or escape, in cases not provided for by section 169.

Of Fraudulent Dealings with Property.

171. Whoever, with intent to prevent any property
of himself or any other person, or any interest therein,
from being taken as a forfeiture or in satisfaction of a
fine, under a sentence which has been pronounced, or
which he knows to be likely to be pronounced, by a Court
of Justice or other competent authority,

or from being taken in execution of a decree or order
which has been made, or which he knows to be likely to
be made, by a Court of Justice in a civil suit,

or from being distributed according to law amongst the
creditors of himself or such other person,

or from being available according to law for payment
of the debts of himself or such other person,

dishonestly or fraudulenty removes or conceals or
assists in removing or concealing such property, or dishonestly or fraudulently transfers, delivers, or releases
such property or any interest therein to any person, or
practices any deception touching the same,

or dishonestly or fraudulently accepts, receives, or
claims such property or any interest therein, knowing that
he has no right or rightful claim thereto, shall be punished
with imprisonment for a term which may extend to two
years, or with fine, or with both.

Fraudulent or dishonest dealing with property to prevent its seizure or its application according to law.

Explanation.—In this section, "property" includes
rights of action, and property of every other description,
whether movable or immovable, and whether corporeal or
incorporeal.

172. Whoever fraudulently causes or suffers a decree
or order to be passed against him at the suit of any person for a sum not due, or for a larger sum than is due to
such person, or for any property or interest in property

Fraudulently suffering decree for sum not due.

to which such person is not entitled, or fraudulently causes or suffers a decree or order to be executed against him after it has been satisfied, or for anything in respect of which it has been satisfied, shall be punished with imprisonment for a term which may extend to two years, or with fine, or with both.

Illustration.

A institutes a suit against Z. Z, knowing that A is likely to obtain a decree against him, fraudulently suffers a judgment to pass against him for a large amount at the suit of B, who has no just claim against him, in order that B, either on his own account or for the benefit of Z, may share in the proceeds of any sale of Z's property which may be made under A's decree. Z has committed an offence under this section.

173. Whoever fraudulently obtains a decree or order against any person for a sum not due, or for a larger sum than is due, or for any property or interest in property to which he is not entitled, or fraudulently causes a decree or order to be executed against any person after it has been satisfied or for anything in respect of which it has been satisfied, or fraudulently suffers or permits any such act to be done in his name, shall be punished with imprisonment for a term which may extend to two years, or with fine, or with both.

Fraudulently obtaining decree for sum not due.

174. Whoever dishonestly or fraudulently signs, executes or becomes a party to any deed or instrument which purports to transfer or subject to any charge any property, or any interest therein, and which contains any false statement relating to the consideration for such transfer or charge, or relating to the person or persons for whose use or benefit it is really intended to operate, shall be punished with imprisonment for a term which may extend to two years, or with fine, or with both.

Dishonest or fraudulent execution of deed of transfer containing false statement of consideration.

Miscellaneous.

175. Whoever, knowing or having reason to believe that an offence has been committed, whether in a part of the Sudan in which this Code is in force or elsewhere, gives any information respecting that offence which he knows or believes to be false, shall be punished with imprisonment for a term which may extend to two years, or with fine, or with both.

Giving false information respecting an offence committed.

68

176. Whoever secretes or destroys any document which he may be lawfully compelled to produce as evidence in a Court of Justice. or in any proceeding lawfully held before a public servant as such, or obliterates or renders illegible the whole or any part of such document with the intention of preventing the same from being produced or used as evidence before such Court or public servant as aforesaid. or after he shall have been lawfully summoned or required to produce the same for that purpose. shall be punished with imprisonment for a term which may extend to two years, or with fine, or with both. Destruction of document to prevent its production as evidence.

177. Whoever falsely personates another, and in such assumed character makes any admission or statement, or causes any process to be issued, or becomes bail or security, or does any other act in any suit or criminal prosecution, shall be punished with imprisonment for a term which may extend to three years, or with fine, or with both. False personation for purpose of act or proceeding in suit or prosecution.

178. Whoever, with intent to cause injury to any person, institutes or causes to be instituted any criminal proceeding against that person, or falsely charges any person with having committed an offence, knowing that there is no just or lawful ground for such proceeding or charge against that person, shall be punished with imprisonment for a term which may extend to two years, or with fine, or with both; False charge of offence made with intent to injure.

and if such criminal proceeding be instituted on a false charge of an offence punishable with death or imprisonment for seven years or upwards, shall be punishable with imprisonment for a term which may extend to seven years, and shall also be liable to fine.

179. Whoever takes or agrees or consents to take any gratification under pretence or on account of helping any person to recover any movable property of which he shall have been deprived by any offence punishable under this Code, shall, unless he uses all means in his power to cause the offender to be apprehended and convicted of the offence. be punished with imprisonment for a term which may extend to two years, or with fine, or with both. Taking gift to help to recover stolen property, etc.

180. Whoever intentionally offers any insult, or causes any interruption, to any public servant, while such public servant is sitting in any stage of a judicial proceeding, Intentional insult or interruption to public servant sitting in judicial proceeding.

shall be punished with imprisonment for a term which may extend to six months, or with fine which may extend to L.E. 20, or with both.

CHAPTER XIV.

OF OFFENCES RELATING TO COIN.

"Coin" defined. **181**. Coin is metal used for the time being as money, and stamped and issued by the authority of some State or Sovereign Power in order to be so used.

Counterfeiting coin. **182**. Whoever counterfeits or knowingly performs any part of the process of counterfeiting coin, shall be punished with imprisonment for a term which may extend to seven years, and shall also be liable to fine.

Explanation.—A person commits this offence who, intending to practise deception, or knowing it to be likely that deception will thereby be practised, causes a genuine coin to appear like a different coin.

Making or selling instrument for counterfeiting coin. **183**. Whoever makes or mends, or performs any part of the process of making or mending, or buys, sells or disposes of, any die or instrument, for the purpose of being used, or knowing or having reason to believe that it is intended to be used, for the purpose of counterfeiting coin, shall be punished with imprisonment for a term which may extend to five years, and shall also be liable to fine.

Possession of instrument or material for the purpose of using the same for counterfeiting coin. **184**. Whoever is in possession of any instrument or material, for the purpose of using the same for counterfeiting coin, or knowing or having reason to believe that the same is intended to be used for that purpose, shall be punished with imprisonment for a term which may extend to five years, and shall also be liable to fine.

Import or export of counterfeit coin. **185**. Whoever imports into the Sudan, or exports therefrom, any counterfeit coin, knowing or having reason to believe that the same is counterfeit, shall be punished with imprisonment for a term which may extend to seven years, and shall also be liable to fine.

186. Whoever performs on any coin any operation which alters the appearance of the coin with the intention that the said coin shall pass as a coin of a different description, or fraudulently or dishonestly performs on any coin any operation which diminishes the weight or alters the composition of that coin, shall be punished with imprisonment for a term which may extend to five years, and shall also be liable to fine. *[Altering appearance of coin or fraudulently or dishonestly diminishing weight or altering composition of coin.]*

Explanation.—A person who scoops out part of a coin and puts anything else into the cavity, alters the composition of that coin.

187. Whoever, having in his possession counterfeit coin or coin with respect to which an offence under section 186 has been committed, and having known at the time when he became possessed of such coin that such coin was counterfeit or that such offence had been committed with respect to it, fraudulently, or with intent that fraud may be committed, delivers such coin to any other person, or attempts to induce any other person to receive the same, shall be punished with imprisonment for a term which may extend to seven years, and shall also be liable to fine. *[Delivery of coin possessed with knowledge that it is counterfeit or altered.]*

188. Whoever, fraudulently or with intent that fraud may be committed, is in possession of counterfeit coin or coin with respect to which an offence under section 186 has been committed, having known at the time of becoming possessed thereof that such coin was counterfeit or that such offence had been committed with respect to it, shall be punished with imprisonment for a term which may extend to five years, and shall also be liable to fine. *[Possession of coin by person who knew it to be counterfeit or altered when he became possessed thereof.]*

189. Whoever delivers to any other person as genuine, or attempts to induce any other person to receive as genuine, any counterfeit coin which he knows to be counterfeit, but which he did not know to be conterfeit at the time when he took it into his possession, shall be punished with imprisonment for a term which may extend to two years, or with fine to an amount which may extend to ten times the value of the coin counterfeited, or with both. *[Delivery of coin as genuine, which, when first possessed, the deliverer did not know to be counterfeit.]*

190. Whoever delivers to any other person as genuine or as a coin of a different description from what it is, or attempts to induce any person to receive as genuine, or as a different coin from what it is, any coin in respect of which he knows that any such operation as is mentioned *[Delivery of coin as genuine, which, when first possessed, the deliverer did not know to be altered.]*

in section 186 has been performed, but in respect of which
he did not, at the time when he took it into his possession,
know that such operation had been performed, shall be
punished with imprisonment for a term which may extend
to two years, or with fine to an amount which may extend
to ten times the value of the coin for which the altered
coin is passed or attempted to be passed, or with both.

CHAPTER XV.

OF OFFENCES RELATING TO REVENUE STAMPS.

"Revenue stamp"
defined.
191. Every stamp issued for the purpose of revenue
by or on behalf of any of the Governments of the Sudan,
Egypt and Great Britain, or, as to stamps issued for postal
purposes, by or on behalf of any Government, is called a
"revenue stamp."

Counterfeiting
revenue stamp.
192. Whoever counterfeits, or knowingly performs
any part of the process of counterfeiting, any revenue
stamp, shall be punished with imprisonment for a term
which may extend to ten years, and shall also be liable
to fine.

Explanation.—A person commits this offence who
counterfeits by causing a genuine stamp of one denomination to appear like a genuine stamp of a different
denomination.

Having pos-
session of instru-
ment or material
for counterfeiting
revenue stamp.
193. Whoever has in his possession any instrument or
material for the purpose of being used, or knowing or
having reason to believe that it is intended to be used,
for the purpose of counterfeiting any revenue stamp, shall
be punished with imprisonment for a term which may
extend to seven years, and shall also be liable to fine.

Making or selling
instrument for
counterfeiting
revenue stamp.
194. Whoever makes or performs any part of the
process of making, or buys, or sells, or disposes of; any
instrument for the purpose of being used, or knowing or
having reason to believe that it is intended to be used,
for the purpose of counterfeiting any revenue stamp, shall
be punished with imprisonment for a term which may
extend to seven years, and shall also be liable to fine.

195. Whoever uses as genuine, sells, or offers for sale, any stamp which he knows or has reason to believe to be a counterfeit of any revenue stamp, shall be punished with imprisonment for a term which may extend to seven years, and shall also be liable to fine. *Use or sale of counterfeit revenue stamp.*

196. Whoever has in his possession any stamp which he knows to be a counterfeit of any revenue stamp, intending to use or dispose of the same as a genuine stamp, or in order that it may be used as a genuine stamp, shall be punished with imprisonment for a term which may extend to seven years, and shall also be liable to fine. *Having possession of counterfeit revenue stamp.*

197. Whoever, fraudulently or with intent to cause loss to any Government, removes or effaces from any substance bearing any revenue stamp, any writing or document for which such stamp has been used, or removes from any writing or document a stamp which has been used for such writing or document, in order that such stamp may be used for a different writing or document, shall be punished with imprisonment for a term which may extend to three years, or with fine, or with both. *Effacing writing from substances bearing revenue stamp, or removing from document a stamp used for it, with intent to cause loss.*

198. Whoever, fraudulently or with intent to cause loss to any Government, uses for any purpose any revenue stamp which he knows to have been before used, shall be punished with imprisonment for a term which may extend to two years, or with fine, or with both. *Using revenue stamp known to have been before used.*

199. Whoever fraudulently or with intent to cause loss to any Government, erases or removes from any revenue stamp, any mark put or impressed upon such stamp for the purpose of denoting that the same has been used, or knowingly has in his possession, or sells or disposes of, any such stamp from which such mark has been erased or removed, or sells or disposes of any such stamp which he knows to have been used, shall be punished with imprisonment for a term which may extend to three years, or with fine, or with both. *Erasure of mark denoting that stamp has been used.*

CHAPTER XVI.

OF OFFENCES RELATING TO WEIGHTS AND MEASURES.

200. Whoever fraudulently uses any instrument for weighing which he knows to be false, shall be punished *Fraudulent use of false instrument for weighing.*

73

with imprisonment for a term which may extend to one year, or with fine, or with both.

Fraudulent use of false weight or measure.

201. Whoever fraudulently uses any false weight or false measure of length or capacity, or fraudulently uses any weight or any measure of length or capacity as a different weight or measure from what it is, shall be punished with imprisonment for a term which may extend to one year, or with fine, or with both.

Being in possession of false weight or measure.

202. Whoever is in possession of any instrument for weighing, or of any weight, or of any measure of length or capacity, which he knows to be false, and intending that the same may be fraudulently used, shall be punished with imprisonment for a term which may extend to one year, or with fine, or with both.

Making or selling false weight or measure.

203. Whoever makes, sells, or disposes of any instrument for weighing, or any weight, or any measure of length or capacity which he knows to be false, in order that the same may be used as true, or knowing that the same is likely to be used as true, shall be punished with imprisonment for a term which may extend to one year, or with fine, or with both.

CHAPTER XVII.

OF OFFENCES AFFECTING THE PUBLIC HEALTH, SAFETY, CONVENIENCE, DECENCY, AND MORALS.

Public nuisance.

204. A person is guilty of a public nuisance who does any act, or is guilty of an illegal omission, which causes any common injury, danger, or annoyance to the public or to the people in general who dwell or occupy property in the vicinity, or which must necessarily cause injury, obstruction, danger, or annoyance to persons who may have occasion to use any public right.

A common nuisance is not excused on the ground that it causes some convenience or advantage.

Explanation.—Whether an act or omission is a public nuisance is a matter of fact, which may depend on the character of the neighbourhood.

Conferring powers of 2nd. Class Magistrates on Mamurs.

++

Kanuni,Cairo.

458 In order to protect natives recommend Mamurs

be given powers 2nd. Class magistrate to sit at

Summary Courts on offences under sections 200 ,
201 & 202 of Penal Code during date harvest namel
1st. Oct: to 30th. Nov: stop All such Summary
Courts to be submitted to Mudir or Inspectors for
approval. (Signed) Mudir
Dongola,9.10.02.

Mudir,Dongola.
555 As special case Hakimam approves conferring
on Mamurs powers Magistrates 2nd. Class sections
200,201 & 202 during date harvest for Summary
Courts Proceedings to be submitted you or Inspector.   (Signed) Bonham Carter.
Cairo,11.10.02.

---

noxious, sells the same, or offers or exposes it for sale, or
issues it from any dispensary for medicinal purposes as
unadulterated, or causes it to be used for medicinal purposes by any person not knowing of the adulteration,
shall be punished with imprisonment for a term which
may extend to six months, or with fine which may extend
to L.E. 20, or with both.

209. Whoever knowingly sells, or offers or exposes
for sale, or issues from a dispensary for medicinal purposes, any drug or medical preparation, as a different drug
or medical preparation, shall be punished with imprisonment for a term which may extend to six months, or
with fine which may extend to L.E. 20, or with both.

Sale of drug as a different drug r prepamtion.

Public nuisance.   **204.** A person is guilty of a public nuisance who does any act, or is guilty of an illegal omission, which causes any common injury, danger, or annoyance to the public or to the people in general who dwell or occupy property in the vicinity, or which must necessarily cause injury, obstruction, danger, or annoyance to persons who may have occasion to use any public right.

A common nuisance is not excused on the ground that it causes some convenience or advantage.

Explanation.—Whether an act or omission is a public nuisance is a matter of fact, which may depend on the character of the neighbourhood.

Illustration.

A powerful steam whistle sounded at intervals during the day, which might be a public nuisance in a residential quarter, may not be a public nuisance in a manufacturing quarter.

205. Whoever adulterates any article of food or drink, so as to make such article noxious as food or drink, intending to sell such article as food or drink, or knowing it to be likely that the same will be sold as food or drink, shall be punished with imprisonment for a term which may extend to six months, or with fine which may extend to L.E. 20, or with both.

Adulteration of food or drink intended for sale.

206. Whoever sells, or offers or exposes for sale, as food or drink, any article which has been rendered or has become noxious, or is in a state unfit for food or drink, knowing or having reason to believe that the same is noxious as food or drink, shall be punished with imprisonment for a term which may extend to six months, or with fine which may extend to L.E. 20, or with both.

Sale of noxious food or drink.

207. Whoever adulterates any drug or medical preparation in such a manner as to lessen the efficacy, or change the operation, of such drug or medical preparation, or to make it noxious, intending that it shall be sold or used for, or knowing it to be likely that it will be sold or used for, any medicinal purpose as if it had not undergone such adulteration, shall be punished with imprisonment for a term which may extend to six months, or with fine which may extend to L.E. 20, or with both.

Adulteration of drugs.

208. Whoever, knowing any drug or medical preparation to have been adulterated in such a manner as to lessen its efficacy, to change its operation, or to render it noxious, sells the same, or offers or exposes it for sale, or issues it from any dispensary for medicinal purposes as unadulterated, or causes it to be used for medicinal purposes by any person not knowing of the adulteration, shall be punished with imprisonment for a term which may extend to six months, or with fine which may extend to L.E. 20, or with both.

Sale of adulterated drugs.

209. Whoever knowingly sells, or offers or exposes for sale, or issues from a dispensary for medicinal purposes, any drug or medical preparation, as a different drug or medical preparation, shall be punished with imprisonment for a term which may extend to six months, or with fine which may extend to L.E. 20, or with both.

Sale of drug as a different drug or preparation.

75

Fouling water of public spring or reservoir.

210. Whoever voluntarily corrupts or fouls the water of any public spring or reservoir, so as to render it less fit for the purpose for which it is ordinarily used, shall be punished with imprisonment for a term which may extend to three months, or with fine which may extend to L.E. 10, or with both.

Making atmosphere noxious to health.

211. Whoever voluntarily vitiates the atmosphere in any place so as to make it noxious to the health of persons in general dwelling or carrying on business in the neighbourhood or passing along a public way, shall be punished with fine which may extend to L.E. 10.

Exhibition of false light, mark or buoy.

212. Whoever exhibits any false light, mark, or buoy, intending or knowing it to be likely that such exhibition will mislead any navigator, shall be punished with imprisonment for a term which may extend to seven years, or with fine, or with both.

Obstruction in public way or line of navigation.

213. Whoever, by doing any act, or by omitting to take order with any property in his possession or under his charge, causes obstruction to any person in any public way or public line of navigation, shall be punished with fine which may extend to L.E. 5.

Negligent conduct causing danger to person or property.

214. Whoever does any act in a manner so rash or negligent as to endanger human life, or to be likely to cause hurt or injury to any person or property,

or knowingly or negligently omits to take such order with any property or substance in his possession or under his control, or with any operations under his control, as is sufficient to guard against probable danger to human life from such property, substance, or operations, shall be punished with imprisonment for a term which may extend to six months, or with fine which may extend to L.E. 20, or with both.

Negligent conduct with respect to animal.

215. Whoever knowingly or negligently omits to take such order with any animal in his possession as is sufficient to guard against any probable danger to human life, or any probable danger of grievous hurt from such animal, shall be punished with imprisonment for a term which may extend to six months, or with fine which may extend to L.E. 20, or with both.

Punishment for public nuisance in cases not otherwise provided for.

216. Whoever commits a public nuisance in any case not otherwise punishable by this Code, shall be punished with fine which may extend to L.E. 5.

217. Whoever repeats or continues a public nuisance, having been enjoined by any public servant who has lawful authority to issue such injunction not to repeat or continue such nuisance, shall be punished with imprisonment for a term which may extend to six months, or with fine, or with both.

Continuance of nuisance after injunction to discontinue.

218. Whoever, to the annoyance of others, does any obscene or indecent act in a public place, shall be punished with imprisonment for a term which may extend to one year, or with fine, or with both.

Obscene or indecent acts.

219. Whoever sells or distributes, imports or prints foresale or hire, or wilfully exhibits to public view, any obscene book, pamphlet, paper, drawing, painting, representation or figure, or attempts, or offers so to do, or has in his possession any such obscene book or other thing for the purpose of sale, distribution, or public exhibition, shall be punished with imprisonment for a term which may extend to three months, or with fine, or with both.

Sale, etc., of obscene books, etc.

220. Whoever, to the annoyance of others, sings, recites or utters any obscene song, ballad or words, in or near any public place, shall be punished with imprisonment for a term which may extend to three months, or with fine, or with both.

Obscene songs, etc.

221. Whoever keeps any office or place for the purpose of drawing any lottery, shall be punished with imprisonment for a term which may extend to six months, or with fine, or with both.

Keeping lottery-office.

And whoever publishes any proposal to pay any sum, or to deliver any goods, or to do or forbear doing anything for the benefit of any person, on any event or contingency relative or applicable to the drawing of any ticket, lot, number or figure in any such lottery, shall be punished with fine which may extend to L.E. 20.

222. Whoever keeps any house or place whereto the public are admitted for the purpose of playing any game of chance, or assists in the conduct of any such house or place, shall be punished with imprisonment for a term which may extend to six months, or with fine, or with both.

Keeping gaming house,

And whoever is found in any such house or place, shall be punished with imprisonment for a term which may extend to one month, or with fine, or with both.

Being found in gaming house.

CHAPTER XVIII.

Of Offences relating to Religion.

Injuring or defiling place of worship, with intent to insult the religion of any class. **223.** Whoever destroys, damages, or defiles any place of worship, or any object held sacred by any class of persons with the intention of thereby insulting the religion of any class of persons, or with the knowledge that any class of persons is likely to consider such destruction, damage or defilement as an insult to their religion, shall be punished with imprisonment for a term which may extend to two years, or with fine, or with both.

Disturbing religious assembly. **224.** Whoever voluntarily causes disturbance to any assembly lawfully engaged in the performance of religious worship, or religious ceremonies, shall be punished with imprisonment for a term which may extend to one year, or with fine, or with both.

Trespassing on burial-places, etc. **225.** Whoever, with the intention of wounding the feelings of any person, or of insulting the religion of any person, or with the knowledge that the feelings of any person are likely to be wounded, or that the religion of any person is likely to be insulted thereby,

commits any trespass in any place of worship or on any place of sepulture, or offers any indignity to any human corpse, or causes disturbance to any persons assembled for the performance of funeral ceremonies, shall be punished with imprisonment for a term which may extend to one year, or with fine, or with both.

CHAPTER XIX.

Of Offences affecting the Human Body.

Of Offences affecting Life.

Culpable homicide. **226.** Whoever causes death by doing an act with the intention of causing death, or with the intention of causing such bodily injury as is likely to cause death, or with the knowledge that he is likely by such act to cause death, commits the offence of culpable homicide.

(*a*) A lays sticks and turf over a pit, with the intention of thereby causing death. or with the knowledge that death is likely to be thereby caused. Z, believing the ground to be firm, treads on it, fall in and is killed. A has committed the offence of culpable homicide.

(*b*) A knows Z to be behind a bush. B does not know it. A intending to cause, or knowing it to be likely to cause Z's death, induces B to fire at the bush. B fires and kills Z. Here B may be guilty of no offence ; but A has committed the offence of culpable homicide.

(*c*) A. by shooting at a fowl with intent to kill and steal it, kills B, who is behind a bush ; A not knowing that he was there. Here, although A was doing an unlawful act, he was not guilty of culpable homicide, as he did not intend to kill B, or cause death by doing an act that he knew was likely to cause death.

Explanation 1.—A person who causes bodily injury to another who is labouring under a disorder, disease or bodily infirmity, and thereby accelerates the death of that other, shall be deemed to have caused his death.

Explanation 2.—Where death is caused by bodily injury, the person who causes such bodily injury shall be deemed to have caused the death, although by resorting to proper remedies and skilful treatment the death might have been prevented.

Explanation 3.—The causing of the death of a child in the mother's womb is not homicide. But it may amount to culpable homicide to cause the death of a living child, if any part of that child has been brought forth, though the child may not have breathed or been completely born.

227. Except in the cases excepted by section 228, culpable homicide is murder, if the act by which the death is caused is done with the intention of causing death, or if the doer of the act knew or had reason to know that death would be the probable consequence of the act, or of any bodily injury which the act was intended to cause. Murder.

• *Explanation.*—Whether death was the probable, or only a likely, consequence of an act, or of any bodily injury, is a question of fact.

(*a*) A shoots Z with the intention of killing him. Z dies in consequence. A commits murder.

(*b*) A, knowing that Z is labouring under such a disease that a blow would probably cause his death, strikes him with the intention of causing bodily injury. Z dies in consequence of the blow. A is guilty of murder, although the blow might not have been sufficient to cause the death of a person in a sound state of health. But if A, not knowing that Z is labouring under any disease, gives him such a blow as would not ordinarily kill a person in a sound state of health, here A, although he may intend to cause bodily injury, is not necessarily guilty of murder.

(*c*) A points a loaded revolver at Z at a distance of ten paces and fires. Z is killed. Here A is guilty of murder. But if Z had been almost out of range. A, unless he intended to kill Z, would not have been guilty of murder.

(*d*) A without any excuse fires a loaded cannon into a crowd of persons and kills one of them. A is guilty of murder, although he may not have had a premeditated design to kill any particular individual.

When culpable homicide is not murder.

228. (*1*) Culpable homicide is not murder if the offender, whilst deprived of the power of self-control by grave and sudden provocation, causes the death of the person who gave the provocation, or causes the death of any other person by mistake or accident.

Explanation.—Whether the provocation was grave and sudden enough to prevent the offence from amounting to murder is a question of fact.

Illustrations.

(*a*) A, under the influence of passion excited by a provocation given by Z, intentionally kills Y, Z's child. This is murder, inasmuch as the provocation was not given by the child, and the death of the child was not caused by accident or misfortune in doing an act caused by the provocation.

(*b*) Y gives grave and sudden provocation to A. A, on this provocation, fires a pistol at Y, neither intending nor knowing himself to be likely to kill Z, who is near him, but out of sight. A kills Z, Here A has not committed murder, but merely culpable homicide. (See section 229.)

(*c*) Z strikes B. B is by this provocation excited to violent rage. A, a bystander, intending to take advantage of B's rage, and to cause him to kill Z, puts a knife into B's hand for that purpose. B kills Z with the knife. Here B may have committed only culpable homicide, but A is guilty of murder.

(*2*) Culpable homicide is not murder if the offender, in the exercise in good faith of the right of private defence of person or property, exceeds the power given to him by law and causes the death of the person against whom he is exercising such right of defence without premeditation, and without any intention of doing more harm than is necessary for the purpose of such defence.

(*3*) Culpable homicide is not murder if the offender, being a public servant or aiding a public servant acting for the advancement of public justice, exceeds the powers given to him by law, and causes death by doing an act which he, in good faith, believes to be lawful and necessary for the due discharge of his duty as such public servant and without ill-will towards the person whose death is caused.

(*4*) Culpable homicide is not murder if it is committed without premeditation in a sudden fight in the heat of passion upon a sudden quarrel and without the offender's having taken undue advantage or acted in a cruel or unusual manner.

Explanation.—It is immaterial in such cases which party offers the provocation or commits the first assault.

(*5*) Culpable homicide is not murder when the person whose death is caused, being above the age of eighteen years, suffers death or takes the risk of death with his own consent.

229. If a person, by doing anything which he intends or knows to be likely to cause death, commits culpable homicide by causing the death of any person whose death he neither intends nor knows himself to be likely to cause, the culpable homicide committed by the offender is of the description of which it would have been if he had caused the death of the person whose death he intended or knew himself to be likely to cause. *Culpable homicide by causing death of person other than person whose death was intended.*

230. Whoever commits murder shall be punished with death, or imprisonment for life, and shall also be liable to fine. *Punishment for murder.*

231. Whoever, being under sentence of imprisonment for life, commits murder, shall be punished with death. *Punishment for murder by life-convict.*

232. Whoever commits culpable homicide not amounting to murder, shall be punished with imprisonment for life or for any less term, or with fine, or with both. *Punishment for culpable homicide not amounting to murder.*

233. Whoever causes the death of any person by doing any rash or negligent act not amounting to culpable homicide, shall be punished with imprisonment for a term which may extend to two years, or with fine, or with both. *Causing death by negligence.*

234. If any person under eighteen years of age, any insane person, any delirious person, any idiot, or any person in a state of intoxication commits suicide, whoever abets the commission of such suicide, shall be punished *Abetment of suicide of child or insane person.*

F

with death, or imprisonment for life or for any less term, and shall also be liable to fine.

Abetment of suicide.

235. If any person commits suicide, whoever abets the commission of such suicide, shall be punished with imprisonment for a term which may extend to ten years, and shall also be liable to fine.

Attempt to murder.

236. Whoever does any act with such intention or knowledge and under such circumstances, that if he by that act caused death, he would be guilty of murder, shall be punished with imprisonment for a term which may extend to ten years, and shall also be liable to fine; and, if hurt is caused to any person by such act, the imprisonment may extend to fourteen years.

Attempts by life-convicts.

When any person offending under this section is under sentence of imprisonment for life, he may, if hurt is caused, be punished with death.

Illustrations.

(*a*) A shoots at Z with intention to kill him, under such circumstances that, if death ensued, A would be guilty of murder. A is liable to punishment under this section.

(*b*) A with the intention of causing the death of a child of tender years exposes it in a desert place. A has committed the offence defined by this section, though the death of the child does not ensue.

(*c*) A, intending to murder Z, buys a gun and loads it. A has not yet committed the offence. A fires the gun at Z. He has committed the offence defined in this section, and if by such firing he wounds Z, he is liable to the punishment provided by the latter part of the first paragraph of this section.

(*d*) A, intending to murder Z by poison, purchases poison and mixes the same with food which remains in A's keeping; A has not yet committed the offence in this section. A places the food on Z's table or delivers it to Z's servants to place it on Z's table. A has committed the offence defined in this section.

Attempt to commit culpable comicide.

237. Whoever does any act with such intention or knowledge, and under such circumstances that, if he by that act caused death, he would be guilty of culpable homicide not amounting to murder, shall be punished with imprisonment for a term which may extend to three years, or with fine, or with both; if hurt is caused to any person by such act, the imprisonment may extend to seven years.

Illustration.

A, on grave and sudden provocation, fires a pistol at Z, under such circumstances that if he thereby caused death he would be guilty of culpable homicide not amounting to murder. A has committed the offence defined in this section.

238. Whoever attempts to commit suicide and does any act towards the commission of such offence, shall be punished with imprisonment for a term which may extend to one year, or with fine, or with both.

Attempt to commit suicide.

Of the Causing of Miscarriage, of Injuries to unborn Children, of the Exposure of Infants, and of the Concealment of Births.

239. Whoever voluntarily causes a woman with child to miscarry, shall, if such miscarriage be not caused in good faith for the purpose of saving the life of the woman, be punished with imprisonment for a term which may extend to three years, or with fine, or with both; and, if the woman be quick with child, shall be punished with imprisonment for a term which may extend to seven years, and shall also be liable to fine.

Causing miscarriage.

Explanation.—A woman who causes herself to miscarry, is within the meaning of this section.

240. Whoever commits the offence defined in the last preceding section without the consent of the woman, whether the woman is quick with child or not, shall be punished with imprisonment for a term which may extend to ten years, and shall also be liable to fine.

Causing miscarriage without woman's consent.

241. Whoever, with intent to cause the miscarriage of a woman with child, does any act which causes the death of such woman, shall be punished with imprisonment for a term which may extend to ten years, and shall also be liable to fine;

Death caused by act done with intent to cause miscarriage;

if the act is done without the consent of the woman, the imprisonment may be for life or for any less term.

if act done without woman's consent.

Explanation.—It is not essential to this offence that the offender should know that the act is likely to cause death.

242. Whoever before the birth of any child does any act with the intention of thereby preventing that child from being born alive or causing it to die after its birth, and does by such act prevent that child from being born alive, or causes it to die after its birth, shall, if such act be not caused in good faith for the purpose of saving the life of the mother, be punished with imprisonment for a

Act done with intent to prevent child being born alive or to die after birth.

term which may extend to ten years, or with fine, or with both.

Causing death of quick unborn child by act amounting to culpable homicide.

243. Whoever does any act under such circumstances, that if he thereby caused death he would be guilty of culpable homicide, and does by such act cause the death of a quick unborn child, shall be punished with imprisonment for a term which may extend to ten years, and shall also be liable to fine.

Illustration.

A, knowing that he is likely to cause the death of a pregnant woman, does an act which, if it caused the death of the woman, would amount to culpable homicide. The woman is injured but does not die; but the death of an unborn quick child with which she is pregnant is thereby caused. A is guilty of the offence defined in this section.

Exposure and abandonment of child under twelve years, by parent or person having care of it.

244. Whoever being the father or mother of a child under the age of twelve years, or having the care of such child, shall expose or leave such child in any place with the intention of wholly abandoning such child, shall be punished with imprisonment for a term which may extend to seven years, or with fine, or with both.

Explanation.—This section is not intended to prevent the trial of the offender for murder or culpable homicide as the case may be, if the child die in consequence of the exposure.

Concealment of birth by secret disposal of dead body.

245. Whoever, by secretly burying or otherwise disposing of the dead body of a child, whether such child die before or after or during its birth, intentionally conceals or endeavours to conceal the birth of such child, shall be punished with imprisonment for a term which may extend to two years, or with fine, or with both.

Of Hurt.

Hurt.

246. Whoever causes bodily pain, disease, or infirmity to any person is said to cause hurt.

Grievous hurt.

247. The following kinds of hurt only are designated as "grievous":—

First.—Emasculation.

Secondly.—Permanent privation of the sight of either eye.

Thirdly.—Permanent privation of the hearing of either ear.

Fourthly.—Privation of any member or joint.

Fifthly.—Destruction or permanent impairing of the powers of any member, or joint.

Sixthly.—Permanent disfiguration of the head or face.

Seventhly.—Fracture or dislocation of a bone or tooth.

Eighthly.—Any hurt which endangers life or which causes the sufferer to be, during the space of twenty days, in severe bodily pain, or unable to follow his ordinary pursuits.

248. Whoever does any act with the intention of thereby causing hurt to any person, or with the knowledge that he is likely thereby to cause hurt to any person, and does thereby cause hurt to any person, is said "voluntarily to cause hurt." *Voluntarily causing hurt.*

249. Whoever voluntarily causes hurt, if the hurt which he intends to cause or knows himself to be likely to cause is grievous hurt, and if the hurt which he causes is grievous hurt, is said "voluntarily to cause grievous hurt." *Voluntarily causing grievous hurt.*

Explanation.—A person is not said voluntarily to cause grievous hurt except when he both causes grievous hurt, and intends or knows himself to be likely to cause grievous hurt. But he is said voluntarily to cause grievous hurt if, intending or knowing himself to be likely to cause grievous hurt of one kind, he actually causes grievous hurt of another kind.

Illustration.

A, intending or knowing himself to be likely permanently to disfigure Z's face, gives Z a blow which does not permanently disfigure Z's face, but which causes Z to suffer severe bodily pain for the space of twenty days. A has voluntarily caused grievous hurt.

250. Whoever voluntarily causes hurt on grave and sudden provocation, if he neither intends nor knows himself to be likely to cause hurt to any person other than the person who gave the provocation, shall be punished with imprisonment for a term which may extend to one month, or with fine which may extend to L.E. 10, or with both. *Voluntarily causing hurt on provocation.*

Voluntarily causing grievous hurt on provocation. **251.** Whoever voluntarily causes grievous hurt on grave and sudden provocation, if he neither intends nor knows himself to be likely to cause grievous hurt to any person other than the person who gave the provocation, shall be punished with imprisonment for a term which may extend to four years, or with fine which may extend to L.E. 50, or with both.

Punishment for voluntarily causing hurt. **252.** Whoever, except in the case provided for by section 250, voluntarily causes hurt, shall be punished with imprisonment for a term which may extend to one year, or with fine which may extend to L.E.20, or with both.

Punishment for voluntarily causing grievous hurt. **253.** Whoever, except in the case provided by section 251, voluntarily causes grievous hurt, shall be punished with imprisonment for a term which may extend to seven years, and shall also be liable to fine.

Voluntarily causing hurt by dangerous weapon or means. **254.** (*1*) Whoever, except in the case provided for by section 250, voluntarily causes hurt by means of any instrument for shooting, stabbing, or cutting, or any instrument, which, used as a weapon of offence, is likely to cause death, or by means of fire or any heated substance, or by means of any corrosive or explosive substance, or by the administration of any poisonous or deleterious substance, or by means of any animal, shall be punished with imprisonment for a term which may extend to three years, or with fine, or with both.

If the hurt be grievous. (*2*) Whoever, except in the case provided by section 251, voluntarily causes grievous hurt by any such means, shall be punished with imprisonment for a term which may extend to fourteen years, and shall also be liable to fine.

Causing hurt by means of poison, etc., with intent to commit an offence. **255** Whoever administers to or causes to be taken by any person any poison or any stupefying, intoxicating, or unwholesome drug or thing, with intent to cause hurt to such person, or with intent to commit or to facilitate the commission of an offence, or knowing it to be likely that he will thereby cause hurt, shall be punished with imprisonment for a term which may extend to ten years, and shall also be liable to fine.

Voluntarily causing hurt to extort property, or to constrain to an illegal act. **256.** (*1*) Whoever voluntarily causes hurt for the purpose of extorting from the sufferer, or from any person interested in the sufferer, any property or valuable security, or of constraining the sufferer or any person interested in the sufferer to do anything which is illegal or which may facilitate the commission of an offence, shall be punished with imprisonment for a term which may extend to ten years, and shall also be liable to fine.

(*2*) Whoever, for the like purpose, voluntarily causes grievous hurt, shall be punished with imprisonment for a term which may extend to fourteen years, and shall also be liable to fine.

[margin: If the hurt be grievous.]

257. (*1*) Whoever voluntarily causes hurt, for the purpose of extorting from the sufferer or any person interested in the sufferer any confession or any information which may lead to the detection of an offence or misconduct, or for the purpose of constraining the sufferer or any person interested in the sufferer to restore, or to cause the restoration of any property or valuable security or to satisfy any claim or demand, or to give information which may lead to the restoration of any property or valuable security, shall be punished with imprisonment for a term which may extend to seven years, and shall also be liable to fine.

[margin: Voluntarily causing hurt to extort confession, or to compel restoration of property.]

(*2*) Whoever, for the like purpose, voluntarily causes grievous hurt, shall be punished with imprisonment for a term which may extend to ten years, and shall also be liable to fine.

[margin: If the hurt be grievous.]

Illustrations.

(*a*) A, a police-officer, tortures Z in order to induce Z to confess that he committed a crime. A is guilty of an offence under this section.

(*b*) A, a police-officer, tortures B to induce him to point out where certain stolen property is deposited. A is guilty of an offence under this section.

(*c*) A, a revenue-officer, tortures Z in order to compel him to pay certain arrears of revenue due from Z. A is guilty of an offence under this section.

(*d*) A, a land-owner, tortures a fellah in order to compel him to pay his rent. A is guilty of an offence under this section.

258. (*1*) Whoever voluntarily causes hurt to any person being a public servant in the discharge of his duty as such public servant, or with intent to prevent or deter that person or any other public servant from discharging his duty as such public servant, or in consequence of anything done or attempted to be done by that person in the lawful discharge of his duty as such public servant, shall

[margin: Voluntarily causing hurt to deter public servant from his duty.]

be punished with imprisonment for a term which may extend to three years, or with fine, or with both.

If the hurt be grievous. (*2*) Whoever, under the like circumstances, with the like intent, or for like reason, voluntarily causes grievous hurt to any person being a public servant, shall be punished with imprisonment for a term which may extend to ten years, and shall also be liable to fine.

Causing hurt by act endangering life or personal safety of others. **259.** (*1*) Whoever causes hurt to any person by doing any act so rashly or negligently as to endanger human life, or the personal safety of others, shall be punished with imprisonment for a term which may extend to six months, or with fine which may extend to L.E. 10, or with both.

If the hurt be grievous. (*2*) Whoever, in like manner, causes grievous hurt to any person, shall be punished with imprisonment for a term which may extend to two years, or with fine which may extend to L.E. 20, or with both.

Of Wrongful Restraint and Wrongful Confinement.

Wrongful restraint. **260.** Whoever voluntarily obstructs any person so as to prevent that person from proceeding in any direction in which that person has a right to proceed, is said "wrongfully to restrain" that person.

Exception.—The obstruction of a private way over land or water which a person in good faith believes himself to have a lawful right to obstruct, is not an offence within the meaning of this section.

Illustration.

A obstructs a path along which Z has a right to pass, A not believing in good faith that he has a right to stop the path. Z is thereby prevented from passing. A wrongfully restrains Z.

Wrongful confinement. **261.** Whoever wrongfully restrains any person in such a manner as to prevent that person from proceeding beyond certain circumscribing limits, is said "wrongfully to confine" that person.

Illustrations.

(*a*) A causes Z to go within a walled space, and locks Z in. Z is thus prevented from proceeding in any direction beyond the circumscribing line of wall. A wrongfully confines Z.

(*b*) A places men with firearms at the outlets of a building, and tells Z that they will fire at Z if Z attempts to leave the building. A wrongfully confines Z.

262. Whoever wrongfully restrains any person, shall be punished with imprisonment for a term which may extend to one month, or with fine which may extend to L.E. 10, or with both. *Punishment for wrongful restraint.*

263. Whoever wrongfully confines any person, shall be punished with imprisonment for a term which may extend to one year, or with fine which may extend to L.E. 20, or with both. *Punishment for wrongful confinement.*

264. Whoever wrongfully confines any person for three days, or more, shall be punished with imprisonment for a term which may extend to two years, or with fine, or with both. *Wrongful confinement for three or more days.*

265. Whoever wrongfully confines any person for ten days, or more, shall be punished with imprisonment for a term which may extend to three years, and shall also be liable to fine. *Wrongful confinement for ten or more days.*

266. Whoever keeps any person in wrongful confinement, knowing that a writ for the liberation of that person has been duly issued, shall be punished with imprisonment for a term which may extend to two years in addition to any term of imprisonment to which he may be liable under any other section of this Chapter. *Wrongful confinement of person for whose liberation writ has been issued.*

267. Whoever wrongfully confines any person in such manner as to indicate an intention that the confinement of such person may not be known to any person interested in the person so confined, or to any public servant, or that the place of such confinement may not be known to or discovered by any such person or public servant as hereinbefore mentioned, shall be punished with imprisonment for a term which may extend to two years in addition to any other punishment to which he may be liable for such wrongful confinement. *Wrongful confinement in secret.*

268. Whoever wrongfully confines any person for the purpose of extorting from the person confined, or from any person interested in the person confined, any property or valuable security, or of constraining the person confined or any person interested in such person to do anything illegal or to give any information which may facilitate the commission of an offence, shall be punished with imprison- *Wrongful confinement to extort property or constraint to illegal act.*

'ment for a term which may extend to three years, and
shall also be liable to fine.

Wrongful confinement to extort confession, or compel restoration of property.

269. Whoever wrongfully confines any person for the
purpose of extorting from the person confined, or any
person interested in the person confined, any confession
or any information which may lead to the detection of an
offence or misconduct, or for the purpose of constraining
the person confined or any person interested in the person
confined to restore or to cause the restoration of any
property or valuable security- or to satisfy any claim or
demand, or to give information which may lead to the
restoration of any property or valuable security, shall be
punished with imprisonment for a term which may extend
to three years, and shall also be liable to fine.

Of Criminal Force and Assault.

Force.

270. A person is said to use force to another if he
causes motion, change of motion, or cessation of motion
to that other, or if he causes any substance to come into
contact with any part of that other's body, or with anything which that other is wearing or carrying, or with
anything so situated that such contact affects that other's
sense of feeling: provided that the person causing any
effect above-mentioned, causes it

First.—By his own bodily power; or

Secondly.—By disposing any substance in such a manner
that the effect takes place without any further voluntary
act on his part, or on the part of any other person, or

Thirdly.—By means of any animal.

Illustrations.

(*a*) A unfastens the moorings of a boat in which Z is sitting, so
that the boats drifts down the river. A has caused motion to Z.

(*b*) A lashes the horse on which Z is riding, so that the horse
quickens his pace. A has caused change of motion to Z.

(*c*) A seizes the rein of Z's horse and stops the horse. A has
caused cessation of motion to Z.

(*d*) A pushes against Z in the street. A has caused his own body
to come into contact with Z.

(*e*) A throws a stone at Z and hits him.

(*f*) A rides past Z on a muddy road and splashes him.

(*g*) A pulls up the veil of Z, a woman.

(*h*) A pours boiling water into the bath in which Z is bathing. A has caused the boiling water to come into contact with the water in the bath, so as to affect Z's sense of feeling.

(*i*) A incites a dog to spring upon Z.

In all the above cases, A has used force to Z.

271. Whoever intentionally uses force to any person, Criminal force. without that person's consent, in order to the committing of any offence, or intending by the use of such force to cause, or knowing it to be likely that by the use of such force he will cause injury, fear, or annoyance to the person to whom the force is used, is said to use criminal force to that other.

272. Whoever makes any gesture, or any preparation, Assault. intending or knowing it to be likely that such gesture or preparation will cause any person present to apprehend that he who makes that gesture or preparation is about to use criminal force to that person, is said to commit an assault.

Explanation.—Mere words do not amount to an assault. But the words which a person uses may give to his gestures or preparations such a meaning as may make those gestures or preparations amount to an assault.

Illustrations.

(*a*) A shakes his fist at Z, intending or knowing it to be likely that he may thereby cause Z to believe that A is about to strike Z. A has committed an assault.

(*b*) A begins to unloose the muzzle of a ferocious dog, intending, or knowing it to be likely that he may thereby cause Z to believe that he is about to cause the dog to attack Z. A has committed an assault upon Z.

(*c*) A takes up a stick, saying to Z, "I will give you a beating." Here, though the words used by A could in no case amount to an assault, and though the mere gesture, unaccompanied by any other circumstances, might not amount to an assault, the gesture explained by the words may amount to an assault.

273. Whoever assaults or uses criminal force to any Punishment for assault or criminal force person otherwise than on grave and sudden provocation otherwise than given by that person, shall be punished with imprison- on grave provocation. ment for a term which may extend to three months, or with fine which may extend to L.E. 10, or with both.

274. Whoever assaults or uses criminal force to any Assault or criminal force person on grave and sudden provocation given by that on grave provocation. person, shall be punished with imprisonment for a term which may extend to one month, or with fine which may extend to L.E. 5, or with both.

Assault or criminal force to deter public servant from discharge of his duty.

275. Whoever assaults or uses criminal force to any person being a public servant in the execution of his duty as such public servant, or with intent to prevent or deter that person from discharging his duty as such public servant, or in consequence of anything done or attempted to be done by such person in the lawful discharge of his duty as such public servant, shall be punished with imprisonment for a term which may extend to two years, or with fine, or with both.

Assault or criminal force to woman with intent to outrage her modesty.

276. Whoever assaults or uses criminal force to any woman, intending to outrage or knowing it to be likely that he will thereby outrage her modesty, shall be punished with imprisonment for a term which may extend to two years, or with fine, or with both.

Assault or criminal force in attempt to commit theft of property carried by a person.

277. Whoever assaults or uses criminal force to any person, in attempting to commit theft on any property which that person is then wearing or carrying, shall be punished with imprisonment for a term which may extend to two years, or with fine, or with both.

Assault or criminal force in attempt wrongfully to confine a person.

278. Whoever assaults or uses criminal force to any person, in attempting wrongfully to confine that person, shall be punished with imprisonment for a term which may extend to one year, or with fine which may extend to L.E. 20, or with both.

Of Kidnapping, Abduction, and Forced Labour.

Kidnapping.

279. Whoever takes or entices any minor under fourteen years of age if a male, or under sixteen years of age if a female, or any person of unsound mind, out of the keeping of the lawful guardian of such minor or person of unsound mind, without the consent of such guardian, or conveys any such minor or any person of unsound mind beyond the limits of the Sudan without the consent of some person legally authorized to consent to such removal, is said to kidnap such minor or person of unsound mind.

Explanation.—The words "lawful guardian" in this section include any person lawfully entrusted with the care or custody of such minor or other person and authorized to consent to the taking.

280. Whoever by force compels, or by any deceitful means induces, any person to go from any place, is said to abduct that person. ^{Abduction.}

Abduction.

281. Whoever kidnaps any person shall be punished with imprisonment for a term which may extend to seven years, and shall also be liable to fine.

Punishment for kidnapping.

282. Whoever kidnaps or abducts any person in order that such person may be murdered or may be so disposed of as to be put in danger of being murdered, shall be punished with imprisonment for a term which may extend to fourteen years, and shall also be liable to fine.

Kidnapping or abducting in order to murder.

283. Whoever kidnaps or abducts any person with intent to cause that person to be secretly and wrongfully confined, shall be punished with imprisonment for a term which may extend to seven years, and shall also be liable to fine.

Kidnapping or abducting with intent secretly and wrongfully to confine person.

284. Whoever kidnaps or abducts any woman with intent that she may be compelled, or knowing it to be likely that she will be compelled, to marry any person against her will, or in order that she may be forced or seduced to illicit intercourse, or knowing it to be likely that she will be forced or seduced to illicit intercourse, shall be punished with imprisonment for a term which may extend to ten years, and shall also be liable to fine.

Kidnapping or abducting woman to compel her marriage, etc.

285. Whoever kidnaps or abducts any person in order that such person may be subjected, or may be so disposed of as to be put in danger of being subjected, to grievous hurt, or to the unnatural lust of any person, or knowing it to be likely that such person will be so subjected or disposed of, shall be punished with imprisonment for a term which may extend to ten years, and shall also be liable to fine.

Kidnapping or abducting in order to subject person to grievous hurt, etc.

286. Whoever, knowing that any person has been kidnapped or has been abducted, wrongfully conceals or confines such person, shall be punished in the same manner as if he had kidnapped or abducted such person with the same intention or knowledge, or for the same purpose as that with or for which he conceals or detains such person in confinement.

Wrongfully concealing or keeping in confinement kidnapped or abducted person.

287. Whoever buys, sells, hires, lets to hire, or otherwise obtains possession or disposes of any minor under the age of sixteen years, with intent that such minor shall

Buying or selling minor for purpose of prostitution, etc.

93

be employed or used for the purpose of prostitution or for any unlawful or immoral purpose, or knowing it to be likely that such minor will be employed or used for any such purpose, shall be punished with imprisonment for a term which may extend to ten years, and shall also be liable to fine.

Unlawful compulsory labour.

288. Whoever unlawfully compels any person to labour against the will of that person, shall be punished with imprisonment for a term which may extend to one year, or with fine, or with both.

Kidnapping or abducting in order to subject or unlawful compulsory labour.

289. Whoever kidnaps or abducts any person, with intent that such person may be unlawfully compelled to labour against his will, shall be punished with imprisonment for a term which may extend to seven years, and shall also be liable to fine.

Transferring control of person with intent to subject to unlawful confinement or unlawful compulsory labour.

290. Whoever, for money or money's worth, transfers or purports to transfer the control of the person of any man or woman to another person, with intent to enable such other person to unlawfully confine such man or woman, or to unlawfully compel him or her to labour against his or her will, shall be punished with imprisonment for a term which may extend to seven years, and shall also be liable to fine.

Of Rape.

Rape.

291. A man is said to commit "rape," who, except in the case hereinafter excepted, has sexual intercourse with a woman against her will, or without her consent.

Explanation.—Penetration is sufficient to constitute the sexual intercourse necessary to the offence of rape.

Exception.—Sexual intercourse by a man with his own wife is not rape, if she has attained to puberty.

Punishment for rape.

292. Whoever commits rape shall be punished with imprisonment for a term which may extend to fourteen years, and shall also be liable to fine.

Of Unnatural Offences.

Unnatural offences.

293. Whoever has carnal intercourse against the order of nature with any man or woman without his or her consent, shall be punished with imprisonment for a term

94

which may extend to fourteen years, and shall also be liable to fine.

Explanation.—Penetration is sufficient to constitute the carnal intercourse necessary to the offence described in this section.

CHAPTER XX.

Of Offences against Property.

Of Theft.

294. Whoever, intending to take dishonestly any Theft. movable property out of the possession of any person without that person's consent, moves that property in order to such taking, is said to commit theft.

Explanation 1.—A thing so long as it is attached to the earth, not being movable property, is not the subject of theft; but it becomes capable of being the subject of theft as soon as it is severed from the earth.

Explanation 2.—A moving effected by the same act which effects the severance, may be a theft.

Explanation 3.—A person is said to cause a thing to move by removing an obstacle which prevented it from moving, or by separating it from any other thing, as well as by actually moving it.

Explanation 4.—A person, who by any means causes an animal to move, is said to move that animal, and to move everything which, in consequence of the motion so caused, is moved by that animal.

Explanation 5.—The consent mentioned in the definition may be express or implied, and may be given either by the person in possession, or by any person having for that purpose authority either express or implied.

Illustrations.

(a) A cuts down a tree on Z's ground, with the intention of dishonestly taking the tree out of Z's possession, without Z's consent. Here, as soon as A has severed the tree, in order to such taking, he has committed theft.

(*b*) A puts a bait for dogs in his pocket, and thus induces Z's dog to follow him. Here, if A's intention be dishonestly to take the dog out of Z's possession without Z's consent, A has committed theft as soon as Z's dog has begun to follow A.

(*c*) A meets a camel carrying a box of treasure. He drives the camel in a certain direction, in order that he may dishonestly take the treasure. As soon as the camel begins to move, A has committed theft of the treasure.

(*d*) A, being Z's servant, and entrusted by Z with the care of Z's jewellery, dishonestly runs away with the jewellery, without Z's consent. A has committed theft.

(*e*) Z, going on a journey, entrusts jewellery to A, till Z shall return. A carries the jewellery to the market and sells it. Here the jewellery was not in Z's possession. It could not therefore be taken out of Z's possession, and A has not committed theft, though he may have committed criminal breach of trust.

(*f*) A finds a ring belonging to Z on a table in the house which Z occupies. Here the ring is in Z's possession, and if A dishonestly removes it, A commits theft.

(*g*) A finds a ring lying on the high-road, not in the possession of any person. A, by taking it, commits no theft, though he may commit criminal misappropriation of property.

(*h*) A sees a ring belonging to Z lying on a table in Z's house. Not venturing to misappropriate the ring immediately for fear of search and detection, A hides the ring in a place where it is highly improbable that it will ever be found by Z, with the intention of taking the ring from the hiding place and selling it when the loss is forgotten. Here A, at the time of first moving the ring, commits theft.

(*i*) A delivers a jewel to Z, a jeweller, to be re-set. Z carries it to his shop. A, not owing to the jeweller any debt for which the jeweller might lawfully detain the jewel as a security, enters the shop openly, takes his jewel by force out of Z's hand, and carries it away. Here A, though he may have committed criminal trespass and assault, has not committed theft, inasmuch as what he did was not done dishonestly.

(*j*) If A owes money to Z for re-setting the jewel, and if Z retains the jewel lawfully as a security for the debt, and A takes the jewel out of Z's possession, with the intention of depriving Z of the property as a security for his debt, he commits theft, inasmuch as he takes it dishonestly.

(*k*) Again if A, having pawned an article to Z, takes it out of Z's possession without Z's consent, not having paid what he borrowed on the article, he commits theft, though the article is his own property, inasmuch as he takes it dishonestly.

(*l*) A takes an article belonging to Z out of Z's possession, without Z's consent, with the intention of keeping it until he obtains money from Z as a reward for its restoration. Here A takes dishonestly; A has therefore committed theft.

(*m*) A, being on friendly terms with Z, goes into Z's house in Z's absence, and takes away a cooking-pot without Z's express consent, with the intention of returning it after use. Here, it is probable that A may have conceived that he had Z's implied consent to use Z's cooking-pot   If this was A's impression, A has not committed theft.

(*n*) A asks charity from Z's wife. She gives A money, food and clothes, which A knows to belong to Z, her husband.   Here it is probable that A may conceive that Z's wife is authorized to give away alms.   If this was A's impression, A has not committed theft.

(*o*) A is the paramour of Z's wife. She gives A valuable property, which A knows to belong to her husband Z, and to be such property as she has not authority from Z to give. If A takes the property dishonestly, he commits theft.

(*p*) A in good faith, believing property belonging to Z to be A's own property, takes that property out of B's possession. Here, as A does not take dishonestly, he does not commit theft.

295. Whoever commits theft shall be punished with imprisonment for a term which may extend to three years, or with fine, or with both. Punishment for theft.

296. Whoever commits theft in any building, tent or vessel, which building, tent or vessel is used as a human dwelling, or used for the custody of property, shall be punished with imprisonment for a term which may extend to seven years, or with fine, or with both. Theft in dwelling-house, etc.

297. Whoever being a clerk or servant, or being employed in the capacity of a clerk or servant, commits theft in respect of any property in the possession of his master or employer, shall be punished with imprisonment for a term which may extend to seven years, or with fine, or with both. Theft by clerk or servant of property in possession of master.

298. Whoever commits theft, having made preparation for causing death, or hurt, or restraint, or fear of death, or of hurt, or of restraint, to any person, in order to the committing of such theft, or in order to the effecting of his escape after the committing of such theft, or in order to the retaining of property taken by such theft, shall be punished with imprisonment for a term which may extend to ten years, and shall also be liable to fine. Theft after preparation made for causing death, hurt or restraint, in order to the committing of the theft.

Illustrations.

(*a*) A commits theft on property in Z's possession; and, while committing this theft, he has a loaded pistol under his garment, having provided this pistol for the purpose of hurting Z in case Z should resist. A has committed the offence defined in this section.

(*b*) A picks Z's pocket, having posted several of his companions near him, in order that they may restrain Z, if Z should perceive what is passing and should resist, or should attempt to apprehend A.   A has committed the offence defined in this section.

Of Extortion.

Extortion. **299.** Whoever intentionally puts any person in fear of any injury to that person, or to any other, and thereby dishonestly induces the person so put in fear to deliver to any person any property or valuable security or anything signed or sealed which may be converted into a valuable security, commits "extortion."

Illustrations.

(a) A threatens to publish a defamatory libel concerning Z, unless Z gives him money. He thus induces Z to give him money. A has committed extortion.

(b) A threatens Z that he will keep Z's child in wrongful confinement, unless Z will sign and deliver to A a promissory note, binding Z to pay certain moneys to A. Z signs and delivers the note. A has committed extortion.

(c) A threatens to send men to pull up Z's crops, unless Z will sign and deliver to B a bond binding Z under a penalty to deliver certain produce to B, and thereby induces Z to sign and deliver the bond. A has committed extortion.

(d) A, by putting Z in fear of grievous hurt, dishonestly induces Z to sign or affix his seal to a blank paper and deliver it to A. Z signs and delivers the paper to A. Here, as the paper so signed may be converted into a valuable security, A has committed extortion.

Punishment for extortion. **300.** Whoever commits extortion shall be punished with imprisonment for a term which may extend to three years, or with fine, or with both.

Putting person in fear of injury in order to commit extortion. **301.** Whoever, in order to the committing of extortion, puts any person in fear, or attempts to put any person in fear, of any injury, shall be punished with imprisonment for a term which may extend to two years, or with fine, or with both.

Extortion by putting a person in fear of death or grievous hurt. **302.** Whoever commits extortion by putting any person in fear of death or of grievous hurt to that person or to any other, shall be punished with imprisonment for a term which may extend to ten years, and shall also be liable to fine.

Putting person in fear of death or of grievous hurt, in order to commit extortion. **303.** Whoever, in order to the committing of extortion, puts or attempts to put any person in fear of death or of grievous hurt to that person or to any other, shall be punished with imprisonment for a term which may extend to seven years, and shall also be liable to fine.

Extortion by threat of accusation of **304.** Whoever commits extortion by putting any person in fear of an accusation against that person or any other, of having committed or attempted to commit any offence punishable with death, or with imprisonment for a term which may extend to ten years, or of having attempted to induce any other person to commit such offence, shall be punished with imprisonment for a term which may extend to ten years, and shall also be liable to fine. *an offence punishable with death.*

305. Whoever, in order to the committing of extortion, puts or attempts to put any person in fear of an accusation, against that person or any other, of having committed or attempted to commit an offence punishable with death or with imprisonment for a term which may extend to ten years, shall be punished with imprisonment for a term which may extend to ten years, and shall also be liable to fine. *Putting person in fear of accusation of offence, in order to commit extortion.*

Of Robbery and Brigandage.

306. In all robbery there is either theft or extortion. *Robbery.*

Theft is "robbery," if, in order to the committing of the theft, or in committing the theft, or in carrying away or attempting to carry away property obtained by the theft, the offender, for that end, voluntarily causes or attempts to cause to any person death or hurt or wrongful restraint, or fear of instant death, or of instant hurt, or of instant wrongful restraint. *When theft is robbery.*

Extortion is "robbery," if the offender, at the time of committing the extortion, is in the presence of the person put in fear, and commits the extortion by putting that person in fear of instant death, of instant hurt, or of instant wrongful restraint to that person, or to some other person, and, by so putting in fear, induces the person so put in fear then and there to deliver up the thing extorted. *When extortion is robbery.*

Explanation.—The offender is said to be present if he is sufficiently near to put the other person in fear of instant death, of instant hurt, or of instant wrongful restraint.

Illustrations.

(a) A holds Z down, and fraudulently takes Z's money and jewels from Z's clothes, without Z's consent. Here A has committed theft, and, in order to the committing of that theft, has voluntarily caused wrongful restraint to Z. A has therefore committed robbery.

(b) A meets Z on the high-road, shows a pistol, and demands Z's purse. Z, in consequence, surrenders his purse. Here A has extorted the purse from Z by putting him in fear of instant hurt, and being at the time of committing the extortion in his presence. A has therefore committed robbery.

(*c*) A meets Z and Z's child on the river bank. A takes the child, and threatens to fling into the river, unless Z delivers his purse. Z, in consequence, delivers his purse. Here A has extorted the purse from Z, by causing Z to be in fear of instant hurt to the child who is there present. A has therefore committed robbery on Z.

(*d*) A obtains property from Z by saying—"Your child is in the hands of my gang, and will be put to death unless you send us L.E. 50." This is extortion, and punishable as such: but it is not robbery, unless Z is put in fear of the instant death of his child.

Brigandage. **307.** When five or more persons conjointly commit or attempt to commit a robbery, or where the whole number of persons conjointly committing or attempting to commit a robbery, and persons present and aiding such commission or attempt, amount to five or more, every person so committing, attempting or aiding, is said to commit "brigandage."

Punishment for robbery. **308.** Whoever commits robbery shall be punished with imprisonment for a term which may extend to ten years, and shall also be liable to fine; and, if the robbery be committed between sunset and sunrise, and on the highway or from a person sleeping or having lain down to sleep in the open air, the imprisonment may be extended to fourteen years.

Attempt to commit robbery. **309.** Whoever attempts to commit robbery shall be punished with imprisonment for a term which may extend to seven years, and shall also be liable to fine.

Voluntarily causing hurt in committing robbery. **310.** If any person, in committing or in attempting to commit robbery, voluntarily causes hurt, such person, and any other person jointly concerned in committing or attempting to commit such robbery, shall be punished with imprisonment for a term which may extend to fourteen years, and shall also be liable to fine.

Punishment for brigandage. **311.** Whoever commits brigandage shall be punished with imprisonment for a term which may extend to fourteen years, and shall also be liable to fine.

Brigandage with murder. **312.** If any one of five or more persons, who are conjointly committing brigandage, commits murder in so committing brigandage, every one of those persons shall be punished with death, or imprisonment for life or for any less term, and shall also be liable to fine.

313. If, at the time of committing robbery or brigandage, the offender uses any deadly weapon, or causes grievous hurt to any person, or attempts to cause death or grievous hurt to any person, the imprisonment with which such offender shall be punished shall not be less than seven years.' Robbery or brigandage, with attempt to cause death or grievous hurt.

314. Whoever makes any preparation for committing brigandage, shall be punished with imprisonment for a term which may extend to ten years, and shall also be liable to fine. Making preparation to commit brigandage.

315. Whoever shall belong to a gang of persons associated for the purpose of habitually committing brigandage, shall be punished with imprisonment for a term which may extend to fourteen years, and shall also be liable to fine. Punishment for gang of brigands.

316. Whoever shall belong to any wandering or other gang of persons associated for the purpose of habitually committing theft or robbery, and not being a gang of brigands, shall be punished with imprisonment for a term which may extend to seven years, and shall also be liable to fine. Punishment for belonging to gang of thieves.

317. Whoever shall be one of five or more persons assembled for the purpose of committing brigandage, shall be punished with imprisonment for a term which may extend to seven years, and shall also be liable to fine. Assembling for purpose of committing brigandage.

Of Criminal Misappropriation of Property.

318. Whoever dishonestly misappropriates or converts to his own use any movable property, shall be punished with imprisonment for a term which may extend to two years, or with fine, or with both. Dishonest misappropriation of property.

Illustrations.

(a). A takes property belonging to Z out of Z's possession, in good faith believing, at the time when he takes it, that the property belongs to himself. A is not guilty of theft; but if A, after discovering his mistake, dishonestly appropriates the property to his own use, he is guilty of an offence under this section.

(b) A, being on friendly terms with Z, goes into Z's house in Z's absence, and takes away a cooking-pot without Z's express consent. Here, if A was under the impression that he had Z's implied consent to take the cooking-pot for the purpose of using it, A has not committed theft. But, if A afterwards sells the cooking-pot for his own benefit he is guilty of an offence under this section.

(c) A and B being joint owners of a horse, A takes the horse out of B's possession, intending to use it. Here, as A has a right to use the horse, he does not dishonestly misappropriate it. But if A sells the horse and appropriates the whole proceeds to his own use, he is guilty of an offence under this section.

Explanation 1.—A dishonest misappropriation for a time only is a misappropriation within the meaning of this section.

Illustration.

A having borrowed Z's property, pledges it as a security for a loan, intending at a future time to restore it to Z. A has committed an offence under this section.

Explanation 2.—A person who finds property not in the possession of any other person, and takes such property for the purpose of protecting it for, or of restoring it to, the owner, does not take or misappropriate it dishonestly, and is not guilty of an offence; but he is guilty of the offence above defined, if he appropriates it to his own use, when he knows or has the means of discovering the owner, or before he has used reasonable means to discover and give notice to the owner and has kept the property a reasonable time to enable the owner to claim it.

What are reasonable means, or what is a reasonable time in such a case, is a question of fact.

It is not necessary that the finder should know who is the owner of the property, or that any particular person is the owner of it: it is sufficient if, at the time of appropriating it, he does not believe it to be his own property, or in good faith believe that the real owner cannot be found.

Illustrations.

(a) A finds a coin on the high-road, not knowing to whom the coin belongs. A picks up the coin. Here A has not committed the offence defined in this section.

(b) A finds a letter on the road, containing a bank note. From the direction and contents of the letter he learns to whom the note belongs. He appropriates the note. He is guilty of an offence under this section.

(c) A finds a cheque payable to bearer. He can form no conjecture as to the person who has lost the cheque. But the name of the person who has drawn the cheque appears. A knows that this person can direct him to the person in whose favour the cheque was drawn. A appropriates the cheque without attempting to discover the owner. He is guilty of an offence under this section.

102

(*d*) A sees Z drop his purse with money in it. A picks up the purse with the intention of restoring it to Z, but afterwards appropriates it to his own use. A has committed an offence under this section.

(*e*) A finds a purse with money, not knowing to whom it belongs; he afterwards discovers that it belongs to Z, and appropriates it to his own use. A is guilty of an offence under this section.

(*f*) A finds a valuable ring, not knowing to whom it belongs. A sells it immediately without attempting to discover the owner. A is guilty of an offence under this section.

319. Whoever dishonestly misappropriates or converts to his own use property, knowing that such property was in the possession of a deceased person at the time of that person's decease, and has not since been in the possession of any person legally entitled to such possession, shall be punished with imprisonment for a term which may extend to three years, and shall also be liable to fine; and, if the offender at the time of such person's decease was employed by him as a clerk or servant, the imprisonment may extend to seven years.

Dishonest misappropriation of property possessed by deceased person at the time of his death.

Illustration.

Z dies in possession of furniture and money. His servant A, before the money comes into the possession of any person entitled to such possession, dishonestly misappropriates it. A has committed the offence defined in this section.

Of Criminal Breach of Trust.

320. Whoever, being in any manner entrusted with property, or with any dominion over property, dishonestly misappropriates or converts to his own use that property, or dishonestly uses or disposes of that property in violation of any direction of law prescribing the mode in which such trust is to be discharged, or of any legal contract, express or implied, which he has made touching the discharge of such trust, or wilfully suffers any other person so to do, commits "criminal breach of trust."

Criminal breach of trust.

Illustrations.

(*a*) A being executor to the will of a deceased person, dishonestly disobeys the law which directs him to divide the effects according to the will, and appropriates them to his own use. A has committed criminal breach of trust.

(*b*) A is a warehouse-keeper. Z, going on a journey, entrusts his furniture to A, under a contract that it shall be returned on payment of a stipulated sum for warehouse-room. A dishonestly sells the goods. A has committed criminal breach of trust.

(*c*) A, residing in Khartoum, is agent for Z, residing at Senar. There is an express or implied contract betwen A and Z, that all sums remitted by Z to A shall be invested by A according to Z's direction. Z remits a sum of money to A, with directions to A to invest the same in Egyptian Government securities. A dishonestly disobeys the directions, and employs the money in his own business. A has committed criminal breach of trust.

(*d*) But if A, in the last illustration, not dishonestly but in good faith, believing that it will be more for Z's advantage to hold Bank shares, disobeys Z's directions and buys Bank shares for Z, instead of buying Government securities, here, though Z should suffer loss, and should be entitled to bring a civil action against A on account of that loss, yet A, not having acted dishonestly, has not committed criminal breach of trust.

(*e*) A, a revenue-officer, is entrusted with public money, and is either directed by law, or bound by a contract, express or implied, with the Government, to pay into a certain treasury all the public money which he holds. A dishonestly appropriates the money. A has committed criminal breach of trust.

(*f*) A, a carrier, is entrusted by Z with property to be carried by land or by water. A dishonestly misappropriates the property. A has committed criminal breach of trust.

Punishment for criminal breach of trust. **321.** Whoever commits criminal breach of trust shall be punished with imprisonment for a term which may extend to three years, or with fine or with both.

Criminal breach of trust by carrier, etc. **322.** Whoever, being entrusted with property as a carrier, wharfinger or warehouse-keeper, commits criminal breach of trust in respect of such property, shall be punished with imprisonment for a term which may extend to seven years, and shall also be liable to fine.

Criminal breach of trust by clerk or servant. **323.** Whoever, being a clerk or servant or employed as a clerk or servant, and being in any manner entrusted in such capacity with property, or with any dominion over property, commits criminal breach of trust in respect of that property, shall be punished with imprisonment for a term which may extend to seven years, and shall also be liable to fine.

Criminal breach of trust by public servant, or by banker, merchant or agent. **324.** Whoever, being in any manner entrusted with property, or with any dominion over property, in his capacity of a public servant or in the way of his business as a banker, merchant, factor, broker, attorney or agent, commits criminal breach of trust in respect of that property, shall be punished with imprisonment for a term which may extend to ten years, and shall also be liable to fine.

Of the Receiving of Stolen Property.

325. Property the possession whereof has been trans- _{Stolen property.} ferred by theft, or by extortion, or by robbery, and property which has been criminally misappropriated or in respect of which criminal breach of trust has been committed, is designated as "stolen property," whether the transfer has been made, or the misappropriation or breach of trust has been committed, within a part of the Sudan in which this Code is in force or elsewhere. But, if such property subsequently comes into the possession of a person legally entitled to the possession thereof, it then ceases to be stolen property.

326. Whoever dishonestly receives or retains any stolen _{Dishonestly receiving stolen property.} property, knowing or having reason to believe the same to be stolen property, shall be punished with imprisonment for a term which may extend to three years, or with fine, or with both.

327. Whoever dishonestly receives or retains any stolen _{Dishonestly receiving property stolen in the commission of brigandage.} property, the possession whereof he knows or has reason to believe to have been transferred by the commission of brigandage, or dishonestly receives from a person, whom he knows or has reason to believe to belong or to have belonged to a gang of brigands, property which he knows or has reason to believe to have been stolen, shall be punished with imprisonment for a term which may extend to fourteen years, and shall also be liable to fine.

328. Whoever habitually receives or deals in property _{Habitually dealing in stolen property.} which he knows or has reason to believe to be stolen property, shall be punished with imprisonment for a term which may extend to fourteen years, and shall also be liable to fine.

329. Whoever voluntarily assists in concealing or dis- _{Assisting in concealment of stolen property.} posing of or making away with property which he knows or has reason to believe to be stolen property, shall be punished with imprisonment for a term which may extend to three years, or with fine, or with both.

Of Cheating.

330. Whoever, by deceiving any person, fraudulently _{Cheating.} or dishonestly induces the person so deceived to deliver any property to any person, or to consent that any person shall retain any property, or intentionally induces the person so deceived to do or omit to do anything which he would not do or omit if he were not so deceived, and which act or omission causes or is likely to cause damage or harm to that person in body, mind, reputation, or property, is said to "cheat."

Explanation.—A dishonest concealment of facts is a deception within the meaning of this section.

Illustrations.

(*a*) A, by falsely pretending to be in the Government service, intentionally deceives Z, and thus dishonestly induces Z to let him have on credit goods for which he does not mean to pay. A cheats.

(*b*) A, by putting a counterfeit mark on an article, intentionally deceives Z into a belief that this article was made by a certain celebrated manufacturer, and thus dishonestly induces Z to buy and pay for the article. A cheats.

(*c*) A, by exhibiting to Z a false sample of an article, intentionally deceives Z into believing that the article corresponds with the sample, and thereby dishonestly induces Z to buy and pay for the article. A cheats.

(*d*) A, by tendering in payment for an article a cheque on a bank with which A keeps no money, and by which A expects that the cheque will be dishonoured, intentionally deceives Z, and thereby dishonestly induces Z to deliver the article, intending not to pay for it. A cheats.

(*e*) A, by pledging as diamonds articles which he knows are not diamonds, intentionally deceives Z, and thereby dishonestly induces Z to lend money. A cheats.

(*f*) A intentionally deceives Z into a belief that A means to repay any money that Z may lend to him, and thereby dishonestly induces Z to lend him money, A not intending to repay it. A cheats.

(*g*) A intentionally deceives Z into a belief that A means to deliver to Z a certain quantity of dhura which A does not intend to deliver, and thereby dishonestly induces Z to advance money upon the faith of such delivery. A cheats; but if A, at the time of obtaining the money, intends to deliver the dhura, and afterwards breaks his contract and does not deliver it, he does not cheat, but is liable only to a civil action for breach of contract.

(*h*) A intentionally deceives Z into a belief that A has performed A's part of a contract made with Z, which he has not performed, and thereby dishonestly induces Z to pay money. A cheats.

(*i*) A sells and conveys an estate to B. A, knowing that in consequence of such sale he has no right to the property, then sells or mortgages the same to Z, without disclosing the fact of the previous sale and conveyance to B, and receives the purchase or mortgage money from Z. A cheats.

331. A person is said to "cheat by personation" if he cheats by pretending to be some other person, or by knowingly substituting one person for another, or

Cheating by personation.

representing that he or any other person is a person other than he or such other person really is.

Explanation.—The offence is committed whether the individual personated is a real or imaginary person.

Illustrations.

(*a*) A cheats by pretending to be a certain rich banker of the same name. A cheats by personation.

(*b*) A cheats by pretending to be B, a person who is deceased. A cheats by personation.

332. Whoever cheats shall be punished with imprisonment for a term which may extend to one year, or with fine, or with both.

Punishment for cheating.

333. Whoever cheats with the knowledge that he is likely thereby to cause wrongful loss to a person whose interest in the transaction to which the cheating relates, he was bound either by law, or by a legal contract, to protect, shall be punished with imprisonment for a term which may extend to three years, or with fine, or with both.

Cheating with knowledge that wrongful loss may ensue to person whose interest offender is bound to protect.

334. Whoever cheats by personation shall be punished with imprisonment for a term which may extend to three years, or with fine, or with both.

Punishment for cheating by personation.

335. Whoever cheats and thereby dishonestly induces the person deceived to deliver any property to any person, or to make, alter, or destroy the whole or any part of a valuable security, or anything which is signed or sealed, and which is capable of being converted into a valuable security, shall be punished with imprisonment for a term which may extend to seven years, and shall also be liable to fine.

Cheating and dishonestly inducing delivery of property.

Of Mischief.

336. Whoever, with intent to cause, or knowing that he is likely to cause wrongful loss or damage to the public or to any person, causes the destruction of any property, or any such change in any property, or in the situation thereof as destroys or diminishes its value or utility, or affects it injuriously, commits "mischief."

Mischief.

Explanation 1.—It is not essential to the offence of mischief that the offender should intend to cause loss or damage to the owner of the property injured or destroyed. It is sufficient if he intends to cause, or knows that he is likely to cause, wrongful loss or damage to any person by injuring any property, whether it belongs to that person or not.

Explanation 2.—Mischief may be committed by an act affecting property belonging to the person who commits the act, or to that person and others jointly.

Illustrations.

(*a*) A voluntary burns a valuable security belonging to Z, intending to cause wrongful loss to Z. A has committed mischief.

(*b*) A voluntarily throws into a river a ring belonging to Z, with the intention of thereby causing wrongful loss to Z. A has committed mischief.

(*c*) A, knowing that his effects are about to be taken in execution in order to satisfy a debt due from him to Z, destroys those effects, with the intention of thereby preventing Z from obtaining satisfaction of the debt, and of thus causing damage to Z. A has committed mischief.

(*d*) A, having joint property with Z in a horse, shoots the horse, intending thereby to cause wrongful loss to Z. A has committed mischief.

(*e*) A causes cattle to enter upon a field belonging to Z, intending to cause or knowing that he is likely to cause damage to Z's crop. A has committed mischief.

Punishment for mischief. **337.** Whoever commits mischief shall be punished with imprisonment for a term which may extend to three months, or with fine, or with both.

Mischief causing damage to the amount of P.T. 200. **338.** Whoever commits mischief and thereby causes loss or damage to the amount of P.T. 200 or upwards, shall be punished with imprisonment for a term which may extend to two years, or with fine, or with both.

Mischief by killing or maiming animal of the value of P.T. 75. **339.** Whoever commits mischief by killing, poisoning, maiming or rendering useless any animal or animals of the value of P.T. 75 or upwards, shall be punished with imprisonment for a term which may extend to two years, or with fine, or with both.

Mischief by killing or maiming cattle, etc., of any value or any animal of the value of P.T. 300. **340.** Whoever commits mischief by killing, poisoning, maiming, or rendering useless, any camel, horse, mule, buffalo, bull, cow or ox, whatever may be the value thereof, or any other animal of the value of P.T. 300 or upwards, shall be punished with imprisonment for a term which may extend to five years, or with fine, or with both.

341. Whoever commits mischief by doing any act which causes, or which he knows to be likely to cause, a diminution of the supply of water for agricultural purposes, or for food or drink for human beings or for animals which are property, or for cleanliness or for carrying on any manufacture, shall be punished with imprisonment for a term which may extend to five years, or with fine, or with both.

Mischief by injury to works of irrigation or by wrongfully diverting water.

342. Whoever commits mischief by doing any act which renders or which he knows to be likely to render any public road, railway, bridge, navigable river, or navigable channel, natural or artificial, impassable or less safe for travelling or conveying property, shall be punished with imprisonment for a term which may extend to five years, or with fine, or with both.

Mischief by rendering road, railway, bridge, river or channel.

343. Whoever commits mischief by doing any act which causes or which he knows to be likely to cause an inundation or an obstruction to any public drainage attended with injury or damage, shall be punished with imprisonment for a term which may extend to five years, or with fine, or with both.

Mischief by causing inundation or obstruction to public drainage attended with damage.

344. Whoever commits mischief by destroying or moving any light-house or other light used as a sea-mark, or any sea-mark or buoy or other thing placed as a guide for navigators, or by any act which renders any such light-house, sea-mark, buoy, or other such thing as aforesaid less useful as a guide for navigators, shall be punished with imprisonment for a term which may extend to seven years, or with fine, or with both.

Mischief by destroying, moving or rendering less useful a light-house or sea-mark.

345. Whoever commits mischief by destroying or moving any land-mark fixed by the authority of a public servant, or by any act which renders such land-mark less useful as such, shall be punished with imprisonment for a term which may extend to one year, or with fine, or with both.

Mischief by destroying or moving, etc., a land-mark fixed by public authority.

346. Whoever commits mischief by fire or any explosive substance, intending to cause, or knowing it to be likely that he will thereby cause damage to any property to the amount of L.E. 5 or upwards (or where the property is agricultural produce, L.E. 1 or upwards), shall be punished with imprisonment for a term which may extend to seven years, and shall also be liable to fine.

Mischief by fire or explosive substance with intent to cause damage to amount of L.E. 5 (or, in case of agricultural produce, L.E. 1).

347. Whoever commits mischief by fire or any explosive substance, intending to cause, or knowing it to be likely that he will thereby cause, the destruction of any building which is ordinarily used as a place of worship or as a human dwelling or as a place for the custody of property, shall be punished with imprisonment for a term which may extend to fourteen years, and shall also be liable to fine.

Mischief by fire or explosive substance with intent to destroy house, etc.

348. Whoever commits mischief to any decked vessel or any vessel of a burden of one hundred ardebs or upwards, intending to destroy or render unsafe, or knowing it to be likely that he will thereby destroy or render unsafe that vessel, shall be punished with imprisonment for a term which may extend to ten years, and shall also be liable to fine.

Mischief with intent to destroy or make unsafe a decked vessel, or one of one hundred ardebs burden.

349. Whoever commits, or attempts to commit, by fire or any explosive substance, such mischief as is described in the last preceding section, shall be punished with imprisonment for a term which may extend to fourteen years, and shall also be liable to fine.

Punishment for the mischief described in section 348 committed by fire or explosive substance.

350. Whoever intentionally runs any vessel aground or ashore, intending to commit theft of any property contained therein or to dishonestly misappropriate any such property, or with intent that such theft or misappropriation of property may be committed, shall be punished with imprisonment for a term which may extend to ten years, and shall also be liable to fine.

Punishment for intentionally running vessel aground or ashore with intent to commit theft, etc.

351. Whoever commits mischief, having made preparation for causing to any person death, or hurt, or wrongful restraint, or fear of death, or of hurt, or of wrongful restraint, shall be punished with imprisonment for a term which may extend to five years, and shall also be liable to fine.

Mischief committed after preparation made for causing death or hurt.

Of Criminal Trespass.

352. Whoever enters into or upon property in the possession of another with intent to commit an offence or to intimidate, insult, or annoy any person in possession of such property,

or having lawfully entered into or upon such property, unlawfully remains there with intent thereby to intimidate, insult, or annoy any such person, or with intent to commit an offence, is said to commit "criminal trespass."

Criminal trespass.

353. Whoever commits criminal trespass by entering House-trespass. into or remaining in any building, tent, or vessel used as a human dwelling, or any building used as a place for worship, or as a place for the custody of property, is said to commit "house-trespass."

Explanation.—The introduction of any part of the criminal trespasser's body is entering sufficient to constitute house-trespass.

354. Whoever commits house-trespass, having taken Lurking house-trespass. precautions to conceal such house-trespass from some person who has a right to exclude or eject the trespasser from the building, tent, or vessel which is the subject of the trespass, is said to commit "lurking house-trespass."

355. Whoever commits lurking house-trespass after Lurking house-trespass sunset and before sunrise, is said to commit "lurking by night. house-trespass by night."

356. A person is said to commit "house-breaking," House-breaking. who commits house-trespass if he effects his entrance into the house or any part of it in any of the six ways hereinafter described; or if, being in the house or any part of it for the purpose of committing an offence, or, having committed an offence therein, he quits the house or any part of it in any of such six ways, that is to say:—

First.—If he enters or quits through a passage made by himself, or by any abettor of the house-trespass, in order to the committing of the house-trespass.

Secondly.—If he enters or quits through any passage not intended by any person, other than himself or an abettor of the offence, for human entrance; or through any passage to which he has obtained access by scaling or climbing over any wall or building.

Thirdly.—If he enters or quits through any passage which he or any abettor of the house-trespass has opened, in order to the committing of the house-trespass, by any means by which that passage was not intended by the occupier of the house to be opened.

Fourthly.—If he enters or quits by opening any lock in order to the committing of the house-trespass, or in order to the quitting of the house after a house-trespass.

Fifthly.—If he effects his entrance or departure by using criminal force or committing an assault, or by threatening any person with assault.

Sixthly.—If he enters or quits by any passage which he knows to have been fastened against such entrance or departure, and to have been unfastened by himself or by an abettor of the house-trespass.

Explanation.—Any out-house, or building occupied with a house and between which and such house, there is an immediate internal communication, is part of the house within the meaning of this section.

Illustrations.

(*a*) A commits house-trespass by making a hole through the wall of Z's house, and putting his hand through the aperture. This is house-breaking.

(*b*) A commits house-trespass by creeping into a ship at a port-hole between decks. This is house-breaking.

(*c*) A commits house-trespass by entering Z's house through a window. This is house-breaking.

(*d*) A commits house-trespass by entering Z's house through the door, having opened a door which was fastened. This is house-breaking.

(*e*) A commits house-trespass by entering Z's house through the door, having lifted a latch by putting a wire through a hole in the door. This is house-breaking.

(*f*) A finds the key of Z's house-door, which Z had lost, and commits house-trespass by entering Z's house, having opened the door with that key. This is house-breaking.

(*g*) Z is standing in his doorway. A forces a passage by knocking Z down, and commits house-trespass by entering the house. This is house-breaking.

(*h*) Z, the boab of Y, is standing in Y's doorway. A commits house-trespass by entering the house, having deterred Z from opposing him by threatening to beat him. This is house-breaking.

House-breaking by night. **357.** Whoever commits house-breaking after sunset and before sunrise, is said to commit "house-breaking by night."

Punishment for criminal trespass. **358.** Whoever commits criminal trespass shall be punished with imprisonment for a term which may extend to three months, or with fine which may extend to L.E. 10, or with both.

Punishment for house-trespass. **359.** Whoever commits house-trespass shall be punished with imprisonment for a term which may extend to one year, or with fine which may extend to L.E. 20, or with both.

House-trespass in order to commit offence punishable with death. **360.** Whoever commits house-trespass in order to the committing of any offence punishable with death, shall be punished with imprisonment for a term not exceeding fourteen years, and shall also be liable to fine.

112

361. Whoever commits house trespass in order to the committing of any offence punishable with fourteen years' imprisonment, shall be punished with imprisonment for a term not exceeding ten years, and shall also be liable to fine.

House-trespass in order to commit offence punishable with fourteen years' imprisonment.

362. Whoever commits house-trespass in order to the committing of any offence punishable with imprisonment, shall be punished with imprisonment for a term which may extend to two years, and shall also be liable to fine ; and, if the offence intended to be committed is theft, the term of the imprisonment may be extended to seven years.

House-trespass in order to commit offence punishable with imprisonment.

363. Whoever commits house-trespass, having made preparation for causing hurt to any person, or for assaulting any person, or for wrongfully restraining any person, or for putting any person in fear of hurt, or of assault, or of wrongful restraint, shall be punished with imprisonment for a term which may extend to seven years, and shall also be liable to fine.

House-trespass after preparation for hurt, assault or wrongful restraint.

364. Whoever commits lurking house-trespass or house-breaking, shall be punished with imprisonment for a term which may extend to two years, and shall also be liable to fine.

Punishment for lurking house-trespass or house-breaking.

365. Whoever commits lurking house-trespass or house-breaking, in order to the committing of any offence punishable with imprisonment, shall be punished with imprisonment for a term which may extend to three years, and shall also be liable to fine ; and, if the offence intended to be committed is theft, the term of the imprisonment may be extended to ten years.

Lurking house-trespass or house-breaking in order to commit offence punishable with imprisonment.

366. Whoever commits lurking house-trespass, or house-breaking, having made preparation for causing hurt to any person, or for assaulting any person, or for wrongfully restraining any person, or for putting any person in fear of hurt or of assault or of wrongful restraint, shall be punished with imprisonment for a term which may extend to ten years, and shall also be liable to fine.

Lurking house-trespass or house-breaking after preparation for hurt, assault or wrongful restraint.

367. Whoever commits lurking house-trespass by night, or house-breaking by night, shall be punished with imprisonment for a term which may extend to three years, and shall also be liable to fine.

Punishment for lurking house-trespass or house-breaking by night.

H

Lurking house-trespass or house-breaking by night, in order to commit offence punishable with imprisonment. **368.** Whoever commits lurking house-trespass by night or house-breaking by night, in order to the committing of any offence punishable with imprisonment, shall be punished with imprisonment for a term which may extend to five years, and shall also be liable to fine; and, if the offence intended to be committed is theft, the term of the imprisonment may be extended to fourteen years.

Lurking house-trespass or house-breaking by night after preparation for hurt, assault or wrongful restraint. **369.** Whoever commits lurking house-trespass by night, or house-breaking by night, having made preparation for causing hurt to any person, or for assaulting any person, or for wrongfully restraining any person, or for putting any person in fear of hurt, or of assault, or of wrongful restraint, shall be punished with imprisonment for a term which may extend to fourteen years, and shall also be liable to fine.

Grievous hurt caused whilst committing lurking house-trespass or house-breaking. **370.** Whoever, whilst committing lurking house-trespass or house-breaking, causes grievous hurt to any person or attempts to cause death or grievous hurt to any person, shall be punished with imprisonment for a term which may extend to fourteen years, and shall also be liable to fine.

All persons jointly concerned in lurking house-trespass or house-breaking by night punishable where death or grievous hurt caused by one of them. **371.** If, at the time of the committing of lurking house-trespass by night or house-breaking by night, any person guilty of such offence shall voluntarily cause or attempt to cause death or grievous hurt to any person, every person jointly concerned in committing such lurking house-trespass by night or house-breaking by night, shall be punished with imprisonment for a term which may extend to fourteen years, and shall also be liable to fine.

Dishonestly breaking open receptacle containing property. **372.** Whoever, dishonestly or with intent to commit mischief, breaks open or unfastens any closed receptacle which contains or which he believes to contain property, shall be punished with imprisonment for a term which may extend to two years, or with fine, or with both.

Punishment for same offence when committed by person entrusted with custody. **373.** Whoever, being entrusted with any closed receptacle which contains or which he believes to contain property, without having authority to open the same, dishonestly, or with intent to commit mischief, breaks open or unfastens that receptacle, shall be punished with imprisonment for a term which may extend to three years, or with fine, or with both.

114

CHAPTER XXI.

Of Offences relating to Documents and to Property or other Marks.

374. Whoever makes any false document or part of a *Forgery* document, with intent to cause damage or injury to the public or to any person, or to support any claim or title, or to cause any person to part with property, or to enter into any express or implied contract, or with intent to commit fraud or that fraud may be committed, commits forgery.

375. A person is said to make a false document— *Making a false document.*

First.—Who dishonestly or fraudulently makes, signs, seals, or executes a document or part of a document, or makes any mark denoting the execution of a document, with the intention of causing it to be believed that such document or part of a document was made, signed, sealed, or executed by or by the authority of a person by whom or by whose authority he knows that it was not made, signed, sealed or executed, or at a time at which he knows, that it was not made, signed, sealed or executed; or

Secondly.—Who, without lawful authority, dishonestly or fraudulently, by cancellation or otherwise, alters a document in any material part thereof, after it has been made or executed either by himself or by any other person, whether such person be living or dead at the time of such alteration; or

Thirdly.—Who dishonestly or fraudulently causes any person to sign, seal, execute, or alter a document, knowing that such person by reason of unsoundness of mind or intoxication cannot, or that by reason of deception practised upon him he does not, know the contents of the document or the nature of the alteration.

Illustrations.

(a) A has a letter of credit upon B for L.E. 100, written by Z. A, in order to defraud B, adds a cipher to the 100, and makes the sum L.E. 1000, intending that it may be believed by B that Z so wrote the letter. A has committed forgery.

(b) A, without Z's authority, affixes Z's seal to a document purporting to be a conveyance of an estate from Z to A, with the intention of selling the estate to B, and thereby of obtaining from B the purchase-money. A has committed forgery.

(c) A picks up a cheque on a banker signed by B, payable to bearer, but without any sum having been inserted in the cheque. A fraudulently fills up the cheque by inserting the sum of L.E. 50. A commits forgery.

(d) A leaves with B, his agent, a cheque on a banker, signed by A, without inserting the sum payable, and authorizes B to fill up the cheque by inserting a sum not exceeding L.E. 200 for the purpose of making certain payments. B fraudulently fills up the cheque by inserting the sum of L.E. 300. B commits forgery.

(e) A draws a bill of exchange on himself in the name of B without B's authority, intending to discount it as a genuine bill with a banker and intending to take up the bill on its maturity. Here, as A draws the bill with intent to deceive the banker by leading him to suppose that he had the security of B, and thereby to discount the bill, A is guilty of forgery.

(f) Z's will contains these words—"I direct that all my remaining property be equally divided between A, B and C." A dishonestly scratches out B's name, intending that it may be believed that the whole was left to himself and C. A has committed forgery.

(g) A sells and conveys an estate to Z. A afterwards, in order to defraud Z of his estate, executes a conveyance of the same estate to B, dated six months earlier than the date of the conveyance to Z, intending it to be believed that he had conveyed the estate to B before he conveyed it to Z. A has committed forgery.

(h) Z dictates his will to A. A intentionally writes down a different legatee from the legatee named by Z, and, by representing to Z that he has prepared the will according to his instructions, induces Z to sign the will. A has committed forgery.

(i) A writes a letter and signs it with B's name without B's authority, certifying that A is a man of good character and in distressed circumstances from unforeseen misfortune, intending by means of such letter to obtain alms from Z and other persons. Here, as A made a false document in order to induce Z to part with property, A has committed forgery.

(j) A without B's authority writes a letter and signs it in B's name, certifying to A's character, intending thereby to obtain employment under Z. A has committed forgery, inasmuch as he intended to deceive Z by the forged certificate, and thereby to induce Z to enter into an express or implied contract for service.

Explanation 1.—A man's signature of his own name may amount to forgery.

Illustrations.

(a) A signs his own name to a bill of exchange, intending that it may be believed that the bill was drawn by another person of the same name. A has committed forgery.

(b) A writes the word "accepted" on a piece of paper and signs it with Z's name, in order that B may afterwards write on the paper a bill of exchange drawn by B upon Z, and negotiate the bill as though it had been accepted by Z. A is guilty of forgery; and if B, knowing the fact, draws the bill upon the paper pursuant to A's intention, B is also guilty of forgery.

(*c*) A picks up a bill of exchange payable to the order of a different person of the same name. A endorses the bill in his own name, intending to cause it to be believed that it was endorsed by the person to whose order it was payable : here A has committed forgery.

(*d*) A purchases an estate sold under execution of a decree against B. B, after the seizure of the estate, in collusion with Z, executes a lease of the estate to Z at a nominal rent and for a long period, and dates the lease six months prior to the seizure, with intent to defraud A, and to cause it to be believed that the lease was granted before the seizure. B, though he executes the lease in his own name, commits forgery by antedating it.

(*e*) A, a trader, in anticipation of insolvency, lodges effects with B for A's benefit, and with intent to defraud his creditors ; and in order to give a colour to the transaction, writes a promissory note binding himself to pay to B a sum for value received, and antedates the note, intending that it may be believed to have been made before A was on the point of insolvency. A has committed forgery under the first head of the definition.

Explanation 2.—The making of a false document in the name of a fictitious person, intending it to be believed that the document was made by a real person, or in the name of a deceased person intending it to be believed that the document was made by the person in his lifetime, may amount to forgery.

Illustration.

A draws a bill of exchange upon a fictitious person, and fraudulently accepts the bill in the name of such fictitious person with intent to negotiate it. A commits forgery.

376. Whoever commits forgery shall be punished with imprisonment for a term which may extend to two years, or with fine, or with both. Punishment for forgery.

377. Whoever forges a document, purporting to be a record or proceeding of or in a Court of Justice, or a register of birth, baptism, marriage, or burial, or a register kept by a public servant as such, or a certificate or document purporting to be made by a public servant in his official capacity, or an authority to institute or defend a suit, or to take any proceedings therein, or a power-of-attorney, shall be punished with imprisonment for a term which may extend to seven years, and shall also be liable to fine. Forgery of record of Court or of public register, etc.

378. Whoever forges a document which purports to be a valuable security or a will, or to give authority to any person to make or transfer any valuable security, or to receive the principal, interest, or dividends thereon, or Forgery of valuable security, will, etc.

117

to receive or deliver any money, movable property or valuable security, or any document purporting to be an acquittance or receipt acknowledging the payment of money, or an acquittance or receipt for the delivery of any movable property or valuable security, shall be punished with imprisonment for a term which may extend to ten years, and shall also be liable to fine.

Forgery for purpose of cheating.
379. Whoever commits forgery, intending that the document forged shall be used for the purpose of cheating, shall be punished with imprisonment for a term which may extend to seven years, and shall also be liable to fine.

Forgery for purpose of harming reputation.
380. Whoever commits forgery, intending that the document forged shall harm the reputation of any party, or knowing that it is likely to be used for that purpose, shall be punished with imprisonment for a term which may extend to three years, and shall also be liable to fine.

Forged document.
381. A false document made wholly or in part by forgery is designated "a forged document."

Using as genuine a forged document.
382. Whoever fraudulently or dishonestly uses as genuine any document which he knows or has reason to believe to be a forged document, shall be punished in the same manner as if he had forged such document.

Making or possessing counterfeit seal, etc., with intent to commit forgery.
383. Whoever makes or counterfeits any seal, plate, or other instrument for making an impression, intending that the same shall be used for the purpose of committing forgery, or with such intent, has in his possession any such seal, plate or other instrument, knowing the same to be counterfeit, shall be punished with imprisonment for a term which may extend to seven years, and shall also be liable to fine.

Having possession of document described in section 377 or 378, knowing it to be forged and intending to use it as genuine.
384. Whoever has in his possession any document of the description mentioned in section 377 or section 378, knowing the same to be forged, and intending that the same shall fraudulently or dishonestly be used as genuine, shall be punished with imprisonment for a term which may extend to seven years, and shall also be liable to fine.

Counterfeiting device or mark used for authenticating documents, or possessing counterfeit marked material.
385. Whoever counterfeits upon, or in the substance of, any material, any device or mark used for the purpose of authenticating any document, intending that such device or mark shall be used for the purpose of giving the appearance of authenticity to any document then forged

or thereafter to be forged on such material, or who with such intent has in his possession any material upon or in the substance of which any such device or mark has been counterfeited, shall be punished with imprisonment for a term which may extend to seven years, and shall also be liable to fine.

386. Whoever, fraudulently or dishonestly, or with intent to cause damage or injury to the public or to any person, cancels, destroys, or defaces, or attempts to cancel, destroy, or deface, or secretes or attempts to secrete any document which is or purports to be a will, or any valuable security, or commits mischief in respect to such document, shall be punished with imprisonment for a term which may extend to seven years, and shall also be liable to fine. *Fraudulent cancellation, destruction, etc., of will, or valuable security.*

387. Whoever, being a clerk, officer, or servant, or employed or acting in the capacity of a clerk, officer or servant, wilfully, and with intent to defraud, destroys, alters, mutilates or falsifies any book, paper, writing, valuable security or account which belongs to or is in the possession of his employer, or has been received by him for or on behalf of his employer, or wilfully, and with intent to defraud, makes or abets the making of any false entry in, or omits or alters or abets the omission or alteration of any material particular from or in, any such book, paper, writing, valuable security or account, shall be punished with imprisonment for a term which may extend to seven years, or with fine or with both. *Falsification of accounts.*

Explanation.—It shall be sufficient in any charge under this section to allege a general intent to defraud without naming any particular person intended to be defrauded or specifying any particular sum of money intended to be the subject of the fraud, or any particular day on which the offence was committed.

Of Property and Other Marks.

388. A mark used for denoting that movable property belongs to a particular person is called a property mark. *Property mark.*

389. Whoever marks any movable property or goods or any case, package or other receptacle containing movable property or goods, or uses any case, package or other receptacle having any mark thereon, in a manner reasonably calculated to cause it to be believed that the property *Using a false property mark.*

or goods so marked, or any property or goods contained in any such receptacle so marked, belong to a person to whom they do not belong, is said to use a false property mark.

Punishment for using a false property mark. **390.** Whoever uses any false property mark shall, unless he proves that he acted without intent to defraud, be punished with imprisonment for a term which may extend to one year, or with fine, or with both.

Counterfeiting a property mark used by another. **391.** Whoever counterfeits any property mark used by any other person shall be punished with imprisonment for a term which may extend to two years, or with fine, or with both.

Counterfeiting a mark used by a public servant. **392.** Whoever counterfeits any property mark used by a public servant, or any mark used by a public servant to denote that any property has been manufactured by a particular person or at a particular time or place, or that the property is of a particular quality or has passed through a particular office, or that it is entitled to any exemption, or uses as genuine any such mark knowing the same to be counterfeit, shall be punished with imprisonment for a term which may extend to three years, and shall also be liable to fine.

Making or possession of any instrument for counterfeiting a property mark. **393.** Whoever makes or has in his possession any die, plate or other instrument for the purpose of counterfeiting a property mark, or has in his possession a property mark for the purpose of denoting that any goods belong to a person to whom they do not belong, shall be punished with imprisonment for a term which may extend to three years, or with fine, or with both.

Selling goods marked with a counterfeit property mark. **394.** Whoever sells or exposes or has in possession for sale or any purpose of trade or manufacture, any goods or things with a counterfeit property mark affixed to or impressed upon the same or to or upon any case, package or other receptacle in which such goods are contained, shall, unless he proves—

> (a) that, having taken all reasonable precautions against committing an offence against this section, he had at the time of the commission of the alleged offence no reason to suspect the genuineness of the mark, and

(*b*) that, on demand made by or on behalf of the prosecutor, he gave all the information in his power
with respect to the person from whom he obtained
such goods or things or,

(*c*) that otherwise he had acted innocently,

be punished with imprisonment for a term which may
extend to one year, or with fine, or with both.

395. Whoever makes any false mark upon any case, package or other receptacle containing goods, in a manner reasonably calculated to cause any public servant or any other person to believe that such receptacle contains goods which it does not contain or that it does not contain goods which it does contain, or that the goods contained in such receptacle are of a nature or quality different from the real nature or quality thereof shall, unless he proves that he acted without intent to defraud, be punished with imprisonment for a term which may extend to three years, or with fine, or with both.

Making a false mark upon any receptacle containing goods.

396. Whoever makes use of any such false mark in any manner prohibited by the last foregoing section shall, unless he proves that he acted without intent to defraud, be punished as if he had committed an offence against that section.

Punishment for making use of any such false mark.

397. Whoever removes, destroys, defaces or adds to any property mark, intending or knowing it to be likely that he may thereby cause injury to any person, shall be punished with imprisonment, for a term which may extend to one year, or with fine or with both.

Tampering with property mark with intent to cause injury.

CHAPTER XXII.

Of the Criminal Breach of Contracts of Service.

398. Whoever, being bound by a lawful contract to render his personal service in conveying or conducting any person, or any property from one place to another place, or to act as servant to any person during a voyage or journey, or to guard any person or property during the voyage or journey, voluntarily omits so to do, except in the case of illness or ill-treatment, shall be punished with imprisonment for a term which may extend to one month, or with fine which may extend to L.E. 5, or with both.

Breach of contract of service during voyage or journey.

Illustrations.

(*a*) A, porter, being bound by lawful contract to carry Z's baggage from one place to another, throws the baggage away, A has committed the offence defined in this section.

(*b*) A, a proprietor of camels, being bound by legal contract to convey goods on his camels from one place to another, illegally omits to do so. A has committed the offence defined in this section.

(*c*) A, by unlawful means, compels B, a porter, to carry his baggage. B in the course of the journey puts down the baggage and runs away. Here, as B was not lawfully bound to carry the baggage, he has not committed any offence.

Explanation.—It is not necessary to this offence that the contract should be made with the person for whom the service is to be performed. It is sufficient, if the contract is legally made with any person, either expressly or impliedly, by the person who is to perform the service.

Illustration.

A contracts with the sheikh of a tribe to provide camels for a journey. B, a member of the tribe, starts in charge of some of the camels and in the middle of the journey voluntarily leaves the camels. B is guilty of an offence under this section.

399. Whoever, being bound by a lawful contract to attend on or to supply the wants of any person who, by reason of youth, or of unsoundness of mind, or of disease or bodily weakness, is helpless or incapable of providing for his own safety or of supplying his own wants, voluntarily omits so to do, shall be punished with imprisonment for a term which may extend to three months, or with fine which may extend to L.E. 10, or with both.

(margin: Breach of contract to attend on and supply wants of helpless person.)

400. Whoever, being bound by a lawful contract in writing to work for another person as an artificer, workman or labourer, for a period not exceeding three years, at any place within the Sudan to which by virtue of the contract he has been or is to be conveyed at the expense of such other, voluntarily deserts the service of that other during the continuance of his contract, or without reasonable cause refuses to perform the service which he has contracted to perform, such service being reasonable and proper service, shall be punished with imprisonment for a term not exceeding one month, or with fine not exceeding double the amount of such expense, or with both; unless the employer has ill-treated him or neglected to perform the contract on his part.

(margin: Breach of contract to serve at distant place to which servant is conveyed at master's expense.)

CHAPTER XXIII.

Of Offences relating to Marriage.

401. Every man who by deceit causes any woman who is not lawfully married to him to believe that she is lawfully married to him and to cohabit or have sexual intercourse with him in that belief, shall be punished with imprisonment for a term which may extend to ten years, and shall also be liable to fine. Cohabitation caused by a man deceitfully inducing a belief of lawful marriage.

402. Whoever, having a husband or wife living, marries in any case in which such marriage is void by reason of its taking place during the life of such husband or wife, shall be punished with imprisonment for a term which may extend to seven years, and shall also be liable to fine. Marrying again during lifetime of husband or wife.

Exception.—This section does not extend to any person whose marriage, with such husband or wife, has been legally dissolved,

nor to any person who contracts a marriage during the life of a former husband or wife, if such husband or wife, at the time of the subsequent marriage shall have been continually absent from such person for the space of seven years, and shall not have been heard of by such person as being alive within that time, provided the person contracting such subsequent marriage shall, before such marriage takes place, inform the person with whom such marriage is contracted of the real state of facts so far as the same are within his or her knowledge.

403. Whoever commits the offence defined in the last preceding section having concealed from the person with whom the subsequent marriage is contracted, the fact of the former marriage, shall be punished with imprisonment for a term which my extend to ten years, and shall also be liable to fine. Same offence with concealment of former marriage from person with whom subsequent marriage is contracted.

404. Whoever, dishonestly or with a fraudulent intention, goes through the ceremony of being married, knowing that he is not thereby lawfully married, shall be punished with imprisonment for a term which may extend to seven years, and shall also be liable to fine. Marriage ceremony fraudulently gone through without lawful marriage.

405. Whoever has sexual intercourse with a person who is and whom he knows or has reason to believe to be the Adultery with married woman.

wife of another man, without the consent or connivance of that man, such sexual intercourse not amounting to the offence of rape, is guilty of the offence of adultery, and shall be punished with imprisonment for a term which may extend to two years, or with fine, or with both.

Adultery by married woman. **406.** Whoever, being the wife of one man, has sexual intercourse with another man without the consent or connivance of her husband, is guilty of the offence of adultery, and shall be punished with imprisonment for a term which may extend to two years, or with fine, or with both.

Enticing or taking away or detaining with criminal intent a married woman. **407.** Whoever takes or entices away any woman who is and whom he knows or has reason to believe to be the wife of any other man, from that man, or from any person having the care of her on behalf of that man, with intent that she may have illicit intercourse with any person, or conceals, or detains with that intent any such woman, shall be punished with imprisonment for a term which may extend to two years, or with fine, or with both.

CHAPTER XXIV.

OF DEFAMATION.

Defamation. **408.** Whoever, by words either spoken or intended to be read, or by signs or by visible representations, makes or publishes any imputation concerning any person, intending to harm, or knowing or having reason to believe that such imputation will harm, the reputation of such person, is said, except in the cases hereinafter, to defame that person.

Explanation 1.—It may amount to defamation to impute anything to a deceased person, if the imputation would harm the reputation of that person if living, and is intended to be hurtful to the feelings of his family or other near relatives.

Explanation 2.—It may amount to defamation to make an imputation concerning a company or an association or collection of persons as such.

Explanation 3.—An imputation in the form of an alternative or expressed ironically, may amount to defamation.

Explanation 4.—No imputation is said to harm a person's reputation, unless that imputation directly or indirectly, in the estimation of others, lowers the moral or intellectual character of that person, or lowers the character of that person in respect of his calling, or lowers the credit of that person, or causes it to be believed that the body of that person is in a loathsome state, or in a state generally considered as disgraceful.

Illustrations.

(*a*) A says—" Z is an honest man; he never stole B's watch:" intending to cause it to be believed that Z did steal B's watch. This is defamation, unless it fall within one of the exceptions.

(*b*) A is asked who stole B's watch. A points to Z, intending to cause it to be believed that Z stole B's watch. This is defamation, unless it fall within one of the exceptions.

(*c*) A draws a picture of Z running away with B's watch, intending it to be believed that Z stole B's watch. This is defamation, unless it fall within one of the exceptions.

First Exception.—It is not defamation to impute anything which is true concerning any person, if it be for the public good that the imputation should be made or published. Whether or not it is for the public good is a question of fact. *[Imputation of truth which public good requires to be made or published.]*

Illustrations.

(*a*) Z opens a school at Khartoum. The fact is that Z has fled from Europe to escape punishment for gross acts of swindling. A is protected by this exception if he publishes that fact.

(*b*) But if the swindling had occurred twenty years ago, and in the meantime Z had been carrying on a school in Cairo and had been living an upright life, A would not be protected by this exception if he raked up the facts and published them.

Second Exception.—It is not defamation to express in good faith any opinion whatever respecting the conduct of a public servant in the discharge of his public functions, or respecting his character, so far as his character appears in that conduct, and no further. *[Public conduct of public servants.]*

Third Exception.—It is not defamation to express in good faith any opinion whatever respecting the conduct of any person touching any public question, and respecting his character, so far as his character appears in that conduct, and no further. *[Conduct of any person touching any public question.]*

Illustration.

It is not defamation in A to express in good faith any opinion whatever respecting Z's conduct in petitioning Government on a public question, in signing a requisition for a meeting on a public question, in presiding or attending at such a meeting, or in forming or joining any society which invites the public support.

Publication of reports of proceedings of Courts.

Fourth Exception.—It is not defamation to publish a substantially true report of the proceedings of a Court of Justice, or of the result of any such proceedings.

Explanation.—An officer holding an enquiry in open Court preliminary to a trial in a Court of Justice, is a Court within the meaning of the above exception.

Merits of case decided in Court, or conduct of witnesses and others concerned.

Fifth Exception.—It is not defamation to express in good faith any opinion whatever respecting the merits of any case, civil or criminal, which has been decided by a Court of Justice, or respecting the conduct of any person as a party, witness, or agent, in any such case, or respecting the character of such person, as far as his character appears in that conduct, and no further.

Illustrations.

(*a*) A says—"I think Z's evidence on that trial is so contradictory that he must be stupid or dishonest." A is within this exception if he says this in good faith, inasmuch as the opinion which he expresses respects Z's character as it appears in Z's conduct as a witness, and no further.

(*b*) But if A says—"I do not believe what Z asserted at that trial, because I know him to be a man without veracity," A is not within this exception, inasmuch as the opinion which he expresses of Z's character, is an opinion not founded on Z's conduct as a witness.

Merits of public performance.

Sixth Exception.—It is not defamation to express in good faith any opinion respecting the merits of any performance which its author has submitted to the judgment of the public, or respecting the character of the author so far as his character appears in such performance, and no further.

Explanation.—A performance may be submitted to the judgment of the public expressly or by acts on the part of the author which imply such submission to the judgment of the public.

Illustrations.

(*a*) A person who publishes a book, submits that book to the judgment of the public.

(*b*) A person who makes a speech in public, submits that speech to the judgment of the public.

(*c*) An actor or singer who appears on a public stage, submits his acting or singing to the judgment of the public.

(d) A says of a book published by Z—"Z's book is foolish, Z must be a weak man. Z's book is indecent, Z must be a man of impure mind." A is within this exception, if he says this in good faith, inasmuch as the opinion which he expresses of Z respects Z's character only so far as it appears in Z's book, and no further.

(e) But if A says—"I am not surprised that Z's book is foolish and indecent, for he is a weak man and a libertine," A is not within this exception, inasmuch as the opinion which he expresses of Z's character is an opinion not founded on Z's book.

Seventh Exception.—It is not defamation in a person having over another any authority, either conferred by law or arising out of a lawful contract made with that other, to pass in good faith any censure on the conduct of that other in matters to which such lawful authority relates. Censure passed in good faith by person having lawful authority over another.

Illustration.

A Magistrate censuring in good faith the conduct of a witness, or of an officer of the Court; a head of a department censuring in good faith those who are under his orders; a parent censuring in good faith a child in the presence of other children; a school-master, whose authority is derived from a parent, censuring in good faith a pupil in the presence of other pupils; a master censuring a servant in good faith for remissness in service; a banker censuring in good faith the cashier of his bank for the conduct of such cashier as such cashier—are within this exception.

Eighth Exception.—It is not defamation to prefer in good faith an accusation against any person to any of those who have lawful authority over that person with respect to the subject-matter of accusation. Accusation preferred in good faith to authorized person.

Illustration.

If A in good faith accuses Z before a Magistrate; if A in good faith complains of the conduct of Z, a servant, to Z's master; if A in good faith complains of the conduct of Z, a child, to Z's father—A is within this exception.

Ninth Exception.—It is not defamation to make an imputation on the character of another, provided that the imputation be made in good faith for the protection of the interests of the person making it, or of any other person, or for the public good. Imputation made in good faith by person for protection of his or other's interests

Illustrations.

(a) A, a shopkeeper, says to B, who manages his business—"Sell nothing to Z unless he pays you ready money, for I have no opinion of his honesty." A is within the exception, if he has made this imputation on Z in good faith for the protection of his own interests.

(*b*) A, a Magistrate, in making a report to his superior officer, casts an imputation on the character of Z. Here, if the imputation is made in good faith, and for the public good, A is within the exception.

(*c*) A, in giving evidence before a Court of Justice, identifies Z as the person whom he saw committing a robbery. Although Z proves that A is mistaken, A is protected by this exception; unless he is giving false evidence (in which case he can be proceeded against under section 157).

Caution intended for good of person to whom conveyed or for public good. *Tenth Exception.*—It is not defamation to convey a caution, in good faith, to one person against another, provided that such caution be intended for the good of the person to whom it is conveyed, or of some person in whom that person is interested, or for the public good.

Punishment for defamation. **409.** Whoever defames another shall be punished with imprisonment for a term which may extend to two years, or with fine, or with both.

Printing or engraving matter known to be defamatory. **410.** Whoever prints or engraves any matter, knowing or having good reason to believe that such matter is defamatory of any person, shall be punished with imprisonment for a term which may extend to two years, or with fine, or with both.

'Sale of printed or engraved substance containing defamatory matter. **411.** Whoever sells or offers for sale any printed or engraved substance containing defamatory matter, knowing that it contains such matter, shall be punished with imprisonment for a term which may extend to two years, or with fine, or with both.

CHAPTER XXV.

OF CRIMINAL INTIMIDATION, INSULT AND ANNOYANCE.

Criminal intimidation. **412.** Whoever threatens another with any injury to his person, reputation or property, or to the person or reputation of any one in whom that person is interested, with intent to cause alarm to that person, or to cause that person to do any act which he is not legally bound to do, or to omit to do any act which that person is legally entitled to do, as the means of avoiding the execution of such threat, commits criminal intimidation.

Explanation.—A threat to injure the reputation of any deceased person in whom the person threatened is interested, is within this section.

Illustration.

A. for the purpose of inducing B to desist from prosecuting a civil suit, threatens to burn B's house.   A is guilty of criminal intimidation.

413. Whoever intentionally insults, and thereby gives provocation to any person, intending or knowing it to be likely that such provocation will cause him to break the public peace, or to commit any other offence, shall be punished with imprisonment for a term which may extend to two years, or with fine, or with both.

Intentional insult with intent to provoke breach of the peace.

414. Whoever circulates or publishes any statement, rumour or report which he knows to be false, with intent to cause an officer, soldier or sailor in any military or naval forces serving in the Sudan to mutiny, or with intent to cause fear or alarm to the public, and thereby to induce any person to commit an offence against the State or against the public tranquility, shall be punished with imprisonment for a term which may extend to two years, or with fine, or with both.

Circulating false report with intent to cause mutiny or an offence against the State, etc.

415. Whoever commits the offence of criminal intimidation shall be punished with imprisonment for a term which may extend to two years, or with fine, or with both;

and if the threat be to cause death or grievous hurt, or to cause the destruction of any property by fire, or to cause an offence punishable with death or with imprisonment for a term which may extend to seven years, or to impute unchastity to a woman, shall be punished with imprisonment for a term which may extend to seven years, or with fine, or with both.

Punishment for criminal intimidation.

If threat be to cause death or grievous hurt, etc.

416. Whoever commits the offence of criminal intimidation by an anonymous communication, or having taken precaution to conceal the name or abode of the person from whom the threat comes, shall be punished with imprisonment for a term which may extend to two years, in addition to the punishment provided for the offence by the last preceding section.

Criminal intimidation by an anonymous communication.

417. Whoever, intending to insult the modesty of any woman, utters any word, makes any sound or gesture, or exhibits any object, intending that such word or sound shall be heard, or that such gesture or object shall be seen, by such woman, or intrudes upon the privacy of

Word, gesture or act intended to insult the modesty of a woman.

129

such woman, shall be punished with imprsonment for a term which may extend to one year, or with fine, or with both.

Misconduct in public by a drunken person. **418.** Whoever, in a state of intoxication, appears in any public place, or in any place which it is a trespass in him to enter, and there conducts himself in such a manner as to cause annoyance to any person, shall be punished with imprisonment for a term which may extend to twenty-four hours, or with fine which may extend to P.T. 100, or with both.

(Signed) KITCHENER OF KHARTOUM,

GOVERNOR GENERAL.

THE

SUDAN CODE OF CRIMINAL PROCEDURE

1899.

CAIRO:

NATIONAL PRINTING OFFICE.

1899.

THE SUDAN CODE OF CRIMINAL PROCEDURE

CONTENTS.

3

PART III.

OF ARREST AND PROCESS.

CHAPTER IV.

OF ARREST.

A.—Arrest.

CHAPTER V.

Of Processes to Compel Appearance.

A.—Summons.

B.—Warrant of Arrest.

C.—Proclamation and Attachment.

D.—Other Rules regarding Processes.

CHAPTER VI.

OF PROCESSES TO COMPEL THE PRODUCTION OF DOCUMENTS AND OTHER MOVABLE PROPERTY AND FOR THE DISCOVERY OF PERSONS WRONGFULLY CONFINED.

PART IV.

OF PROCEEDINGS IN PROSECUTIONS.

CHAPTER VII.

OF INFORMATION TO THE POLICE AND THEIR POWERS TO INVESTIGATE.

CHAPTER VIII.

PLACE OF INQUIRY AND TRIAL.

CHAPTER IX.

OF THE TAKING COGNIZANCE OF OFFENCES BY MAGISTRATES.

CHAPTER X.

OF THE SANCTIONS NECESSARY FOR THE INITIATION OF CERTAIN PROCEEDINGS.

.CHAPTER XI.

OF INQUIRY INTO CASES TRIABLE BY A MINOR DISTRICT COURT OR THE MUDIR'S COURT.

CHAPTER XII.

OF CHARGES.

A.—*Form of Charges.*

B.—*Joinder of Charges.*

CHAPTER XVII.

OF THE JUDGMENT.

CHAPTER XVIII.

OF REFERENCE FOR CONFIRMATION, APPEAL AND REVISION.

CHAPTER XIX.

OF EXECUTION.

CHAPTER XX.

OF SUSPENSIONS, REMISSIONS AND COMMUTATIONS OF SENTENCES.

CHAPTER XXI.

OF PREVIOUS ACQUITTALS OR CONVICTIONS.

PART V.

SPECIAL PROCEEDINGS.

CHAPTER XXII.

PROCEEDINGS IN CASE OF CERTAIN OFFENCES AFFECTING THE ADMINISTRATION OF JUSTICE.

CHAPTER XXIII.

OF LUNATICS.

PART VI.

SUPPLEMENTARY.

CHAPTER XXIV.

OF THE COMPOUNDING OF OFFENCES.

CHAPTER XXV.

OF BAIL.

CHAPTER XXVI.

PROVISIONS AS TO BONDS.

Criminal Procedure.

CHAPTER XXVII.

Of the Disposal of Property.

Sections.

CHAPTER XXVIII.

Of Unlawful Assemblies.

CHAPTER XXIX.

Of the Preventive Action of the Police.

CHAPTER XXX.

Of the Application of this Code to Second-class Districts.

CHAPTER XXXI.

Miscellaneous.

THE

SUDAN CODE OF CRIMINAL PROCEDURE.

It is hereby enacted as follows:—

PART I.

PRELIMINARY.

CHAPTER I.

1. (*1*) This Ordinance may be called the Code of Short title. Criminal Procedure.

(*2*) It shall take effect in such parts of the Sudan as Extent. the Governor General may, from time to time, by notice published in the "Sudan Gazette," order.

2. (*1*) All offences under the Sudan Penal Code shall Trial of offences be investigated, inquired into, tried, and otherwise dealt Code. with according to the provisions hereinafter contained.

(*2*) All offences under any other law shall be investi- Trial of gated, inquired into, tried and otherwise dealt with other laws. according to the same provisions, but subject to any enactment for the time being in force regulating the manner or place of investigating, inquiring into, trying or otherwise dealing with such offences.

(*3*) Nevertheless, this Code shall take effect subject to Saving of the exigencies of martial law, wherever and so far as the martial law. same may, for the time being, be in force.

3. (*1*) In this Code the following words and expressions Definitions. have the following meanings, unless a different intention appears from the subject or context:—

15

"Charge."   (*a*) "charge" includes any head of charge when the charge contains more heads than one:

"Complaint."   (*b*) "complaint" means the allegation made orally or in writing to a Magistrate, with a view to his taking action, under this Code, that some person, whether known or unknown, has committed an offence, but it does not include the report of a police-officer:

Inquiry."   (*c*) "inquiry" includes every inquiry, other than a trial, conducted under this Code by a Magistrate or Court:

"Investigation."   (*d*) "investigation" includes all the proceedings under this Code for the collection of evidence conducted by a police-officer or by any person (other than a Magistrate) who is authorised by a Magistrate in this behalf:

"Judicial proceeding."   (*e*) "judicial proceeding" includes any proceeding in the course of which evidence is or may be legally taken on oath:

"Officer in charge of a police-station."   (*f*) "officer in charge of a police-station" includes, when the officer in charge of the police-station is absent from the station-house or unable from illness or other cause to perform his duties, the police-officer present at the station-house who is next in rank to such officer and is above the rank of constable: and

"Pleader."   (*g*) "pleader" used with reference to any proceeding in any Court, means a pleader authorised under any law for the time being in force to practise in such Court, and includes any person appointed with the permission of the Court to act in such proceeding.

Words referring to acts.   (*2*) Words which refer to acts done, extend also to illegal omissions; and

Words to have same meaning as in Penal Code.   all words and expressions used herein and defined in the Sudan Penal Code shall have the meanings respectively attributed to them by that Code.

PART II.

CONSTITUTION AND POWERS OF CRIMINAL COURTS AND OFFICES.

CHAPTER II.

OF THE CONSTITUTION OF CRIMINAL COURTS.

4. There shall be five classes of Criminal Courts in the Sudan, namely:— Classes of Criminal Courts
- (i) Mudir's Courts:
- (ii) Minor District Courts:
- (iii) Courts of Magistrates of the first class:
- (iv) Courts of Magistrates of the second class:
- (v) Courts of Magistrates of the third class.

5. A Mudir's Court shall consist of three Magistrates, inclusive of the Mudir or other Magistrate of the first class nominated by him to preside. Constitution of Mudir's Court.

6. A Minor District Court shall consist of three Magistrates, of whom one at least shall be a Magistrate of the second class or a Magistrate of the first class other than the Mudir. Constitution of Minor District Court.

7. By virtue of office Ex-officio Magistrates.
- a Mamur is a Magistrate of the third class:
- an Inspector is a Magistrate of the second class, but may be nominated a Magistrate of the first class:
- a Mudir is a Magistrate of the first class.

8. Any military officer serving or employed in the Sudan and qualified to sit on Courts-Martial may be nominated by the Governor-General a Magistrate for the purpose of constituting Mudir's Courts and Minor District Courts. Special Magistrates.

9. All Magistrates exercising their functions within any Province shall be subordinate to the Mudir of the Province, who shall, subject to any directions from the Governor-General, provide for the constitution of Mudir's Courts and Minor District Courts, and for the distribution of business amongst the Magistrates subordinate to him. Subordination of Magistrates to Mudir.

B

17

Officer temporarily acting as Mudir.

10. All the powers and duties of a Mudir under this Code shall be exercised and performed by any officer temporarily acting as Mudir during a vacancy or during the absence of the Mudir.

CHAPTER III.

Powers of Courts and Offices.

A.—*Description of Offences triable by each Court.*

Offences under Penal Code.

11. Subject to the other provisions of this Code, any offence under the Sudan Penal Code may be tried by any Court by which such offence is shewn in the sixth column of the first section to be triable, or by any Court with greater powers.

Offences under other laws.

12. (*1*) Any offence under any other law may be tried by any Court mentioned in that behalf in the law, or by any Court with greater powers.

(*2*) When no Court is so mentioned it may be tried by any Court constituted under this Code other than a Summary Court; provided that

(*a*) a Minor District Court shall not try an offence punishable with imprisonment for a term which may exceed ten years, or with fine exceeding L.E. 100;

(*b*) a Magistrate of the first class shall not try an offence punishable with imprisonment for a term which may exceed three years, or with fine exceeding L.E. 50;

(*c*) a Magistrate of the second class shall not try an offence punishable with imprisonment for a term which may exceed two years, or with fine exceeding L.E. 25; and

(*d*) an offence punishable with death shall be tried by a Mudir's Court.

Trial of juvenile offenders.

13. A male offender who, in the opinion of the Court, is under sixteen years of age may be tried summarily by the Court of a Magistrate of the first or second class, for any offence not punishable with death.

18

*B.—Sentences which may be passed by Courts
of various classes.*

14. A Mudir's Court may pass any sentence authorised by law. Powers of
Mudir's Court.

15. A Minor District Court may pass any sentence of imprisonment for a term not exceeding seven years, or of fine not exceeding L.E. 50. Powers of Minor
District Court.

16. The Court of a Magistrate of the first class may pass the following sentences, namely :— Powers of Court
of Magistrate
of first class.

> Imprisonment for a term not exceeding one year:
> Fine not exceeding L.E. 20:

or, when sitting as a Summary Court,

> Imprisonment for a term not exceeding two calendar months:
> Fine not exceeding L.E. 5:
> Flogging:
> Whipping.

17. The Court of a Magistrate of the second class may pass the following sentences, namely :— Powers of Court
of Magistrate
of second class.

> Imprisonment for a term not exceeding six calendar months:
> Fine not exceeding L.E. 10:

or, when sitting as a Summary Court,

> Imprisonment for a term not exceeding fifteen days:
> Fine not exceeding P.T. 200:
> Flogging:
> Whipping.

18. The Court of a Magistrate of the third class shall sit only as a Summary Court, and may pass the following sentences, namely :— Powers of Court
of Magistrate
of third class.

> Imprisonment for a term not exceeding two days, or such higher limit, not exceeding seven days, as the Mudir may in the case of each Magistrate direct:
> Fine not exceeding P.T. 20.

19. Any Court may pass any lawful sentence combining any of the sentences which it is authorised by law to pass. Combination of
sentences.

20. Any criminal Court may award any term of imprisonment in default of payment of fine which is authorised by sections 47 and 48 of the Sudan Penal Code in case of such default;

Imprisonment in default of payment of fine.

provided that—

(*a*) the term shall not be in excess of the powers of the Court under sections 15 to 18 ;

(*b*) in any case decided by a Minor District Court in which imprisonment is awarded as part of the substantive sentence, the combined term of imprisonment shall not exceed seven years ;

(*c*) in any case decided by a Magistrate in which imprisonment is awarded as part of the substantive sentence, the term of imprisonment awarded in default of payment of fine shall not exceed

(i) if the Magistrate be a Magistrate of the first class, the period of three months, or, if the case is tried summarily, the period of two months : and

(ii) if he be a Magistrate of the second class, the period of six weeks, or, if the case is tried summarily, the period of fifteen days.

Sentences in case of conviction of several offences at one trial.

21. (*1*) When a person is convicted at one trial of two or more distinct offences, the Court may sentence him, for such offences, to the several punishments prescribed therefor which such Court is competent to inflict ; such punishments, when consisting of imprisonment, to commence the one after the expiration of the other in such order as the Court may direct, unless the Court directs that such punishments shall run concurrently.

(*2*) In cases falling under this section, it shall not be necessary for the Court, by reason only of the aggregate punishment for the several offences being in excess of the punishment which it is competent to inflict on conviction of a single offence, to send the offender for trial before a higher Court ;

provided as follows—

(*a*) in no case shall a person be sentenced under this section to imprisonment for a longer period than ten years :

20

(*b*) if the case is tried by a Magistrate, the aggregate punishment shall not exceed twice the amount of punishment which he is, in the exercise of his ordinary jurisdiction, competent to inflict.

Explanation.—Separable offences which come within the provisions of section 51 of the Sudan Penal Code are not distinct offences within the meaning of this section.

C.—Powers of Magistrates.

22. All Mudirs and Magistrates of the first, second and third class, have ordinarily the powers hereinafter respectively conferred on them and specified in the third schedule.

Ordinary powers of Magistrates.

23. (*1*) The Governor-General may confer on any military officer serving or employed in the Sudan and qualified to sit on Courts-Martial, all, or any, of the powers of a Magistrate of the first, second, or third class, and may confer on any Magistrate of the second or third class, all, or any, of the powers of a Magistrate of the first or second class respectively, either for particular cases or classes of cases, or generally.

Power of Governor-General to confer special powers.

(*2*) The Governor-General may delegate this power to a Mudir in respect of his Province.

Delegation to Mudir.

PART III.

ARREST AND PROCESS.

CHAPTER IV.

OF ARREST.

A.—Arrest.

24. Any police-officer, omdeh, or sheikh may arrest— *first* —any person for whose arrest he has a warrant: *secondly*—any person who has been concerned in an offence for which, according to the third column of the first schedule, a police-officer may arrest without warrant, or against whom a reasonable

When police may arrest.

complaint has been made, or credible information has been received, or reasonable suspicion exists, of his having been so concerned:

thirdly—any person who has been proclaimed an offender under this Code or any other law:

fourthly—any person in whose possession property is found which may reasonably be suspected to be stolen property, or who may reasonably be suspected of having committed an offence with reference to such property:

fifthly—any person who obstructs a police-officer while in the execution of his duty:

sixthly—any person who has escaped or attempts to escape from lawful custody:

seventhly—any person reasonably suspected of being a deserter from any military or naval forces for the time being serving in the Sudan: and

eighthly—any person who in the presence of such officer has committed or been accused of committing any offence for which a police-officer may not, according to the third column of the first schedule, arrest without a warrant if, on the demand of such officer, such person refuses to give his name and address, or gives a name or address which the officer believes to be a false one.

Power to arrest vagabonds, etc.

25. An officer in charge of a police-station may also arrest, or cause to be arrested, without a warrant—

first—any person found taking precautions to conceal his presence, within the limits of such officer's jurisdiction, under suspicious circumstances: and

secondly—any person within the limits of such officer's jurisdiction who has no ostensible means of subsistence, or who cannot give a satisfactory account of himself.

Order to subordinate to arrest.

26. An order by an officer in charge of a police-station to a subordinate to arrest any person without a warrant (otherwise than in his presence) shall be in writing, and shall specify the person to be arrested and the cause of the arrest.

When private person may arrest.

27. A gaffir or any private person may arrest—

first—any person for whose arrest he has a warrant, or whom he is directed to arrest by a Magistrate, under section 28 or section 29:

secondly—any person who has escaped from his custody:
thirdly—any person proclaimed an offender; and
fourthly—any person committing, in his presence, an
offence for which a police-officer is authorised to
arrest without a warrant.

28. Any Magistrate may arrest or direct the arrest of any person committing any offence in his presence, within the local limits of his jurisdiction, and may thereupon commit the offender to custody. _{Arrest for offence committed in Magistrate's presence.}

29. Any Magistrate may at any time arrest or direct the arrest, in his presence, within the local limits of his jurisdiction, of any person for whose arrest he is competent at the time and in the circumstances to issue a warrant. _{Arrest by or in presence of Magistrate.}

30. (*1*) If a person liable to arrest resists the endeavour to arrest him or attempts to evade the arrest, the person authorised to arrest him may use all means necessary to affect the arrest. _{Resisting endeavour to arrest.}

(*2*) Provided that this section shall not give the right to cause the death of a person who is not accused of an offence punishable with death or with imprisonment for a term which may extend to ten years.

31. The officer or other person making an arrest may take from the person arrested any offensive weapons which he has about his person, and shall deliver all weapons so taken to the Court or officer before whom the person arrested is required by the warrant of arrest or by this Code to be produced. _{Power to seize offensive weapons.}

32. Every person is bound to assist a Magistrate, police-officer, omdeh, or sheikh reasonably demanding his aid, in the arresting or preventing the escape of any other person whom such Magistrate, police-officer, omdeh, or sheikh is authorised to arrest. _{When public are bound to assist Magistrates, etc.}

33 (*1*) If a police-officer or other person has reason to believe that any person whom he is authorised to arrest has entered into, or is within, any place, he may enter such place and there search for the person to be arrested. _{Search of place entered by person sought to be arrested.}

(*2*) The person residing in, or being in charge of, such place shall, on demand, allow free ingress thereto and afford all reasonable facilities for search.

. (*3*) If, on demand, such ingress is refused, the police-officer or other person as aforesaid may effect an entry by force.

Pursuit of offenders into other jurisdictions.

34. A police-officer or other person may, for the purpose of effecting the arrest of any person whom he is authorised to arrest, pursue such person into any part of the Sudan.

No unnecessary restraint.

35. An arrested person shall not be subjected to more restraint than is necessary to prevent his escape.

B.—*Procedure after Arrest.*

Procedure after arrest by private person.

36. (*1*) A gaffir or private person making an arrest without a warrant or a Magistrate's order shall, without unnecessary delay, take the person arrested to the nearest police-station, or make him over to a police-officer.

(*2*) If the arrested person appears to be one whom the officer in charge of the police-station or other police-officer is authorised to arrest, he shall re-arrest him: otherwise, the arrested person shall be at once released.

Procedure when offender has refused to give his name and address.

37. Any person arrested for refusing to give his name and address, or for giving a false name or address, shall—

(i) if he be found to have given his true name and address, be released:

(ii) when his true name and address are ascertained, be released on his executing a bond, with or without sureties, to appear before a Magistrate if required:

(iii) should his true name and address not be ascertained within twenty-four hours from the time of arrest, or should he fail to execute the bond, or, if so required, to furnish sufficient sureties, be forthwith forwarded to the nearest Magistrate having jurisdiction.

Person arrested to be taken before Magistrate or officer in charge of police-station.

38. A police-officer, omdeh, or sheikh making an arrest without warrant shall, without unnecessary delay, take or send the person arrested before a Magistrate having jurisdiction in the case, or before the officer in charge of a police-station.

Person arrested without warrant not to be detained more than twenty-four hours.

39. No police-officer shall detain in custody a person arrested without warrant for a longer period that, in the circumstances of the case, is reasonable; and such period shall not, in the absence of a Magistrate's order under

section 85, exceed twenty-four hours exclusive of the
time necessary for the journey from the place of arrest to
the Magistrate's Court.

40. Officers in charge of police-stations shall report to the Mudir, through the Mamur, all cases of arrest without warrant within their respective districts. *Police to report apprehensions.*

41. (*1*) A police-officer making an arrest, or receiving an arrested person from a person by whom the arrest has been made, may search the arrested person or cause him to be searched, and place in safe custody all articles, other than necessary wearing apparel, found upon him. *Search of arrested person.*

(*2*) When the arrested person is a woman, the search shall not be made except by a woman. *Searching woman.*

42. No person who has been arrested by a police-officer shall be discharged except on his own bond, or on bail, or under the special order of a Magistrate. *Discharge of arrested person.*

- - -

CHAPTER V.

OF PROCESSES TO COMPEL APPEARANCE.

A.—*Summons.*

43. (*1*) Every summons issued by a Court under this Code shall be in writing, in duplicate, signed or sealed by the presiding officer of the Court. *Form of summons.*

(*2*) Such summons shall be served by a police-officer, sheikh, or gaffir, or by any officer of the Court issuing it or other public servant who, under any rule for the time being in force, may be authorized to serve summonses. *Summons, by whom served.*

44. (*1*) The summons shall, if practicable, be served personally on the person summoned, by delivering or tendering to him one of the duplicates of the summons. *Summons, how served.*

(*2*) The person served shall, if so required by the serving officer, sign or seal a receipt therefor on the back of the other duplicate. *Signature of receipt for summons.*

45. Service of a summons on an incorporated company or other body corporate may be effected by serving it on the secretary, local manager, or other principal officer of the corporation, at any office of the corporation in the Sudan. *Service on company.*

25

Service when person summoned cannot be found. **46.** Where the person summoned cannot by the exercise of due diligence be found, the summons may be served by leaving one of the duplicates for him with some adult male member of his family, who shall, if so required by the serving officer, sign a receipt therefor on the back of the other duplicate, or by affixing one of the duplicates of the summons to some conspicuous part of the house or homestead in which the person summoned ordinarily resides.

Inability of person served to sign or seal. **47.** Where the person on or with whom a summons is served or left is unable to sign his name or affix his seal, the summons shall be served or left in the presence of two witnesses.

Service of summons outside local limits. **48.** A summons requiring to be served outside the local limits of the jurisdiction of the Court issuing it, shall ordinarily be sent in duplicate to a Magistrate within the local limits of whose jurisdiction the person summoned resides or is, to be there served.

Proof of service. **49.** An affidavit or declaration purporting to be made before a Magistrate by the serving officer or by a witness to the service that a summons has been served, and a duplicate of the summons purporting to be endorsed (in manner provided by section 44 or section 46) by the person to whom it was delivered or tendered or with whom it was left, shall be admissible in evidence, and the statements made therein shall be deemed to be correct unless and until the contrary is proved.

B.—*Warrant of Arrest.*

Form of warrant of arrest. **50.** (*1*) Every warrant of arrest issued by a Court under this Code shall be in writing, signed or sealed by the presiding officer of the Court.

Continuance of warrant of arrest. (*2*) Every such warrant shall remain in force until it is cancelled by the Court which issued it, or until it is executed.

Court may direct security to be taken. **51.** (*1*) A Court issuing a warrant for the arrest of any person may, in its discretion, direct by endorsement on the warrant, that, if such person executes a bond with sufficient sureties for his attendance before the Court at a specified time and thereafter until otherwise directed, the officer to whom the warrant is directed shall, on receiving security, release such person from custody.

(2) The endorsement shall state—

(*a*) the number of sureties;

(*b*) the amount in which they and the person for whose arrest the warrant is issued, are to be respectively bound; and

(*c*) the time at which he is to attend before the Court.

(3) Whenever security is taken under this section, the officer to whom the warrant is directed, shall forward the bond to the Court. <small>Bond to be forwarded.</small>

52. (*1*) A warrant of arrest shall ordinarily be directed to one or more police-officers, omdehs, or sheikhs; but the Court issuing the warrant may, if its immediate execution is necessary and no police-officer or suitable omdeh or sheikh is immediately available, direct it to any other person or persons. <small>Warrants, to whom directed.</small>

(2) When a warrant is directed to more officers or persons than one, it may be executed by all, or by any one or more, of them. <small>Warrant to several persons.</small>

53. A warrant directed to a police-officer may also be executed by any other police-officer whose name is endorsed upon the warrant by the officer to whom it is directed or endorsed. <small>Warrant directed to a police-officer.</small>

54. The police-officer or other person executing a warrant of arrest shall notify the substance thereof to the person to be arrested, and, if so required, shall show him the warrant. <small>Notification of substance of warrant.</small>

55. The police-officer or other person executing a warrant of arrest shall (subject to the provisions of section 51 as to security) without unnecessary delay bring the person arrested before the Court before which he is required by law to produce such person. <small>Person arrested to be brought before Court without delay.</small>

56. A warrant of arrest may be executed at any place in the Sudan. <small>Where warrant may be executed.</small>

57. (*1*) When a warrant is to be executed outside the local limits of the jurisdiction of the Court issuing the same, such Court may, instead of directing such warrant to a police-officer, forward the same by post or otherwise to any Magistrate within the local limits of whose jurisdiction it is to be executed. <small>Warrant forwarded for execution outside jurisdiction.</small>

(*2*) Such Magistrate shall endorse his name thereon and, if practicable, cause it to be executed in manner hereinbefore provided within the local limits of his jurisdiction.

Warrant directed to police-officer for execution outside jurisdiction.

58. When a warrant directed to a police-officer is to be executed beyond the local limits of the jurisdiction of the Court issuing the same, he shall, unless he believes that delay would prevent its execution, take it for endorsement either to a Magistrate or to a police-officer in charge of a station, within the local limits of whose jurisdiction the warrant is to be executed.

Procedure on arrest under warrant outside jurisdiction.

59. When a warrant of arrest is executed outside the Province in which it was issued, the person arrested shall, unless security is taken under section 51, be taken before a Magistrate within the local limits of whose jurisdiction the arrest was made, and such Magistrate shall, if the person arrested appears to be the person intended by the Court which issued the warrant, direct his removal in custody to such Court.

C.—*Proclamation and Attachment.*

Proclamation for person absconding.

60. (*1*) If a Mudir has reason to believe (whether after taking evidence or not) that a person against whom a warrant has been issued by the Mudir or by any Court within his Province, has absconded, or is concealing himself, so that such warrant cannot be executed, the Mudir may publish a written proclamation requiring him to appear at a specified place and a specified time not less than thirty days from the date of publishing the proclamation.

(*2*) The proclamation shall be published as follows:—

(*a*) it shall be publicly read in some conspicuous place of the town or village in which such person ordinarily resides;

(*b*) it shall be affixed to some conspicuous part of the house or homestead in which such person ordinarily resides, or to some conspicuous place of such town or village; and

(*c*) a copy thereof shall be affixed to some conspicuous part of the Mudirieh.

(*3*) A statement in writing by the Mudir to the effect that the proclamation was duly published on a specified

28

day shall be conclusive evidence that the requirements of this section have been complied with, and that the proclamation was published on such day.

61. (*1*) The Mudir may at any time thereafter order the attachment of any property, movable or immovable, or both, belonging to the proclaimed person. *Attachment of property of person absconding.*

(*2*) Such order shall authorize any officer named in it to attach any property belonging to such person within the Province in which it is made by seizure, or in any other manner in which for the time being property may be attached by way of civil process; and it shall authorize the attachment in like manner of any property belonging to such person outside the Province, when endorsed by the Mudir within whose Province it is situate.

(*3*) If the proclaimed person does not appear within the time specified in the proclamation, the property under attachment shall be at the disposal of Government; but it shall not be sold until the expiration of three months from the date of the attachment, unless it is subject to speedy and natural decay or the Mudir considers that the sale would be for the benefit of the owner, in either of which cases the Mudir may cause it to be sold whenever he thinks fit.

62. If, within one year from the date of the attachment, any person whose property is or has been at the disposal of Government under section 61, appears voluntarily or, being apprehended, is brought before the Mudir, and proves to the satisfaction of the Mudir that he did not abscond or conceal himself for the purpose of avoiding execution of the warrant, and that he had not such notice of the proclamation as to enable him to attend within the time specified therein, such property, so far as it has not been sold, and the nett proceeds of any part thereof which has been sold shall, after satisfying thereout all costs incurred in consequence of the attachment, be delivered to him. *Restoration of attached property.*

D. — Other Rules regarding Processes.

63. A Court empowered by this Code to issue a summons for the appearance of any person may, after recording its reasons in writing, issue a warrant for his arrest in addition to or in place of the summons— *Issue of warrant in lieu of, or in addition to, summons.*

29

(a) if, whether before or after the issue of such summons, the Court sees reason to believe that he has absconded or will not obey the summons; or

(b) if at the time fixed for his appearance he fails to appear, and the summons is proved to have been duly served in time to admit of his appearing, and no reasonable excuse is offered for his failure.

Power to take bond for appearance.

64. When any person for whose appearance or arrest a Court is empowered to issue a summons or warrant is present in the Court, the Court may require him to execute a bond, with or without sureties, for his appearance before the Court.

Arrest on breach of bond for appearance.

65. When a person who is bound by any bond taken under this Code to appear before a Court does not so appear, the Court may issue a warrant directing that he be arrested and produced before the Court.

Provisions of this chapter generally applicable to summons and warrants.

66. The provisions contained in this Chapter relating to summonses and warrants, and their issue, service and execution, shall, so far as may be, apply to every summons and every warrant issued under this Code.

CHAPTER VI.

OF PROCESSES TO COMPEL THE PRODUCTION OF DOCUMENTS AND OTHER MOVABLE PROPERTY AND FOR THE DISCOVERY OF PERSONS WRONGFULLY CONFINED.

A.—Summons to Produce.

Summons to produce document or other thing.

67. When a Court or an officer in charge of a police-station considers that the production of any document or other thing is necessary or desirable for the purpose of any investigation, inquiry, trial, or other proceeding under this Code by or before such Court or officer, the Court may issue a summons, or the officer a written order, to any person in whose possession or power the document or thing is believed to be, requiring him to attend and produce it, or to cause it to be produced, at the time and place stated in the summons or order.

B.—Searches.

68. Where for any reason it appears to a Court that it is impossible or inadvisable to proceed under the last preceding section, or that a general search or inspection would further the purposes of any investigation, inquiry, trial or other proceeding under this Code, the Court may issue a search-warrant authorising the person to whom it is addressed to search or inspect generally or in the place or places mentioned in the warrant, for any document or thing specified, or for any purpose described in the warrant.

Issue of search-warrant by Court.

69. Where an investigation under this Code is being prosecuted by an officer in charge of a police-station, he may apply to any Court or Magistrate within the local limits of whose jurisdiction his station is situate for the issue of a search-warrant under section 68.

Application of police-officer for search-warrant.

70. Where upon information, and after such inquiry as he thinks necessary, a Magistrate of the first or second class has reason to believe that any place is used for the deposit or sale of stolen property, or that there is kept or deposited in any place any property in respect of or by means of which an offence has been committed, or which is intended to be used for any illegal purpose—

Search for stolen property, etc.

he may issue a search-warrant addressed to an officer in charge of a police-station, or to an omdeh, or sheikh, authorising the person to whom it is addressed:—

(*1*) to search the place in accordance with the terms of the warrant and to seize any property appearing to be of any description above mentioned, and to dispose of it in accordance with the terms of the warrant; and.

(*2*) to arrest any person found in the place and appearing to have been or to be a party to any offence committed or intended to be committed in connection with the property.

71. Where a Magistrate of the first or second class, upon information and after such inquiry as he thinks necessary, has reason to believe that any person is confined under such circumstances that the confinement amounts to an offence, he may issue a search-warrant authorising the person to whom it is addressed to search for the

Search for person illegally confined.

31

confined person and to bring him before the Magistrate: upon the confined person being brought before him the Magistrate shall make such order as seems proper.

Search to be made in presence of witnesses.
72. Searches under this Chapter shall, unless the Magistrate owing to the pressing nature of the case otherwise directs, be made in the presence of two omdehs, sheikhs or other respectable inhabitants of the neighbourhood, to be summoned by the person to whom the search-warrant is addressed. A list of all things seized and of the places in which they are found shall be drawn up by the person carrying out the search and shall be signed or sealed by the witnesses.

Occupant of place searched may attend.
73. The occupant of any placed searched, or some person on his behalf, shall be permitted to be present at the search and shall, if he so require, receive a copy of the list of things seized therein signed or sealed by the witnesses.

Search of persons found in place.
74. (*1*) Where any person in or about a place which is being searched is reasonably suspected of concealing about his person any article for which search should be made, such person may be searched.

(*2*) A list of all things found on his person and seized shall be prepared and witnessed in manner mentioned in section 72, and a witnessed copy of the list shall be delivered to the person, if he so require.

Execution of search-warrant outside jurisdiction.
75. Every person executing a search-warrant beyond the local limits of the jurisdiction of the Court by which it was issued, shall before doing so apply to some Magistrate within the local limits of whose jurisdiction search is to be made, and shall act under his directions.

Provisions as to warrants of arrest to apply to search-warrant.
76. The provisions of section 33 as to ingress, and all other provisions hereinbefore contained as to warrants of arrest, shall, so far as applicable, apply to search warrants.

Magistrate may direct search in his presence.
77. Any Magistrate may direct a search to be made in his presence of any place for the search of which he is competent to issue a search-warrant.

PART IV.

OF PROCEEDINGS IN PROSECUTIONS.

CHAPTER VII.

Of Information to the Police and their Powers to Investigate.

78. If an officer in charge of a police-station receive information of the commission of an offence for which a police-officer is authorized to arrest without a warrant and which, under the provisions of Chapter VIII, may be tried by a Court within the local limits of whose jurisdiction his station is situate, or if for any other reason he suspects that such an offence has been committed, he shall proceed to the spot to investigate the case and take such steps as may be necessary for the discovery and the arrest of the offender, or may depute one of his subordinate officers so to do, and to report to him.

Investigation in cases where police-officer may arrest without warrant.

79. Every information received by an officer in charge of a police-station relating to the commission of such an

Information in such cases.

[handwritten annotation:] Jaafi   ) Please see penal opponents Sec: 81 (1) of Criminal

Sudan Government Order.

---●●●---

378. DEATH UNDER SUSPICIOUS CIRCUMSTANCES.

Whenever a Death is reported to the Local Authorities, which has not been certified by a Doctor or Sanitary Barber to be due to natural causes, or in places where there are no Doctors or Sanitary Authorities, and not seen so certified by the Sheikh, or as to which there are suspicious circumstances, the Mamur or a higher Magistrate shall hold an investigation under Section 81 (1) of the Criminal Procedure Code and report.

In the case of the death of an European the enquiry should be held by a Magistrate of the first or second class.

C.S./456   (6th Jan. 1905)

confined person and to bring him before the Magistrate: upon the confined person being brought before him the Magistrate shall make such order as seems proper.

Search to be made in presence of witnesses.

72. Searches under this Chapter shall, unless the Magistrate owing to the pressing nature of the case otherwise directs, be made in the presence of two omdehs, sheikhs or other respectable inhabitants of the neighbourhood, to be summoned by the person to whom the search-warrant is addressed. A list of all things seized and of the places in which they are found shall be drawn up by the person carrying out the search and shall be signed or sealed by the witnesses.

Occupant of place searched may attend.

73. The occupant of any placed searched, or some person on his behalf, shall be permitted to be present at the search and shall, if he so require, receive a copy of the list of things seized therein signed or sealed by the witnesses.

Search of persons found in place.

74. (*1*) Where any person in or about a place which is being searched is reasonably suspected of concealing about his person any article for which search should be made, such person may be searched.

(*2*) A list of all things found on his person and seized shall be prepared and witnessed in manner mentioned in section 72, and a witnessed copy of the list shall be delivered to the person, if he so require.

PART IV.

OF PROCEEDINGS IN PROSECUTIONS.

___

CHAPTER VII.

Of Information to the Police and their Powers to Investigate.

78. If an officer in charge of a police-station receive information of the commission of an offence for which a police-officer is authorized to arrest without a warrant and which, under the provisions of Chapter VIII, may be tried by a Court within the local limits of whose jurisdiction his station is situate, or if for any other reason he suspects that such an offence has been committed, he shall proceed to the spot to investigate the case and take such steps as may be necessary for the discovery and the arrest of the offender, or may depute one of his subordinate officers so to do, and to report to him.

Investigation in cases where police-officer may arrest without warrant.

79. Every information received by an officer in charge of a police-station relating to the commission of such an offence as is mentioned in section 78 shall, if given orally, be reduced to writing by him or under his direction, and the substance of every information, whether oral or written, shall be entered in a book to be kept in prescribed form by the officer.

Information in such cases.

80. If information is given to an officer in charge of a police-station of the commission of an offence for which a police-officer is not authorized to arrest without a warrant, he shall enter the substance of the information in a book to be kept as aforesaid and refer the informant to the proper Magistrate.

Information in other cases.

81. (*1*) Before entering upon an investigation under this Chapter, an officer in charge of a police-station shall send a report of the information or of his suspicion that an offence has been committed to the Mudir or to an Inspector, through the Mamur.

Report to be made.

C

33

<small>Magistrate receiving report may make preliminary inquiry.</small>

(*2*) Any of such Magistrates may himself make or direct a Magistrate subordinate to him to make, a preliminary inquiry, or may give any directions to the police-officer as to the conduct of the investigation.

<small>Cases in which investigation may be omitted.</small>

82. (*1*) If information is given under section 78 against a person by name and the alleged offence is not of a serious character, the officer need not make or direct an investigation on the spot ; and

(*2*) If it appears to the officer that there is no sufficient ground for entering on an investigation, he need not investigate the case.

(*3*) In each of the cases mentioned in this section, the officer shall record in the information book the reasons for his action, and shall report as under section 81.

<small>Power of police-officer to summon and examine witnesses.</small>

83. (*1*) A police-officer making an investigation under this Chapter, may require the attendance before him of any person being within the limits of his own or any adjoining police-station whose evidence appears likely to be of assistance in the case, and may examine such person orally.

(*2*) Such person shall be bound to answer the questions put to him, save so far as his answers would tend to expose him to a criminal charge or to a penalty.

(*3*) No person giving evidence in an investigation under this Chapter shall be required to sign his evidence if it be reduced to writing, nor shall such writing be used as evidence.

<small>No inducement to be offered.</small>

84. (*1*) No police-officer or person in authority shall make use of any threat or of any promise of an advantage towards a witness in an investigation under this Chapter in order to influence the evidence he may give.

(*2*) But no police-officer or other person shall prevent any person, by any caution or otherwise, from making in the course of the investigation any statement which of his own free will he may be disposed to make.

<small>Procedure when investigation cannot be completed in twenty-four hours.</small>

85. (*1*) Whenever it appears that an investigation under this Chapter cannot be completed within twenty-four hours of the arrest of the accused or suspected person, the officer in charge of the police-station shall forward the arrested person to the nearest Magistrate, with a report on the investigation so far as it has proceeded.

(2) The Magistrate, whether he has or has not juris-diction to try the case, may, from time to time, authorise the detention of the person under arrest in such custody as the Magistrate thinks fit, for a time not exceeding fifteen days in the whole, and shall record his reasons for so doing.

86. Whenever in the course of an investigation under this Chapter any person has been arrested and the officer in charge of the police-station is of opinion that there is not sufficient evidence or reasonable ground of suspicion to justify the forwarding of such person to a Magistrate, the officer may release him on his executing a bond, with or without sureties, to appear, if and when required, before a competent Magistrate. *Release of accused when evidence deficient.*

87. (*1*) If, upon an investigation under this Chapter, it appears to the officer in charge of the police-station that there is sufficient evidence or reasonable ground of suspicion to justify him in so doing, he may forward the accused person to a Magistrate competent to try the case or commit it for trial. *Case to be sent to Magistrate when evidence is sufficient.*

(2) When the officer in charge of a police-station forwards a person in custody under this section, he shall require the complainant (if any) and so many of the persons who appear to be acquainted with the circumstances of the case as he may think necessary, to execute bonds, without sureties, to appear before a Magistrate as thereby directed, and prosecute or give evidence in the matter of the charge against the accused.

(3) The day fixed for appearance shall be the day on which the accused person may be expected to arrive at the Court of the Magistrate.

(4) The bonds shall be forwarded to the Magistrate.

(5) If any person required to execute a bond under this section refuse to do so, he may be forwarded in custody to the Magistrate and detained until he executes the bond, or until the hearing of the case is concluded.

88. So soon as an investigation under this Chapter is completed, the officer in charge of the police-station shall forward his report to a Magistrate competent to try the case or commit it for trial. If it appear from the report that the accused has been released on his bond, the Magistrate shall make such order for the discharge of the bond or otherwise as he thinks fit. *Final report of police-officer.*

35

Powers of Magistrate holding preliminary inquiry under section 81.   **89.** All or any of the powers of an officer in charge of a police-station under sections 83 to 87 may be exercised by a Magistrate not having power to try a case or commit it for trial, who holds a preliminary inquiry under section 81 (2) or to whom a person under arrest is forwarded under section 85.

CHAPTER VIII.

PLACE OF INQUIRY AND TRIAL.

Ordinary place of inquiry and trial.   **90.** Every offence shall ordinarily be inquired into and tried by a Court within the local limits of whose jurisdiction

(i) the offence was wholly or in part committed, or some act forming part of the offence was done; or

(ii) some consequence of the offence has ensued; or

(iii) some offence was committed by reference to which the offence is defined; or

(iv) some person against whom, or property in respect of which, the offence was committed is found, having been transported thither by the offender or by some person knowing of the offence.

Illustrations.

(*a*) A posts, in Dongola, a letter addressed to B in Khartoum, threatening to accuse B of an offence, in order to extort money from him.

(*b*) A stabs B at Dongola, and B dies ten days later at Khartoum in consequence of the wound.

(*c*) A, in Dongola, abets an offence committed by B at Khartoum.

(*d*) A abducts B at Dongola and carries him to Khartoum, where he is found.

(*e*) A steals property at Dongola, and the property is taken by B, who knows it to be stolen, to Khartoum, where it is found.

In all the above cases, A may be tried either at Dongola or at Khartoum.

Place of inquiry or trial when scene of offence is uncertain.   **91.** When it is uncertain in which of several local areas an offence was wholly or in part committed, the offence may be inquired into or tried by a Court having jurisdiction over any of such local areas.

Offences committed elsewhere than in a place where Penal Code is in force.   **92.** Every offence which by virtue of section 3 of the Sudan Penal Code may be punished under that Code, although committed elsewhere than in a part of the Sudan in which that Code is in force, may be dealt with as if it had been committed at any place (being in a part of the Sudan in which this Code is in force) at which the offender may be found.

93. The Mudir shall, where it is doubtful which is the competent Court within his Province under section 90, direct by what Magistrate an inquiry shall be made or before what Court a trial shall take place, within his Province. *Powers of Mudir in cases of doubt.*

94. (*1*) The Mudir may, whenever it appears to him that such transfer will promote the ends of justice, transfer any case from one Court within his Province to another, at any stage of the proceedings. *Power to transfer.*

(*2*) The Governor-General may make the like transfer from one Province to another.

95. When a Magistrate of the first or second class sees reason to believe that any person within the local limits of his jurisdiction has committed without such limits an offence which cannot, under the provisions of section 90 or any other law for the time being in force, be inquired into or tried within such local limits, but is, under some law for the time being in force, triable in the Sudan, he may inquire into the offence as if it had been committed within such local limits, and compel such person in manner hereinbefore provided to appear before him, and send such person to the Mudir, to be by him forwarded to the Court having jurisdiction to inquire into or try the offence. *Power to issue summons or warrant for offence committed beyond local jurisdiction. Magistrate's procedure on arrest.*

96. No proceeding before any Court, nor any order passed nor judgment delivered therein, shall be invalid by reason of the fact that, according to the rules contained in this Chapter, such proceeding ought to have been taken before some other Court. *Proceedings before wrong Court not to be invalid.*

CHAPTER IX.

Of the Taking Cognizance of Offences by Magistrates.

97. A Magistrate competent to try an offence or commit for trial in respect of it may (subject to the provisions of Chapter X) take cognizance of it— *Cognizance of offences by Magistrates.*

(*a*) upon receiving a police report under Chapter VII;
(*b*) upon receiving a complaint of facts which constitute the offence;
(*c*) if, from information received from any person other than a police-officer, or from his own knowledge, he has reason to believe or suspect that the offence has been committed.

Examination of complainant.

98. A Magistrate taking cognizance of an offence on complaint shall, subject to the provisions of section 211, at once examine the complainant and reduce his complaint and the substance of the examination to writing. The writing shall be signed or sealed by the complainant if he is able so to do.

Procedure by Magistrate not competent to take cognizance of the case.

99. If a complaint is made to a Magistrate who is not competent to take cognizance of the case, he shall direct the complainant to the proper Court, and, if the complaint has been made in writing, shall endorse the complaint and return it.

Transfer of cases by Magistrates.

100. If an offence complained of is one which, under any general regulations for the distribution of business issued by the Mudir, ought to be tried or inquired into by another Magistrate, or if in the opinion of the Magistrate receiving the complaint the offence might, consistently with such general regulations, be more conveniently tried or inquired into by another Magistrate, the Magistrate receiving the complaint shall, either before or after examining the complainant, transfer the case to such other Magistrate.

Postponing issue of process.

101. If a Magistrate upon receiving a complaint and examining the complainant is not satisfied as to its truth, or if a Magistrate takes cognizance of an offence under section 97 (*c*), he may, before causing process to issue for compelling the attendance of the person accused or suspected, either himself make a preliminary inquiry into the case or direct any officer subordinate to him or a police-officer to do so. Such preliminary inquiry shall be conducted so far as may be in the manner, and with the powers, in and with which an investigation under Chapter VII is conducted.

Dismissal of complaint.

102. The Magistrate before whom a complaint is made may dismiss the complaint, if, after examining the complainant and considering the result of the preliminary inquiry (if any) under section 101, there is, in his judgment, no sufficient ground for proceeding. In such case he shall briefly record his reasons for so doing.

103. (*1*) When a Magistrate taking cognizance of a case is satisfied that there is sufficient ground for proceeding, he shall cause process to issue for compelling the attendance of the accused person.

Issue of process.

(*2*) Such process shall ordinarily be a summons or a warrant according as, in his opinion, a summons or a warrant should, according to the fourth column of the first schedule, issue in the first instance. But a Magistrate may issue a summons in place of a warrant if he think fit.

(*3*) When by law any process-fees or other fees are payable, no process shall issue until the fees are paid, and, if such fees are not paid within a reasonable time, the Magistrate may dismiss the complaint.

104. Whenever a Magistrate issues a summons, he may, if he sees reason so to do, dispense with the personal attendance of the accused and permit him to appear by his pleader or other permissible agent.

Magistrate may dispense with personal attendance of accused.

In such case the Magistrate may in his discretion, at any future stage of the proceedings, direct the personal attendance of the accused and, if necessary, enforce his attendance in manner hereinbefore provided.

CHAPTER X.

OF THE SANCTIONS NECESSARY FOR THE INITIATION OF CERTAIN PROCEEDINGS.

105. (*1*) No Magistrate or Court shall take cognizance:—

Prosecution for contempts of lawful authority of public servants.

(*a*) of any offence punishable under sections 137 to 152 (both inclusive) of the Sudan Penal Code, except with the previous sanction, or on the complaint, of the public servant concerned or of some public servant to whom he is subordinate;

(*b*) of any offence punishable under sections 157, 158, 159, 160, 163, 164, 171, 172, 173, 177, 178 or 180 of the same Code, when such offence is committed

Prosecution for certain offences against public justice.

in, or in relation to, any proceeding in any Court, except with the previous sanction, or on the complaint of such Court, or of the Magistrate who presided over the Court, or of the Mudir;

Prosecution for certain offences relating to documents given in evidence.

(*c*) of any offence described in section 374 or punishable under section 382 or 385 of the same Code, when such offence has been committed by a party to any proceeding in any Court in respect of a document produced or given in evidence in such proceeding, except with the previous sanction, or on the complaint, of such Court or of the Magistrate who presided over the Court, or of the Mudir.

(*2*) In clauses (*b*) and (*c*) of sub-section (*1*) the term "Court" includes every Civil, Revenue or Criminal Court.

(*3*) The provisions of sub-section (*1*), with reference to the offences named therein, apply also to the abetment of such offences, and attempts to commit them.

Nature of sanction necessary.

(*4*) The sanction referred to in this section may be expressed in general terms, and need not name the accused person; but it shall, so far as practicable, specify the Court or other place in which, and the occasion on which, the offence was committed.

(*5*) When sanction is given in respect of any offence referred to in this section, the Court taking cognizance of the case may frame a charge of any other offence so referred to which is disclosed by the facts.

(*6*) Any sanction given or refused under this section may be revoked or granted by any authority to which the authority giving or refusing it is subordinate.

Prosecution for offences against the State.

106. No Magistrate or Court shall take cognizance of any offence punishable under Chapter VIII of the Sudan Penal Code, or punishable under section 91 or section 414 of the same Code, unless upon complaint made by order of, or under authority from, the Mudir or Governor-General.

Prosecution of public servants.

107. When any public servant, not removable from his office without the sanction of the Governor-General, is accused as such public servant of any offence, no Magistrate or Court shall take cognizance of such offence, except with the previous sanction of the Governor-General, or of some Court or other authority to which such public servant is subordinate. and whose power to give such sanction has not been limited by the Governor-General.

108. No Court shall take cognizance of an offence falling under Chapter XXII or Chapter XXIV of the Sudan Penal Code or under sections 401 to 404 (both inclusive) of the same Code. except upon a complaint made by some person aggrieved by such offence. Prosecution for breach of contract, defamation and offences against marriage.

109. No Court shall take cognizance of an offence under section 105, 106, or 407 of the Sudan Penal Code, except upon a complaint made by the husband of the woman, or, in his absence, by some person who had care of such woman on his behalf at the time when such offence was committed. Prosecution for adultery or enticing a married woman.

CHAPTER XI.

OF INQUIRY INTO CASES TRIABLE BY A MINOR DISTRICT COURT OR THE MUDIR'S COURT.

110. Any Magistrate of the first or second class may (subject to any directions to be issued by the Mudir) commit any person for trial to a Minor District Court or the Mudir's Court. Power to commit for trial.

111. The following procedure shall be adopted in inquiries before Magistrates. where the case is triable exclusively by a Minor District Court or the Mudir's Court. or, in the opinion of the Magistrate, ought to be tried by one of such Courts. Procedure in inquires preparatory to commitment.

112. (*1*) The Magistrate shall. when the accused appears or is brought before him. proceed to hear the complainant (if any). and take in manner hereinafter provided all such evidence as may be produced in support of the prosecution or in behalf of the accused, or as may be called for by the Magistrate. Taking of evidence produced.

(*2*) The accused shall be at liberty to cross-examine the witnesses for the prosecution, and in such case the prosecutor may re-examine them.

(*3*) If the complainant or officer conducting the prose-cution, or the accused. applies to the Magistrate to issue process to compel the attendance of any witness or the Process for the production of further evidence.

production of any document or thing, the Magistrate shall issue such process unless, for reasons to be recorded, he deems it unnecessary to do so.

Power to examine accused.

(*4*) The Magistrate may, if he think proper, examine the accused for the purpose of enabling him to explain any circumstances appearing in the evidence against him.

When accused person to be discharged.

113. (*1*) If after hearing the evidence the Magistrate finds that there are not sufficient grounds for committing the accused for trial, he shall record his reasons and discharge him, unless it appears to the Magistrate that the accused should be tried before himself or some other Magistrate, in which case he shall proceed accordingly.

(*2*) The Magistrate may discharge the accused at any previous stage of the case if, for reasons to be recorded, he considers the charge to be groundless.

When charge to be framed.

114. If upon hearing the evidence the Magistrate is satisfied that there are sufficient grounds for committing the accused for trial, he shall frame a charge under his hand, declaring with what offence the accused is charged.

Charge to be explained, and copy furnished, to accused.

(*2*) As soon as the charge has been framed, it shall be read and explained to the accused, and a copy of it shall, if he so requires, be given to him free of cost.

List of witnesses for defence on trial.

115. (*1*) The accused shall be required at once to give in, orally or in writing, a list of the persons (if any) whom he wishes to be summoned to give evidence on his trial.

Further list.

(*2*) The Magistrate may, in his discretion, allow the accused to give in any further list of witnesses at a subsequent time.

Power of Magistrate to examine such witnesses.

116. The Magistrate may, in his discretion, summon and examine any witness named in any list given in to him under section 115.

Order of commitment.

117. (*1*) If the Magistrate, after hearing the witnesses summoned under section 116, is satisfied that there are not sufficient grounds for committing the accused, he may cancel the charge and discharge the accused.

(*2*) Otherwise he shall make an order committing the accused for trial by a Minor District Court or the Mudir's Court (as the case may be), and shall briefly record his reasons for the commitment.

118. When the accused has given in any list of witnesses under section 115 and has been committed for trial, the Magistrate shall summon such of the witnesses included in the list as have not appeared before himself to appear before the Court to which the accused has been committed :

provided that, if the Magistrate thinks that any witness is included in the list for the purpose of vexation or delay, or of defeating the ends of justice, the Magistrate may require the accused to satisfy him that there are reasonable grounds for believing that the evidence of such witness is material, and if he is not so satisfied, may refuse to summon the witness (recording his reasons for such refusal), or may before summoning him require such sum to be deposited as he thinks necessary to defray the expense of obtaining the attendance of the witness and all other proper expenses.

Summons to witnesses for defence when accused is committed.

119. Complainants and witnesses for the prosecution and defence whose attendance at the trial is necessary and who appear before a Magistrate, shall execute before him bonds binding themselves to be in attendance when called upon at the trial to prosecute or give evidence, as the case may be.

Bonds of complainants and witnesses.

120. If any complainant or witness refuse to execute the bond above directed, the Magistrate may detain him in custody until he executes the bond, or until his attendance at the trial is required, when the Magistrate shall send him in custody to the Minor District Court or Mudir's Court, as the case may be.

Detention in custody in case of refusal to execute bond.

121. When the accused is committed for trial by a Magistrate, other than the Mudir, the Magistrate shall send the charge, the record of the inquiry and any weapon or other thing which is to be produced in evidence, to the Mudir or to the officer prescribed by the Mudir.

Charge, etc., to be forwarded.

122. (*1*) The Magistrate may, if he thinks fit, summon and examine supplementary witnesses after the committment and before the commencement of trial, and bind them over in manner hereinbefore provided to appear and give evidence.

Power to summon supplementary witnesses.

(*2*) Such examination shall, if possible, be taken in the presence of the accused, and a copy of the evidence of such witnesses shall, if the accused so require, be given to him free of cost.

Custody of accused pending trial.

123. Until and during the trial, the Magistrate shall, subject to the provisions of this Code regarding the taking of bail, commit the accused, by warrant, to custody.

CHAPTER XII.

OF CHARGES.

A.—Form of Charges.

Charge to state offence.

124. (*1*) Every charge under this Code shall state the offence with which the accused is charged.

Specific name of offence sufficient description.

(*2*) If the law which creates the offence gives it any specified name, the offence may be described in the charge by that name only.

How stated where offence has no specific name.

(*3*) If the law which creates the offence does not give it any specific name, so much of the definition of the offence must be stated as to give the accused notice of the matter with which he is charged.

(*4*) The law and section of the law against which the offence is said to have been committed shall be mentioned in the charge.

What implied in charge.

(*5*) The fact that the charge is made is equivalent to a statement that every legal condition required by law to constitute the offence charged was fulfilled in the particular case.

Language of charge.

(*6*) The charge shall be written either in English or in Arabic.

Particulars as to time, place and person.

125. The charge shall contain such particulars as to the time and place of the alleged offence, and the person (if any) against whom, or the thing (if any) in respect of which, it was committed, as are reasonably sufficient to give the accused notice of the matter with which he is charged.

Charge of criminal breach of trust, etc.

126. When the accused is charged with criminal breach of trust or dishonest misappropriation of money, it shall be sufficient to specify the gross sum in respect of which the offence is alleged to have been committed, and the dates between which the offence is alleged to have been committed, without specifying particular items or exact dates, and the charge so framed shall be deemed to be a charge of one offence within the meaning of section 136: provided that the time included between the first and last of such dates shall not exceed one year.

127. When the nature of the case is such that the particulars mentioned in sections 124 and 125 do not give the accused sufficient notice of the matter with which he is charged, the charge shall also contain such particulars of the manner in which the alleged offence was committed as will be sufficient for that purpose.

When manner of committing offence must be stated.

Illustrations.

(*a*) A is accused of the theft of a certain article at a certain time and place. The charge need not set out the manner in which the theft was effected.

(*b*) A is accused of cheating B at a given time and place. The charge must set out the manner in which A cheated B.

(*c*) A is accused of giving false evidence at a given time and place. The charge must set out that portion of the evidence given by A which is alleged to be false.

128. No error in stating either the offence or the particulars required to be stated in the charge, and no omission to state the offence or those particulars, shall be regarded at any stage of the case as material, unless the accused was in fact misled by such error or omission, and it has occasioned a failure of justice.

Effect of errors.

Illustrations.

(*a*) A is charged with cheating B, and the manner in which he cheated B is not set out in the charge, or is set out incorrectly. A defends himself, calls witnesses, and gives his own account of the transaction. The Court may infer from this that the omission to set out the manner of the cheating is not material.

(*b*) A is charged with cheating B, and the manner in which he cheated B is not set out in the charge. There were many transactions between A and B, and A had no means of knowing to which of them the charge referred, and offered no defence. The Court may infer from such facts that the omission to set out the manner of the cheating was, in this case a material error.

(*c*) A is charged with the murder of Ahmed Mahmoud on the 21st January, 1899. In fact, the murdered person's name was Abdul Mahmoud, and the date of the murder was the 20th January, 1899. A was never charged with any murder but one, and had heard the inquiry before the Magistrate, which referred exclusively to the case of Abdul Mahmoud. The Court may infer from these facts that A was not misled, and that the error in the charge was immaterial.

(*d*) A was accused of murdering Ahmed Mahmoud on the 20th January, 1899, and Abdul Mahmoud (who tried to arrest him for that murder) on the 21st January, 1899. He was, upon a charge referring to the murdered man as Ahmed Mahmoud, tried for the murder of Abdul Mahmoud. The witnesses present in his defence were witnesses in the case of Ahmed Mahmoud. The confirming authority may infer from this that A was misled and that the error was material.

Procedure on commitment without charge, or on imperfect charge.

129. When any person is committed for trial without a charge, or with an imperfect or erroneous charge, the Court may frame a charge, or add to or otherwise alter the charge, as the case may be, having regard to the rules contained in this Code as to the form of charges.

Court may alter charge.

130. (*1*) Any Court may alter or add to any charge at any time before judgment is pronounced.

(*2*) Every such alteration or addition shall be read and explained to the accused.

When trial may proceed immediately after alteration.

131. If the charge framed or alteration or addition made under section 129 or section 130 is such that proceeding immediately with the trial is not likely, in the opinion of the Court, to prejudice the accused in his defence or the prosecutor in the conduct of the case, the Court may, in its discretion, after such charge or alteration or addition has been framed or made, proceed with the trial as if the new or altered charge had been the original charge.

When new trial may be directed, or trial suspended.

132. If the new or altered or added charge is such that proceeding immediately with the trial is likely, in the opinion of the Court, to prejudice the accused or the prosecutor as aforesaid, the Court may either direct a new trial or adjourn the trial for such period as may be necessary.

Recall of witnesses when charge altered.

133. Whenever a charge is altered or added to by the Court after the commencement of the trial, the prosecutor and the accused shall be allowed to recall or re-summon, and examine with reference to such alteration or addition, any witness who may have been examined, and also to call any further witness whom the Court may think to be material.

Effect of material error.

134. (*1*) If the Mudir or the Governor-General, in the exercise of any power under Chapter XVIII, is of opinion that any person convicted of an offence was misled in his defence by the absence of a charge or by an error in the charge, he shall direct a new trial to be had upon a charge framed in whatever manner he thinks fit.

(2) If the Mudir or Governor-General is of opinion that the facts of the case are such that no valid charge could be preferred against the accused in respect of the facts proved, he shall quash the conviction.

B.—Joinder of Charges.

135. For every distinct offence of which any person is accused there shall be a separate charge, and every such charge shall be tried separately, except in the cases mentioned in sections 136, 137, 138 and 141.

Separate charges for distinct offences.

Illustration.

A is accused of a theft on one occasion, and of causing grievous hurt on another occasion. A must be separately charged and separately tried for the theft and for causing grievous hurt.

136. (*1*) When a person is accused of more offences than one of the same kind committed within the space of twelve months from the first to the last of such offences, he may be charged with, and tried at one trial for, any number of them not exceeding three.

Three offences of same kind within year may be charged together.

(2) Offences are of the same kind when they are punishable with the same amount of punishment under the same section of the same law.

137. If a series of acts are alleged, so connected together as to form the same transaction, the accused may be charged with, and tried at one trial for, every offence which he would have committed if the whole of such acts, or some one or more of them without the rest were proved.

Acts forming the same transaction.

[*Note.*—In passing sentence, the Court must, nevertheless, have regard to section 51 of the Sudan Penal Code.]

138. If a single act or series of acts is of such a nature that it is doubtful which of several offences the facts which can be proved will constitute, the accused may be charged with having committed all or any of such offences, and any number of such charges may be tried at once; or he may be charged in the alternative with having committed some one of the said offences.

When it is doubtful what offence has been committed.

Illustrations.

(*a*) A is accused of an act which may amount to theft, or receiving stolen property, or criminal breach of trust, or cheating. He may be charged with theft, receiving stolen property, criminal breach of trust and cheating, or he may be charged with having committed theft, or receiving stolen property, or criminal breach of trust, or cheating.

(*b*) A states on oath before the Magistrate that he saw B hit C with a club. Before a Minor District Court A states on oath that B never hit C. A may be charged in the alternative and convicted of intentionally giving false evidence, although it cannot be proved which of these contradictory statements was false.

When person charged with one offence can be convicted of another. **139.** (*1*) If, in the case mentioned in section 138, the accused is charged with one offence, and it appears in evidence that he committed a different offence for which he might have been charged under the provisions of that section, he may be convicted of the offence which he is shown to have committed, although he was not charged with it.

(*2*) When the accused is charged with an offence, he may be convicted of having attempted to commit that offence, although the attempt is not separately charged.

When offence proved included in that charged. **140.** (*1*) When a person is charged with an offence consisting of several particulars, a combination of some only of which constitutes a complete minor offence, and such combination is proved, but the remaining particulars are not proved, he may be convicted of the minor offence, though he was not charged with it.

(*2*) When a person is charged with an offence and facts are proved which reduce it to a minor offence, he may be convicted of the minor offence, although he is not charged with it.

What persons may be charged jointly. **141.** When more persons than one are accused of the same offence or of diffent offences committed in the same transaction, or when one person is accused of committing an offence, and another of abetment of, or attempt to commit, such offence, they may be charged and tried together or separately, as the Court thinks fit; and the provisions contained in the former part of this Chapter shall apply to all such charges.

Illustrations.

(*a*) A and B are accused of the same murder. A and B may be charged and tried together for the murder.

48

(*b*) A and B are accused of a robbery, in the course of which A commits a murder with which B has nothing to do. A and B may be tried together on a charge, charging both of them with the robbery and A alone with the murder.

(*c*) A and B are both charged with theft, and B is charged with two other thefts committed by him in the course of the same transaction. A and B may be tried together on a charge, charging both with the one theft and B alone with the two other thefts.

142. When a charge containing more heads than one is framed against the same person, and when a conviction has been had on one or more of them, the complainant, or the officer conducting the prosecution, may, with the consent of the Court, withdraw the remaining charge or charges, or the Court of its own accord may stay the inquiry into, or trial of, such charge or charges. Such withdrawal shall have the effect of an acquittal on such charge or charges, unless the conviction be set aside, in which case the Court (subject to the order setting aside the conviction) may proceed with the inquiry into or trial of the charge or charges so withdrawn.

Withdrawal of remaining charges on conviction on one of several charges.

CHAPTER XIII.

Of Summary Trials by Magistrates.

143. Every Magistrate of the first, second and third class, respectively, may try summarily the offences specified in that behalf in the third schedule.

What cases may be tried summarily.

144. The procedure in a summary trial shall, so far as may be, be the same as that on the hearing of a charge in a summary manner by a Commanding Officer under Egyptian Military Law.

Procedure in summary trial.

145. (*1*) In summary trials the Magistrate need not record the evidence of the witnesses or frame a formal charge; but he shall enter in a form to be prescribed the following particulars—

Record in summary trial.

  (*a*) the serial number;
  (*b*) the date of the commission of the offence;
  (*c*) the date of the report or complaint;
  (*d*) the name of the complainant (if any);
  (*e*) the name, parentage and residence of the accused;

(*f*) the offence complained of and the offence (if any) proved, with the value of the property in respect of which the offence has been committed if the value is material as shewing that he had jurisdiction in the case;

(*g*) the plea of the accused and his examination (if any);

(*h*) the finding, and, in the case of a conviction, a brief statement of the reason therefor;

(*i*) the sentence, or other final order; and

(*j*) the date on which the proceedings terminated.

(*2*) The record shall be in English or in Arabic, and shall be signed or sealed by the Magistrate.

CHAPTER XIV.

Of Trials by Magistrates other than Summary Trials.

Procedure in non-summary trial by Magistrate.

146. The following procedure shall be observed by Magistrates in the trial of cases otherwise than summarily.

Evidence for prosecution.

147. (*1*) When the accused appears or is brought before him, the Magistrate shall proceed to hear the complainant (if any) and take all such evidence as may be produced in support of the prosecution.

(*2*) The Magistrate shall ascertain, from the complainant or otherwise, the name of any persons likely to be acquainted with the facts of the case and to be able to give evidence for the prosecution, and shall summon to give evidence before himself such of them as he thinks necessary.

Discharge of accused.

148. (*1*) If, upon taking all the evidence referred to in section 147, and making such examination (if any) of the accused as the Magistrate thinks necessary, he finds that no case against the accused has been made out which, if unrebutted, would warrant his conviction, the Magistrate shall discharge him.

(*2*) The Magistrate may discharge the accused at any previous stage of the case if, for reasons to be recorded by him, he considers the charge to be groundless.

149. If, when such evidence and examination have been taken and made, or at any previous stage of the case, the Magistrate is of opinion that there is ground for presuming that the accused has committed an offence triable under this Chapter, which such Magistrate is competent to try, and which, in his opinion, could be adequately punished by him, he shall frame in writing a charge against the accused. *Charge to be framed when offence appears to have been committed.*

150. (*1*) The charge shall then be read and explained to the accused and he shall be asked whether he is guilty or has any defence to make. *Plea.*

(*2*) If the accused pleads guilty, the Magistrate shall record the plea, and may, in his discretion, convict him thereon.

151. (*1*) If the accused refuses to plead, or does not plead, or claims to be tried, he shall be required to state whether he wishes to cross-examine any, and if so which, of the witnesses for the prosecution whose evidence has been taken. If he says he does so wish, the witnesses named by him shall be recalled, and, after cross-examination and re-examination (if any), they shall be discharged. The evidence of any remaining witnesses for the prosecution shall next be taken, and, after cross-examination and re-examination (if any), they also shall be discharged. The accused shall then be called upon to enter upon his defence and produce his evidence. *Defence.*

(*2*) If the accused puts in any written statement, the Magistrate shall file it with the record.

152. (*1*) The accused may, after entering upon his defence, apply to the Magistrate to issue any process for compelling the attendance of any witness for the purpose of examination or the production of any document or other thing, and the Magistrate shall issue such process unless, for reasons to be recorded by him in writing, he considers that the application is made for the purpose of vexation or delay or for defeating the ends of justice. *Process for compelling production of evidence at instance of accused.*

(*2*) The Magistrate may, before summoning any witness on such application, require that his reasonable expenses incurred in attending for the purposes of the trial be deposited in Court.

153. (*1*) If in any case under this Chapter in which a charge has been framed the Magistrate finds the accused not guilty, he shall record an order of acquittal. *Acquittal.*

Conviction.

(*2*) If in any such case the Magistrate finds the accused guilty, he shall pass sentence upon him according to law.

Absence of complainant.

154. When the proceedings have been instituted upon complaint, and upon any day fixed for the hearing of the case the complainant is absent, the Magistrate may, in his discretion, notwithstanding anything hereinbefore contained, at any time before the charge has been framed, discharge the accused.

Frivolous or vexatious accusations.

155. (*1*) If, in any case instituted by complaint as defined in this Code or upon information given to a police-officer or Magistrate and heard under this Chapter, the Magistrate discharges or acquits the accused and is satisfied that the accusation against him was frivolous or vexatious, the Magistrate may, in his discretion, by his order of discharge or acquittal, direct the complainant or informant to pay to the accused, or to each of the accused where there are more than one, such compensation, not exceeding L.E. 3, as the Magistrate thinks fit:

Provided that, before making any such direction, the Magistrate shall—

(*a*) record and consider any objection which the complainant or informant if present at the hearing may urge against the making of the direction, and,

(*b*) if the Magistrate directs any compensation to be paid, state in writing, in his order of discharge or acquittal, his reasons for awarding the compensation.

(*2*) Compensation awarded as above shall be recoverable as if it were a fine:

provided that if imprisonment be awarded in default of payment, the term of such imprisonment shall not exceed thirty days.

CHAPTER XV.

OF TRIALS BY MINOR DISTRICT COURTS AND MUDIR'S COURTS.

Procedure that of Court-Martial.

156. Subject to any other provision of this Code, the procedure, and the rules as to the appointment and functions of a prisoner's friend, shall, so far as may be, be the same as in a trial, by Court-Martial under Egyptian Military Law:

provided that Provisos.

(1) the members of the Court shall not be sworn;

(2) no objection shall be taken to the constitution of the Court, otherwise than on the ground that it violates some provision of this Code;

(3) there shall be no Judge Advocate; and

(4) judgment shall be pronounced, in accordance with Chapter XVII, before submission to the confirming authority.

CHAPTER XVI.

General Provisions as to Inquiries and Trials.

157. Subject to any other provision of this Code, evidence shall be admissible and shall be recorded in every inquiry and trial, and the evidence taken on an inquiry into an offence shall be admissible at the trial, according to the rules applicable at a trial by Court-Martial under Egyptian Military Law. Admissibility and recording of evidence. Evidence taken on inquiry available at trial.

158. Any Court may, if it thinks fit, impound any document or thing produced before it under this Code. Power to impound documents, etc.

159. (*1*) In the case of any offence triable exclusively by a Minor District Court or the Mudir's Court, the Mudir, or the Magistrate inquiring to into the offence with the sanction of the Mudir, may at any time, with the view of obtaining the evidence of any person supposed to have been directly or indirectly concerned in, or privy to the offence, tender a pardon to such person on condition of his making a full and true disclosure of the whole of the circumstances within his knowledge relative to such offence, and to every other person concerned, whether as principal or abettor, in the commission thereof. Tender of pardon

(*2*) Every person accepting a tender under this section shall be examined as a witness in the case.

(*3*) Such person, if not on bail, shall be detained in custody until the termination of the trial.

(*4*) Every Magistrate, who tenders a pardon under this section, shall record his reasons for so doing.

Power to direct tender of pardon during trial. **160.** At any time after the commencement of the trial, but before judgment is passed, the Court before which the trial takes place may, with the view of obtaining the evidence of any person supposed to have been directly or indirectly concerned in, or privy to, any such offence, tender a pardon on the same condition to such person.

When pardon may be revoked. **161.** (*1*) Where a pardon has been tendered under section 159 or section 160, and any person who has accepted such tender has, either by wilfully concealing anything essential or by giving false evidence, not complied with the condition on which the tender was made, he may be tried for the offence in respect of which the pardon was so tendered, or for any other offence of which he appears to have been guilty in connection with the same matter.

(*2*) The statement made by a person who has accepted a tender of pardon may be given in evidence against him when the pardon has been forfeited under this section.

Prosecutions, by whom conducted. **162.** Prosecutions may be conducted by the complainant, or by a police-officer, pleader, or other person appointed by the Mudir or by the presiding Magistrate.

Right to be defended by pleader. **163.** Every person accused before any Criminal Court may of right be defended by a pleader.

Procedure when accused does not understand proceedings. **164.** If the accused, though not insane, cannot be made to understand the proceedings, the Court may proceed with the inquiry or trial; and if the accused is ultimately convicted, the proceedings shall be forwarded to the confirming authority under Chapter XVIII with a report of the circumstances of the case, and the confirming authority shall pass thereon such order as he thinks fit.

Power to examine the accused. **165.** (*1*) For the purpose of enabling the accused to explain any circumstances appearing in the evidence against him, the Court may, at any stage of an inquiry or trial, without previously warning the accused, put such questions to him as the Court considers necessary, and shall, for the purpose aforesaid, question him generally on the case after the witnesses for the prosecution have been examined and before he is called on for his defence.

(*2*) The accused shall not render himself liable to punishment by refusing to answer such questions, or by giving false answers to them; but the Court may draw such inference from such refusal or answers as it thinks just.

(*3*) The answers given by the accused may be taken into consideration in the inquiry or trial, and put in evidence for or against him in any other inquiry into, or trial for, any other offence which such answers may tend to show he has committed.

(*4*) No oath shall be administered to the accused.

166. Except as provided in sections 159 and 160, no influence, by means of any promise or threat or otherwise, shall be used to an accused person to induce him to disclose or withhold any matter within his knowledge. *No influence to be used to induce disclosure.*

167. (*1*) If, from the absence of a witness, or any other reasonable cause, it becomes necessary or advisable to postpone the commencement of, or adjourn, any inquiry or trial, the Court may, if it thinks fit, by order in writing, stating the reasons therefor, from time to time, postpone or adjourn the same on such terms as it thinks fit, for such time as it considers reasonable, and may by a warrant remand the accused, if in custody. *Power to postpone or adjourn proceedings.*

(*2*) Provided that no Magistrate shall remand an accused person to custody under this section for a term exceeding fifteen days at a time.

Explanation.—If sufficient evidence has been obtained to raise a suspicion that the accused may have committed an offence, and it appears likely that further evidence may be obtained by a remand, this is reasonable cause for a remand. *Reasonable cause for demand.*

168. (*1*) If, in the course of an inquiry or a trial before a Magistrate the evidence appears to him to warrant a presumption that the case is one which should be tried or committed for trial by some other Magistrate, he shall stay proceedings and submit the case, with a brief report explaining its nature, to any Magistrate to whom he is subordinate, or to such other Magistrate, having jurisdiction, as the Mudir directs. *Procedure of Magistrate in cases which he cannot dispose of.*

(*2*) The Magistrate to whom the case is submitted may either try the case himself (if he has jurisdiction so to do), or refer it to any Magistrate subordinate to him having jurisdiction, or commit the accused for trial.

Procedure when, after commencement of trial, Magistrate finds case should be committed.

169. If in any trial before a Magistrate, it appears to him, at any stage of the proceedings before the signing of judgment, that the case is one which ought to be tried by a Minor District Court or the Mudir's Court, he shall stop further proceedings and commit the accused.

Reference on points of law.

170. (*1*) A Court other than the Mudir's Court may refer for the opinion of the Mudir any question of law which arises in the hearing of any case pending before it, or may give judgment in any such case subject to the Mudir's decision, and, pending such decision, may either commit the accused to jail or release him on bail to appear for judgment when called on. Upon the Mudir's notifying his decision, the case shall be disposed of conformably to it.

(*2*) The Mudir's Court may in like manner refer any point of law to the Governor-General.

Transfer of case by Magistrate to his successor.

171. Whenever any Magistrate, after having heard and recorded the whole or any part of the evidence in an inquiry or a trial, is succeeded, or temporarily replaced, in his office by another Magistrate, the Magistrate so succeeding may act on the evidence so recorded by his predecessor, or partly recorded by his predecessor and partly recorded by himself; or he may of his own motion or on the reasonable demand of the accused re-summon all or any of the witnesses or recommence the inquiry or trial.

Courts to be open.

172. The place in which any Criminal Court is held for the purpose of inquiring into or trying any offence shall be deemed an open Court, to which the public generally may have access, so far as the same can conveniently contain them ;

provided that the presiding Magistrate may, if he thinks fit, order at any stage of any inquiry into, or trial of, any particular case that the public generally, or any particular person shall not have access to, or be or remain in, the room or building used by the Court.

CHAPTER XVII.

Of the Judgment.

Language and mode of delivering judgment.

173. (*1*) The Judgment in every trial in a Criminal Court other than a summary Court shall be written in English or in Arabic; and the judgment shall be pronounced, or the substance of it explained, in open Court, either immediately after the termination of the trial, or at some subsequent time of which notice shall be given to the parties or their pleaders.

Provided that the whole judgment shall be read out by the presiding Magistrate, if he is requested so to do either by the prosecution or the defence.

(2) The accused shall, if in custody, be brought up, to hear judgment delivered.

174. (*1*) Every judgment shall contain the point or points for determination, the decision thereon and the reasons for the decision; and shall be dated and signed or sealed by the presiding Magistrate in open Court at the time of pronouncing it. *Contents of judgment.*

(*2*) It shall specify the offence (if any) of which, and the section of the Sudan Penal Code or other law under which, the accused is convicted, and the punishment to which he is sentenced.

(*3*) When the conviction is under the Sudan Penal Code, and it is doubtful under which of two sections or under which of two parts of the same section of that Code the offence falls, the Court shall distinctly express the same, and pass judgment in the alternative.

(*4*) If it be a judgment of acquittal, it shall state the offence of which the accused is acquitted, and direct that he be set at liberty.

175. If the accused is convicted of an offence punishable with death, and the Court sentences him to any punishment other than death, the Court shall in its judgment state the reason why sentence of death was not passed. *Reason for not passing death sentence to be stated.*

176. When a person is sentenced to death, the sentence shall direct that he be hanged by the neck till he is dead. *Sentence of death.*

177. When a person is sentenced to death, the presiding Magistrate shall inform him within what time his petition of appeal, if he desire to present one, should be presented. *Case of person sentenced to death.*

178. No Court, when it has signed its judgment, shall alter or review the same, except as provided in section 215 or to correct a clerical error. *Court not to alter judgment.*

179. On the application of the accused, a copy of the judgment or, when he so desires, a translation in his own *Copy of judgment, etc., to be given to accused on application.*

language, if practicable, or in Arabic shall be given to him without delay. Such copy shall be given free of cost.

Original judgment to be filed. **180.** The original judgment shall be filed with the record of the proceedings.

CHAPTER XVIII.

Of Reference for Confirmation, Appeal and Revision.

Submission for confirmation of judgment of Minor District Court. **181.** Every judgment of a Minor District Court shall be submitted to the Mudir for confirmation.

Submission for confirmation of judgment of Mudir's Court. **182.** Every judgment of a Mudir's Court shall be submitted to the Governor-General for confirmation.

Right of convicted person to present petition of appeal to conforming authority. **183.** When a judgment of conviction is submitted for confirmation under section 181 or 182, the convicted person may submit to the confirming authority, by way of petition of appeal, a statement in writing of his reasons why such judgment should not be confirmed.

Appeal to Mudir' from subordinate Magistrates in certain cases. **184.** An appeal to the Mudir, by petition in writing, shall lie from every judgment of the Court of a Magistrate of the second class, or of a Magistrate of the first class other than the Mudir, whereby a sentence is passed of imprisonment for a term exceeding two months, or of fine exceeding P.T. 200, or of imprisonment and fine.

Petition of appeal when and how presented. **185.** (*1*) Every petition of appeal under section 183 or 184 shall be presented within seven days after the passing of sentence.

(*2*) The petition shall be presented to the Mudir, who, if the sentence was passed by the Mudir's Court, shall forward it to the Governor-General.

(*3*) If the appellant is in jail, he may present his petition to the officer in charge of the jail, to be forwarded to the Mudir.

Summary dismissal of appeal or confirmation of sentence. **186.** If the Mudir or Governor-General, upon receiving a petition of appeal or upon a judgment being submitted to him for confirmation, sees no reason for questioning the decision of the Court, he shall dismiss the appeal or confirm the sentence.

187. If the Mudir or Governor-General, under the like circumstances, considers it right to send for the record of the case, he may do so; and thereupon he shall be entitled to exercise in respect of the case all the powers of a confirming authority to whom the decision of a Court-Martial is sent for confirmation under Egyptian Military Law. Powers of confirming or appellate authority.

188. (*1*) The Governor-General may, on his own motion, call for and examine the record of any proceedings before any Criminal Court, and a Mudir may in like manner call for and examine the record of any proceedings before a Criminal Court within his Province other than the Mudir's Court, for the purpose of satisfying himself as to the correctness, legality, or propriety of any finding, sentence or order recorded or passed, and as to the regularity of the proceedings of the Court. Governor-General's and Mudir's powers of revision.

(*2*) The Governor-General or the Mudir, as the case may be, shall have, in respect of the proceedings the record of which is called for under this section, all the powers of a confirming authority under section 187; provided that no judgment shall be sent back under the powers conferred by this section to the Court by which it was delivered, with a view to the conviction of an acquitted person or to the increase of a sentence, unless the record was called for within one month of the date of the delivery of the judgment.

189. (*1*) Whenever, under section 187 or section 188, the record of a case comes before the Governor-General or a Mudir, the Governor-General or the Mudir, as the case may be, may, in ordering the Court to rehear the case, also order, for reason to be recorded by him in writing, that the convicted person, if in confinement, be released on bail or on his own bond, pending the re-hearing, or that an acquitted person be re-arrested. Power of confirming authority to pass interim order.

(*2*) Subject to any order of the Governor-General or Mudir passed under this Chapter, a sentence other than a sentence of death shall take effect notwithstanding an appeal or a submission for confirmation. Sentence to take effect pending appeal or confirmation.

190. The Governor-General or Mudir shall not, in the exercise of his appellate or confirming jurisdiction, interfere with the finding or sentence of the Court on the ground, only that evidence has been wrongly admitted, or that Confirming authority not to send back judgment for technical error in procedure.

there has been a technical irregularity in procedure, if he be satisfied that the accused has not been prejudiced in his defence and that the finding and sentence are correct.

Vacancies in Court to which judgment is sent back.

191. Whenever a finding or sentence is sent back by the confirming or appellate authority under this chapter, and, owing to death, transfer, or other cause, it is impossible to reconstitute the Court as originally constituted, the Mudir shall nominate an officer or officers to fill the vacancy or vacancies.

Magistrate not to hear appeals from, or confirm his own sentences or judgments.

192. When a Magistrate is appointed to act as Mudir while an appeal from a sentence passed by him is still pending or a judgment of a Court of which he has been a member is still unconfirmed, the appeal shall be heard by the Governor-General or the judgment shall be submitted to him for confirmation.

CHAPTER XIX.

OF EXECUTION.

Execution of death sentence.

193. When a sentence of death passed by a Mudir's Court is confirmed, the Mudir shall, on receiving the order of confirmation, issue a warrant directing such order to be carried into effect.

Pending confirmation of the sentence, the person sentenced shall be committed to jail.

Postponement of death sentence on pregnant woman.

194. If a woman sentenced to death is found to be pregnant, the Mudir shall order the execution of the sentence to be postponed, and shall report the case to the Governor-General.

Execution of sentence of imprisonment.

195. When an accused person is sentenced to imprisonment, the Court passing the sentence shall forthwith forward a warrant to the jail in which he is, or is to be, confined, and, unless the accused is already confined in such jail, shall forward him to such jail, with the warrant.

Direction of warrant for execution.

196. Every warrant for the execution of a sentence of imprisonment shall be directed to the officer in charge of the jail or other place in which the prisoner is, or is to be, confined.

197. When the prisoner is to be confined in jail, the warrant shall be lodged with the jailor.

Warrant, with whom to be lodged.

198. Whenever an offender is sentenced to pay a fine, the Court passing the sentence may, in its discretion, issue a warrant for the levy of the amount by distress and sale of any movable property belonging to the offender, although the sentence directs that, in default of payment of the fine, the offender shall be imprisoned.

Warrant for levy of fine.

199. Such warrant may be executed within the local limits of the jurisdiction of the Court, and it shall authorise the distress and sale of any such property outside such limits, when endorsed by the Mudir within the local limits of whose jurisdiction such property is found.

Effect of such warrant.

200. When an offender has been sentenced to fine only and to imprisonment in default of payment of the fine, and the Court issues a warrant under section 198, it may suspend the execution of the sentence of imprisonment and may release the offender on his executing a bond, with or without sureties, as the Court thinks fit, conditioned for his appearance before the Court or before the presiding Magistrate, on the day appointed for the return to such warrant, such day not being more than fifteen days from the time of executing the bond; and in the event of the fine not having been then realized the Court or the presiding Magistrate may direct the sentence of imprisonment to be carried into execution at once.

Suspension of execution of sentence of imprisonment.

201. (*1*) When the accused is sentenced to flogging or whipping, the sentence shall be executed at such place and time as the Court may direct.

Execution of sentence of flogging or whipping

(*2*) The flogging or whipping shall be inflicted in the presence of the officer in charge of the jail, unless the Magistrate orders it to be inflicted in his own presence.

(*3*) No sentence of flogging or whipping shall be executed by instalments.

(*4*) The sentence shall be inflicted with such instrument and in such manner as the Mudir shall, by a general order, direct.

202. If, during the execution of a sentence of flogging or whipping, it appears to the Magistrate or officer present, that the offender is not in a fit state of health to undergo

Stay of execution.

the remainder of the sentence, the flogging or whipping shall be finally stopped and the remainder of the sentence remitted.

Who may issue warrant. **203.** Every warrant for the execution of a sentence or order may be issued either by the Magistrate who, or the presiding officer of the Court which, passed the sentence or order, or by his successor in office.

Execution of sentence on escaped convict. **204.** When sentence of imprisonment is passed on an escaped convict, such sentence shall take effect after he has suffered imprisonment for a further period equal to that which, at the time of his escape, remained unexpired of his former sentence.

Sentence on an offender already sentenced for another offence. **205.** When a person already undergoing a sentence of imprisonment is sentenced to imprisonment, such imprisonment shall commence at the expiration of the imprisonment to which he has been previously sentenced.

Return of warrant on execution of sentence. **206.** When a sentence has been fully executed, the officer executing it shall return the warrant to the Court or Magistrate from which it issued, with an endorsement under his hand certifying the manner in which the sentence has been executed.

CHAPTER XX.

Of Suspensions, Remissions and Commutations of Sentences.

Power to suspend or remit sentences. **207.** (*1*) When any person has been sentenced to punishment for an offence, the Governor-General may at any time, without conditions or upon any conditions which the person sentenced accepts, suspend the execution of his sentence or remit the whole or any part of the punishment to which he has been sentenced.

(*2*) If any condition on which a sentence has been suspended or remitted, is in the opinion of the Governor-General, not fulfilled, the Governor-General may cancel the suspension or remission, and thereupon the person in whose favour the sentence has been suspended or remitted, may, if at large, be arrested by any police-officer without warrant and remanded to undergo the unexpired portion of the sentence.

(*3*) The condition on which a sentence is suspended or remitted under this section, may be one to be fulfilled by the person in whose favour the sentence is suspended or remitted, or one independent of his will.

208. The Governor-General may, without the consent of the person sentenced, commute a sentence of death into any other sentence allowed by law, or a sentence of imprisonment into one of fine. *Power to commute punishment.*

CHAPTER XXI.

OF PREVIOUS ACQUITALS OR CONVICTIONS.

209. (*1*) A person who has once been tried by a Court of competent jurisdiction for an offence and convicted or acquitted of that offence shall, while such conviction or acquittal remains in force, not be liable to be tried again for the same offence, nor on the same facts for any other offence for which a different charge from the one made against him might have been made under section 138, or for which he might have been convicted under section 139. *Person once convicted or acquitted not to be tried for same offence.*

(*2*) A person convicted of any offence constituted by any act causing consequences which, together with such act, constituted a different offence from that of which he was convicted, may be afterwards tried for such last-mentioned offence, if the consequences had not happened, or were not known to the Court to have happened, at the time when he was convicted.

(*3*) A person acquitted or convicted of any offence constituted by any acts, may notwithstanding such acquittal or conviction, be subsequently charged with, and tried for, any other offence constituted by the same acts which he may have committed, if the Court by which he was first tried was not competent to try the offence with which he is subsequently charged.

Illustrations.

(*a*) A is tried upon a charge of theft as a servant and acquitted. He cannot afterwards, while the acquittal remains in force, be charged with theft as a servant, or, upon the same facts, with theft simply, or with criminal breach of trust.

. (*b*) A is tried upon a charge of murder and acquitted. There is no charge of robbery; but it appears from the facts that A committed robbery at the time when the murder was committed; he may afterwards be charged with, and tried for, robbery.

(*c*) A is tried for causing grievous hurt and convicted. The person injured afterwards dies. A may be tried again for culpable homicide.

(*d*) A is charged before the Mudir's Court and convicted of the culpable homicide of B. A may not afterwards be tried on the same facts for the murder of B.

(*e*) A is charged by a Magistrate of the first class with, and convicted by him of, voluntarily causing hurt to B. A may not afterwards be tried for voluntarily causing grievous hurt to B on the same facts, unless the case comes within paragraph 3 of the section.

(*f*) A is charged by a Magistrate of the second class with, and convicted by him of, theft of property from the person of B. A may be subsequently charged with, and tried for, robbery on the same facts.

(*g*) A, B and C are charged by a Magistrate of the first class with, and convicted by him of, robbing D. A, B and C may afterwards be charged with, and tried for, brigandage on the same facts.

Previous acquittal or conviction, when to be proved. **210.** A previous acquittal or conviction may be pleaded or proved at any stage of an inquiry into, or trial for, the same offence or any other offence to a charge of which it is a bar; upon its being proved, the accused shall be discharged.

PART V.

SPECIAL PROCEEDINGS.

CHAPTER XXII.

PROCEEDINGS IN CASE OF CERTAIN OFFENCES AFFECTING THE ADMINISTRATION OF JUSTICE.

Procedure in cases mentioned in section 105. **211.** (*1*) When any Civil, Criminal or Revenue Court is of opinion that there is ground for inquiring into any offence referred to in section 105 and committed before it or brought under its notice in the course of a judicial proceeding, such Court, after making any preliminary inquiry that may be necessary, may send the case for inquiry or trial to the nearest Magistrate of the first or second class, and may send the accused in custody, or take sufficient security for his appearance, before such Magistrate; and may bind over any person to appear and give evidence on such inquiry or trial.

(2) Such Magistrate shall thereupon proceed according to law, and as if upon complaint made and recorded under section 97.

212. (*1*) When any such offence as is described in section 140, section 144, section 145, section 146, or section 180 of the Sudan Penal Code is committed in the view or presence of any Civil, Criminal or Revenue Court, the Court may cause the offender to be detained in custody; and at any time before the rising of the Court on the same day may, if it thinks fit, take cognizance of the offence and sentence the offender to fine not exceeding L.E. 5, and, in default of payment, to imprisonment for a term which may extend to one month, unless such fine be sooner paid. *Procedure in certain cases of contempt.*

(2) Nevertheless, no Criminal Court shall impose a sentence under this section which it is not competent to impose under the provisions of Chapter II.

213. (*1*) In every such case the Court shall record the facts constituting the offence, with the statement (if any) made by the offender, as well as the finding and sentence. *Record in such cases.*

(2) If the offence is under section 180 of the Sudan Penal Code, the record shall show the nature and stage of the judicial proceeding in which the Court interrupted or insulted was sitting, and the nature of the interruption or insult.

214. (*1*) If the Court in any case considers that a person accused of any of the offences referred to in section 212 and committed in its view or presence should be imprisoned otherwise than in default of payment of fine, or that a fine exceeding L.E. 5 should be imposed upon him, or the Court is for any other reason of opinion that the case should not be disposed of under section 212, the Court, after recording the facts constituting the offence and the statement of the accused as hereinbefore provided, may forward the case to a Magistrate having jurisdiction to try the same, and may require security to be given for the appearance of the accused person before the Magis- *Procedure where Court considers that case should not be dealt with under section 212.*

E   65

trate, or, if sufficient security is not given, shall forward the accused person in custody to the Magistrate.

(2) The Magistrate to whom any case is forwarded under this section, shall proceed to hear the complaint against the accused person in manner hereinbefore provided.

Discharge of offender on submission or apology.

215. When any Court has under section 212 adjudged an offender to punishment for refusing or omitting to do anything which he was lawfully required to do, or for any intentional insult or interruption, the Court may, in its discretion, discharge the offender or remit the punishment on his submission to the order or requisition of the Court, or on apology being made to its satisfaction.

Imprisonment or committal of person refusing to answer or produce document.

216. If any witness or person called to produce a document or thing before a Criminal Court refuses to answer such questions as are put to him or to produce any document or thing in his possession or power which the Court requires him to produce, and does not offer any reasonable excuse for such refusal, the Court may, for reasons to be recorded in writing, sentence him to imprisonment, or by warrant under the hand of the presiding Magistrate commit him to the custody of an officer of the Court, for any term not exceeding seven days, unless in the meantime he consents to be examined and to answer, or to produce the document or thing. In the event of his persisting in his refusal, he may be dealt with according to the provisions of section 212 or section 214.

Appeals from convictions in contempt cases.

217. Any person sentenced by any Court under section 212 or section 216 may, notwithstanding anything hereinbefore contained, appeal to the Court to which decrees or orders made in that Court are ordinarily appealable or are ordinarily sent for confirmation.

CHAPTER XXIII.

OF LUNATICS.

Person incapable of making his defence by reason of unsoundness of mind,

218. (*1*) When in the course of an inquiry or trial there is reason to believe that the accused is of unsound mind and consequently incapable of making his defence, the inquiry or trial shall be adjourned and the facts shall be reported to the Mudir, and the Mudir shall cause the accused to be examined by one or more medical officers who shall report to him.

(*2*) If the unsoundness of mind be established, the inquiry or trial shall be further adjourned until such time as the accused shall have sufficiently recovered to make his defence, and, in the meantime, subject to any general or special regulations or order to be issued or passed by the Governor-General, the accused shall be placed in such custody as the Mudir may think desirable.

(*3*) If in the judgment of the Mudir the circumstances permit of it, the custody may, subject as aforesaid, be that of any relatives or friends of the accused willing to take charge of him. In such case, the Mudir may, if he thinks fit, take security from the custodians for proper care being given to the lunatic.

219. If at the time of his trial an accused person appears to be of sound mind, and it appears from the evidence that he has done an act which, had he been of such unsound mind, would have constituted an offence, but that, at the time of doing it, he was, by reason of unsoundness of mind, incapable of judging of the nature and consequence of the act, the Court shall record its finding that he was at the time of unsound mind and shall forward him to the Mudir to be dealt with as under the preceding section.

Person of unsound mind doing an act which but for such unsoundness would be an offence.

PART VI.

SUPPLEMENTARY.

CHAPTER XXIV.

OF THE COMPOUNDING OF OFFENCES.

220. (*1*) The offences punishable under the sections of the Sudan Penal Code described in the first two columns of the table next following may be compounded

Compounding offences.

by the persons mentioned in the third column of that table :—

Offence.	Sections of Sudan Penal Code applicable.	Person by whom offence may be compounded.
Causing hurt	250, 252	The person to whom the hurt is caused.
Assault or use of criminal force .	273, 271	The person assaulted or to whom criminal force is used.
Mischief, when the only loss or damage caused is loss or damage to a private person .	337, 338	The person to whom the loss or damage is caused.
Criminal trespass	358	The person in possession of the property trespassed upon.
House-trespass	359	
Criminal breach of contract of service.	398, 399, 400	The person with whom the offender has contracted.
Adultery	405, 406	The husband of the woman.
Enticing or taking away or detaining with a criminal intent a married woman.	407	
Defamation	409	
Printing or engraving matter knowing it to be defamatory.	410	
Sale of printed or engraved substance containing defamatory matter, knowing it to contain such matter.	411	The person defamed.
Insult intended to provoke a breach of the peace.	413	The person insulted.
Criminal intimidation, except when the offence is punishable with imprisonment for seven years.	415	The person intimidated.
And, with the permission of the Court before which any prosecution for such offence is pending:—		
Hurt or grievous hurt . . .	251, 253, 254 (i), 259	The person to whom the hurt has been caused.
Wrongfully restraining or confining any person.	262, 263	The person restrained or confined.
Unlawful compulsory labour. .	288	The person compelled to labour.

(*2*) When any offence is compoundable under this section, the abetment of such offence or an attempt to commit such offence (when such attempt is itself an offence) may be compounded in like manner.

(*3*) When the person who would otherwise be competent to compound an offence under this section is a minor, an idiot or a lunatic, any person competent to contract on his behalf may compound the offence.

(*4*) When the accused has been committed for trial or when he has been convicted and an appeal is pending, no composition for the offence shall be allowed without the leave of the committing Magistrate or the Magistrate before whom he was convicted.

(*5*) The composition of an offence under this section shall have the effect of an acquittal of the accused.

(*6*) No offence shall be compounded except as provided by this section.

CHAPTER XXV.

Of Bail.

221. When any person other than a person accused of an offence punishable with imprisonment which may extend to two years is arrested or detained without warrant by an officer in charge of a police-station, or appears or is brought before a Court, and is prepared at any time while in the custody of such officer or at any stage of the proceedings before such Court to give bail, such person shall be released on bail: provided that such officer or Court, if he or it thinks fit, may, instead of taking bail from such person, discharge him on his executing a bond without sureties for his appearance as hereinafter provided. *In what cases bail to be taken.*

222. (*1*) When any person accused of any offence punishable with imprisonment exceeding two years is arrested or detained without warrant by an officer in charge of a police-station, or appears or is brought before a Court, he may be released on bail, but he shall not be so released if there appear reasonable grounds for believing that he has been guilty of the offence of which he is accused. *When bail may be taken in case of non-bailable offence.*

(*2*) If it appears to such officer or Court at any stage of the investigation, inquiry or trial, as the case may be, that there are not reasonable grounds for believing that the accused has committed such offence, but that there are sufficient grounds for further inquiry into his guilt, the accused shall, pending such inquiry, be released on bail, or, at the discretion of such officer or Court, on the execution by him of a bond without sureties for his appearance as hereinafter provided.

(*3*) Any Court may, at any subsequent stage of any proceeding under this Code, cause any person who has been released under this section to be arrested, and may commit him to custody.

223. The amount of every bond executed under this Chapter shall be fixed with due regard to the circumstances of the case, and shall not be excessive; and the Mudir may, in any case, direct that any person be admitted to bail, or that the bail required by a police-officer or Magistrate be reduced.

Power to direct admission to bail or reduction of bail.

224. (*1*) Before any person is released on bail or released on his own bond, a bond for such sum of money as the police-officer or Court, as the case may be, thinks sufficient shall be executed by such person, and, when he is released on bail, by one or more sufficient sureties, conditioned that such person shall attend at the time and place mentioned in the bond, and shall continue so to attend until otherwise directed by the police-officer or Court, as the case may be.

Bond of accused and sureties.

(*2*) If the case so require, the bond shall also bind the person released on bail to appear when called upon before the Mudir's Court, Minor District Court, or other Court to answer the charge.

225. (*1*) As soon as the bond has been executed, the person for whose appearance it has been executed shall be released; and, when he is in jail, the Court admitting him to bail shall issue an order of release to the officer in charge of the jail, and such officer on receipt of the order shall release him.

Discharge from custody.

(*2*) Nothing in this section, section 221 or section 222 shall be deemed to require the release of any person liable to be detained for some matter other than that in respect of which the bond was executed.

226. If, through mistake, fraud or otherwise, insufficient sureties have been accepted, or if they afterwards become insufficient, the Court may issue a warrant of arrest directing that the person released on bail be brought before it and may order him to find sufficient sureties; and, on his failing so to do, may commit him to jail.

Power to order sufficient bail when that first taken is insufficient.

227. (*1*) All or any sureties for the attendance and appearance of a person released on bail may at any time

Discharge of sureties.

apply to the Court which caused the bond to be taken or to any Magistrate of the first or second class to discharge the bond, either wholly or so far as relates to the applicants.

(2) On such application being made, the Magistrate shall issue his warrant of arrest directing that the person so released be brought before him.

(3) On the appearance of such person pursuant to the warrant, or on his voluntary surrender, the Magistrate shall direct the bond to be discharged either wholly or so far as relates to the applicants, and shall call upon such person to find other sufficient sureties, and, if he fails to do so, may commit him to custody.

CHAPTER XXVI.

PROVISIONS AS TO BONDS.

228. When any person is required by any Court or officer to execute a bond, with or without sureties, such Court or officer may permit him to deposit a sum of money to such amount as the Court or officer may fix, in lieu of executing such bond. *Deposit instead of recognisance.*

229. (*1*) Whenever it is proved to the satisfaction of the Court by which a bond under this Code has been taken, or of the Court of a Magistrate of the first or second class, *Procedure on forfeiture of bond.*

or, when the bond is for appearance before a Court, to the satisfaction of such Court,

that such bond has been forfeited, the Court shall record the grounds of such proof, and may call upon any person bound by the bond to pay the penalty thereof, or to show cause why it should not be paid.

(2) If sufficient cause is not shown and the penalty is not paid, the Court may proceed to recover the same by issuing a warrant for the attachment and sale of the movable property belonging to such person, or to his estate if he be dead.

(3) Such warrant may be executed within the local limits of the jurisdiction of the Court which issued it; and

it shall authorise the distress and sale of any movable property belonging to such person outside such limits, when endorsed by the Mudir within the local limits of whose jurisdiction such property is found.

(*4*) If the penalty is not paid and cannot be recovered by attachment and sale, the person bound shall be liable, by order of the Court which issued the warrant, to imprisonment for a term which may extend to six months.

(*5*) The Court may, at its discretion, remit any portion of the penalty mentioned and enforce payment in part only.

(*6*) Where a surety to a bond dies before the bond is forfeited, his estate shall be discharged from all liability in respect of the bond, but the party who gave the bond may be required to find a new surety.

Appeal from, and revision of, orders under section 229.

230. All orders passed under section 229 by any Magistrate other than the Mudir shall be appealable to the Mudir, or, if not so appealed, may be revised by him.

Power to direct levy of amount due on certain recognisances.

231. The Mudir's Court or a Minor District Court may direct any Magistrate to levy the amount due on a bond to appear and attend at such Court.

CHAPTER XXVII.

OF THE DISPOSAL OF PROPERTY.

Order for disposal of property regarding which offence committed.

232. (*1*) When an inquiry or a trial in any Criminal Court is concluded, the Court may make such order as it thinks fit for the disposal of any property or document produced before it or in its custody or regarding which any offence appears to have been committed, or which has been used for the commission of any offence.

(*2*) When the Mudir's Court or a Minor District Court makes such order and cannot through its own officers conveniently deliver the property to the person entitled thereto, such Court may direct that the order be carried into effect by the presiding Magistrate.

(*3*) When an order is made under this section in a case in which an appeal lies, or which requires confirmation, such order shall not (except when the property is livestock or is subject to speedy and natural decay) be carried out until the period allowed for presenting such appeal has passed, or, when such appeal is presented within such period, until such appeal has been disposed of or until the order is confirmed.

Explanation.—In this section the term "property" includes, in the case of property regarding which an offence appears to have been committed, not only such property as has been originally in the possession or under the control of any party, but also any property into or for which the same may have been converted or exchanged, and anything acquired by such conversion or exchange, whether immediately or otherwise.

233. In lieu of itself passing an order under section 232, the Court may direct the property to be delivered to the Mudir, who shall in such case deal with it as if it had been seized by the police and the seizure had been reported to him in the manner hereinafter mentioned.
[Order may take form of reference to Mudir.]

234. When any person is convicted of any offence which includes, or amounts to, theft or receiving stolen property, and it is proved that any other person has bought the stolen property from him without knowing or having reason to believe that the same was stolen, and that any money has on his arrest been taken out of the possession of the convicted person, the Court may, on the application of such purchaser and on the restitution of the stolen property to the person entitled to the possession thereof, order that out of such money a sum not exceeding the price paid by the purchaser be delivered to him.
[Payment to innocent purchaser of money found on accused.]

235. (*1*) On a conviction under the Sudan Penal Code, section 219, section 410 or section 411, the Court may order the destruction of all the copies of the thing in respect of which the conviction was had, and which are in the custody of the Court or remain in the possession or power of the person convicted.
[Destruction of libellous and other matter.]

(*2*) The Court may, in like manner, on a conviction under the Sudan Penal Code, section 206, section 207, section 208 or section 209, order the food, drink, drug or medical preparation in respect of which the conviction was had, to be destroyed.

236. (*1*) Whenever a person is convicted of an offence attended by criminal force and it appears to the Court
[Power to restore possession of immovable property.]

that by such force any person has been dispossessed of any immovable property, the Court may, if it thinks fit, order such person to be restored to the possession of the same.

(2) No such order shall prejudice any right or interest to or in such immovable property which any person may be able to establish in a civil suit.

Procedure by police upon seizure of property taken under section 41 or stolen.

237. (*1*) The seizure by any police-officer of property taken under section 41, or alleged or suspected to have been stolen, or found under circumstances which create suspicion of the commission of an offence, shall be forthwith reported to a Magistrate, who shall make such order as he thinks fit respecting the disposal of such property or the delivery of such property to the person entitled to the possession thereof, or, if such person cannot be ascertained, respecting the custody and production of such property.

Procedure where owner of property seized unknown.

(2) If the person so entitled is known, the Magistrate may order the property to be delivered to him on such conditions (if any) as the Magistrate thinks fit. If such person is unknown, the Magistrate may detain it and shall, in such case, issue a proclamation specifying the articles of which such property consists, and requiring any person who may have a claim thereto, to appear before him and establish his claim within six months from the date of such proclamation.

Procedure where no claimant appears within six months.

238. If no person within such period establishes his claim to such property, and if the person in whose possession such property was found, is unable to show that it was legally acquired by him, such property shall be at the disposal of the Government, and may be sold under the orders of the Mudir.

Power to sell perishable property.

239. If the person entitled to the possession of such property is unknown or absent and the property is subject to speedy and natural decay, or the Magistrate to whom its seizure is reported is of opinion that its sale would be for the benefit of the owner, the Magistrate may at any time direct it to be sold; and the provisions of sections 237 and 238 shall, as nearly as may be practicable, apply to the nett proceeds of such sale.

CHAPTER XXVIII.

OF UNLAWFUL ASSEMBLIES.

240. Any Magistrate or officer in charge of a police-station may command any unlawful assembly, or any assembly of five or more persons likely to cause a disturbance of the public peace, to disperse; and it shall thereupon be the duty of the members of such assembly to disperse accordingly.

Assembly to disperse on command of Magistrate or police-officer.

241. If, upon being so commanded, any such assembly does not disperse, or if, without being so commanded, it conducts itself in such a manner as to show a determination not to disperse, any Magistrate or officer in charge of a police-station may proceed to disperse such assembly by force, and may require the assistance of any male person, not being a military officer or soldier acting as such, for the purpose of dispersing such assembly, and, if necessary, arresting and confining the persons who form part of it, in order to disperse such assembly or that they may be punished according to law.

Use of civil force to disperse.

242. If any such assembly cannot be otherwise dispersed, and if it is necessary for the public security that it should be dispersed, the Magistrate of the highest rank who is present may cause it to be dispersed by military force.

Use of military force.

243. (*1*) When a Magistrate determines that any such assembly ought to be dispersed by military force, he may require any commissioned or non-commissioned officer in command of any troops to disperse such assembly by military force, and to arrest and confine such persons forming part of it as the Magistrate may direct, or as it may be necessary to arrest and confine in order to disperse the assembly or to have them punished according to law.

Duty of officer commanding troops required by Magistrate to disperse assembly.

(*2*) Every such officer shall obey such requisition in such manner as he thinks fit, but in so doing he shall use as little force, and do as little injury to person and property, as may be consistent with dispersing the assembly and arresting and detaining such persons.

(*3*) If the Magistrate be himself a commissioned officer, due regard shall be had, in the application of this section, to the obligations of military obedience between the Magistrate and the officer commanding the troops.

244. When the public security is manifestly endangered by any such assembly, and when no Magistrate can be communicated with, any commissioned officer in command of any troops may disperse such assembly by military force, and may arrest and confine any persons forming part of it, in order to disperse such assembly or that they may be punished according to law ; but if, while he is acting under this section, it becomes practicable for him to communicate with a Magistrate he shall do so, and shall thenceforward obey the instructions of such Magistrate (unless such Magistrate be a commissioned officer junior to him in rank) as to whether he shall or shall not continue such action.

Power of commissioned military officer to disperse assembly.

245. No prosecution against any person for any act purporting to be done under this Chapter shall be instituted in any Criminal Court, except with the sanction of the Governor-General; and

Protection against prosecution for acts done under this Chapter.

(*a*) no Magistrate or police-officer acting under this Chapter in good faith,

(*b*) no officer acting under section 244 in good faith,

(*c*) no person doing any act in good faith, in compliance with a requisition under section 241 or section 243, and

(*d*) no inferior officer or soldier doing any act in obedience to any order which he was bound to obey, shall be deemed to have thereby committed an offence.

CHAPTER XXIX.

OF THE PREVENTIVE ACTION OF THE POLICE.

246. Every police-officer may interpose for the purpose of preventing, and shall, to the best of his ability, prevent, the commission of any offence for which a police-officer is authorized to arrest without a warrant.

Police to prevent offences for which police may arrest without warrant.

247. Every police-officer receiving information of a design to commit any such offence shall communicate such information to the police-officer to whom he is subordinate, and to any other officer whose duty it is to prevent or take cognizance of the commission of any such offence.

Information of design to commit such offences.

248. A police-officer knowing of a design to commit any such offence may arrest, without orders from a Magistrate and without a warrant, the person so designing, if it appears to such officer that the commission of the offence cannot be otherwise prevented.

Arrest to prevent such offences.

249. A police-officer may of his own authority interpose to prevent any injury attempted to be committed in his view to any public property, movable or immovable, or the removal or injury of any public landmark or buoy or other mark used for navigation.

Prevention of injury to public property.

CHAPTER XXX.

OF THE APPLICATION OF THIS CODE TO SECOND-CLASS DISTRICTS.

250. Whenever this Code shall have been declared to take effect in a second-class District, the Governor of the District shall be *ex-officio* a Magistrate of the first class, and, subject to the provisions of section 251 and to any general or special orders of the Governor-General, shall exercise and perform within his District all the powers by this Code given to a Mudir within his Province.

Powers of Governor.

251. Subject to such general or special orders as may be passed by the Governor-General from time to time, the judgments of Minor District Courts within a second-class District shall be submitted to the Governor-General for confirmation.

Confirmation of judgments of Minor District Courts.

CHAPTER XXXI.

MISCELLANEOUS.

252. Any Court may, at any stage of any inquiry, trial or other proceeding under this Code, summon any person as a witness, or examine any person in attendance though not summoned as a witness, or recall and re-examine any person already examined; and the Court shall summon and examine or recall and re-examine any such person if his evidence appears to it essential to the just decision of the case.

Power to summon material witness, or examine person present.

Prisoner in jail, how brought up for examination. **253.** (*1*) No person confined in any jail under a sentence of imprisonment shall be brought before a Magistrate or Court for examination, whether as a witness or as an accused person, except upon an order of the Mudir within whose Province the jail is situate.

(*2*) Such order may be issued upon the request of the Magistrate before whom, or the presiding officer of the Court before which, the prisoner is to be brought, and shall be directed to the officer in charge of the jail, who shall cause the prisoner to be produced in custody at the time and place named in the order and shall provide for the safe custody of the prisoner during his absence from the jail.

Interpreter bound to interpret truthfully. **254.** When the services of an interpreter are required by any Criminal Court for the interpretation of any evidence or statement, he shall be bound to state the true interpretation of such evidence or statement.

Expenses of complainants and witnesses. **255.** Subject to any rules made by the Governor-General, any Criminal Court may, if it think fit, order payment, on the part of Government, of the reasonable expenses of any complainant or witness attending for the purposes of any inquiry, trial or other proceeding before such Court under this Code.

Power of Court to pay expenses or compensation out of fine. **256.** (*1*) Whenever under any law in force for the time being a Criminal Court imposes a fine, the Court may, when passing judgment, order the whole or any part of the fine recovered to be applied—

(*a*) in defraying expenses properly incurred in the prosecution;

(*b*) in compensation for the injury caused by the offence committed, where substantial compensation is, in the opinion of the Court, recoverable by civil suit.

(*2*) If the fine is imposed in a case which is subject to appeal or requires confirmation, no such payment shall be made before the period allowed for presenting the appeal has elapsed, or, if an appeal be presented, before the decision of the appeal, or before the sentence is confirmed.

Payments to be taken into account in subsequent suit. **257.** At the time of awarding compensation in any subsequent civil suit relating to the same matter, the Court shall take into account any sum paid or recovered as compensation under section 256.

258. Payment of any money (other than a fine) payable by virtue of any order made under this Code may be enforced as if it were a fine.

259. If any person affected by a judgment or order passed by a Criminal Court desires to have a copy of any order or deposition or other part of the record, he shall, on applying for such copy, be furnished therewith: provided that he pays for the same, unless the Court, for some special reason, thinks fit to furnish it free of cost.

260. Any police-officer may seize any property which may be alleged or suspected to have been stolen, or which may be found under circumstances which create suspicion of the commission of any offence. Such police-officer, if subordinate to the officer in charge of a police-station, shall forthwith report the seizure to that officer.

Detention Allowance
for
Witnesses

_____

To Governer Merewé.

390-1314 No rates have been fixed or rules made
not provided for in Budget so may what you think
reasonable under section 255 Criminal Procedure
cost should be charged against Central informing
Malisudca of amount when paid.

Khartoum, 16.10.05   (Sd) Kanuni.

thinks fit.

Prisoner in Jail, how brought up for examination.

253. (*1*) No person confined in any jail under a sentence of imprisonment shall be brought before a Magistrate or Court for examination, whether as a witness or as an accused person, except upon an order of the Mudir within whose Province the jail is situate.

(*2*) Such order may be issued upon the request of the Magistrate before whom, or the presiding officer of the Court before which, the prisoner is to be brought, and shall be directed to the officer in charge of the jail, who shall cause the prisoner to be produced in custody at the time and place named in the order and shall provide for the safe custody of the prisoner during his absence from the jail.

Interpreter bound to interpret truthfully.

254. When the services of an interpreter are required by any Criminal Court for the interpretation of any evidence or statement, he shall be bound to state the true interpretation of such evidence or statement.

as compensation under section 256.

258. Payment of any money (other than a fine) payable by virtue of any order made under this Code may be enforced as if it were a fine. Moneys ordered to be paid recoverable as fines.

259. If any person affected by a judgment or order passed by a Criminal Court desires to have a copy of any order or deposition or other part of the record, he shall, on applying for such copy, be furnished therewith: provided that he pays for the same, unless the Court, for some special reason, thinks fit to furnish it free of cost. Copies of proceedings.

260. Any police-officer may seize any property which may be alleged or suspected to have been stolen, or which may be found under circumstances which create suspicion of the commission of any offence. Such police-officer, if subordinate to the officer in charge of a police-station, shall forthwith report the seizure to that officer. Power of police to seize property suspected to be stolen.

261. Police-officers superior in rank to an officer in charge of a police-station may exercise the same powers, throughout the local area to which they are appointed, as may be exercised by such officer within the limits of his station. Powers of superior officers of police.

262. Upon complaint made to a Magistrate of the first class on oath of the abduction or unlawful detention of a woman, or of a female child under the age of fourteen years, for any unlawful purpose, he may make an order for the immediate restoration of such woman to her liberty, or of such female child to her husband, parent, guardian or other person having the lawful charge of such child, and may compel compliance with such order, using such force as may be necessary. Power to compel restoration of abducted females.

263. (*1*) Whenever any person causes a police-officer to arrest another person, if it appears to the Magistrate by whom the case is inquired into or tried (being a Magistrate of the first or second class), that there was no sufficient ground for causing such arrest, the Magistrate may award such compensation, not exceeding L.E. 3, to be paid by the person so causing the arrest to the person so arrested, for his loss of time and expenses in the matter, as the Magistrate thinks fit. Compensation to persons groundlessly given in charge.

(*2*) In such cases, if more persons than one are arrested the Magistrate may, in like manner, award to each of them such compensation not exceeding L. E. 3, as he thinks fit.

(3) Payment of compensation awarded under this section may be enforced as if it were a fine; provided that the term of imprisonment (if any) imposed in default of payment shall not exceed 30 days.

Forms.

264. The forms set forth in the fourth schedule, with such variation as the circumstances of each case require, may be used for the respective purposes therein mentioned, and if used shall be sufficient.

Case in which Magistrate is personally interested.

265. No Magistrate shall try or commit for trial, or form part of the Court which tries, any case to or in which he is a party, or personally interested, without the consent of the Mudir or (in the case of a Mudir) the Governor-General.

Explanation.—A Magistrate shall not be deemed to be a party or personally interested, within the meaning of this section, to or in any case by reason only that he is concerned therein in a public capacity, or by reason only that he has viewed the place in which an offence is alleged to have been committed, or any other place in which any other transaction material to the case is alleged to have occured, or made or held an inquiry in connection with the case.

Arabic to be language of Courts.

266. Subject to any order which may be passed by the Governor-General, the proceedings of every Court under this Code shall be conducted in Arabic.

Officers concerned in sales not to be purchase or bid for property.

267. A public servant having any duty to perform in connection with the sale of any property under this Code shall not purchase or bid for the property.

SCHEDULES.

81

SCHEDULE I.

Tabular Statement of Offences.

EXPLANATORY NOTE.—The entries in the second and fifth columns of this schedule, headed respectively "Offence" and "Punishment under the Sudan Penal Code," are not intended as definitions of the offences and punishments described in the several corresponding sections of the Sudan Penal Code, or even as abstracts of those sections, but merely as references to the subject of the section, the number of which is given in the first column.

An offence may be tried by a Mudir's Court, although that Court be not mentioned in the sixth column of this schedule, (s. 11 of this Code.)

The provisions of this Code and of the Sudan Penal Code as to summary trials by Magistrates of the third class (see third schedule), summary trial of juvenile offenders (s. 13 of this Code) and flogging and whipping, are not incorporated in this schedule.

CHAPTER VI.—ABETMENT.

Section.	Offence.	Whether the police may arrest without, warrant or not.	Whether a warrant or a summons shall ordinarily issue in the first instance.	Punishment under the Sudan Penal Code.	By what Court triable.
82	Abetment of any offence, if the act abetted is committed in consequence, and where no express provision is made for its punishment.	May arrest without warrant if arrest for the offence abetted may be made without warrant, but not otherwise.	According as a warrant or summons may issue for the offence abetted.	The same punishment as for the offence abetted.	The Court by which the offence abetted is triable.
83	Abetment of any offence, if the person abetted does the act with a different intention from that of the abettor.	Ditto.	Ditto.	Ditto.	Ditto.
84	Abetment of any offence, when one act is abetted and a different act is done; subject to the proviso.	Ditto.	Ditto.	The same punishment as for the offence intended to be abetted.	Ditto.
80	Abetment of any offence, when an effect is caused by the act abetted different from that intended by the abettor.	Ditto.	Ditto.	The same punishment as for the offence committed.	Ditto.

82

No.	Offence		Punishment		Court
87	Abetment of any offence, if abettor is present when offence is committed.	Ditto.	Ditto.		Ditto.
88	Abetment of an offence punishable with death or imprisonment for life, if the offence be not committed in consequence of the abetment.	Ditto.	Imprisonment for 7 years and fine.		Ditto.
	If the abettor be a public servant whose duty it is to prevent the offence.	Ditto.	Imprisonment for 10 years and fine.		Ditto.
89	Abetment of an offence punishable with imprisonment, if the offence be not committed in consequence of the abetment.	Ditto.	Imprisonment extending to a quarter part of the longest term provided for the offence, or fine, or both.		Ditto.
	If the abettor be a public servant whose duty it is to prevent the offence.	Ditto.	Imprisonment extending to half of the longest term provided for the offence, or fine, or both.		Ditto.
90	Abetting the commission of an offence by the public, or by more than ten persons.	Ditto.	Imprisonment for 3 years, or fine, or both.		Ditto.

CHAPTER VII.—ATTEMPTS TO COMMIT OFFENCES.

No.	Offence	Arrest	Punishment	Court
92	Attempting to commit offences punishable with imprisonment, and in such attempt doing any act towards the commission of the offence.	According as the offence is one in respect of which a summons or warrant shall ordinarily issue.	Imprisonment not exceeding half of the longest term provided for the offence, or fine, or both.	The Court by which the offence attempted is triable.

83

SCHEDULE I—*continued.*
CHAPTER VIII.—OFFENCES AGAINST THE STATE.

Section.	Offence.	Whether the police may arrest without warrant or not.	Whether a warrant or a summons shall ordinarily issue in the first instance.	Punishment under the Sudan Penal Code.	By what Court triable.
93	Waging or attempting to wage war, or abetting the waging of war, against the Government or the Khedive.	Shall not arrest without warrant.	Warrant.	Death or imprisonment for life, and forfeiture of property.	Mudir's Court.
94	Conspiring to commit certain offences against the State.	Ditto.	Ditto.	Imprisonment for 14 years.	Ditto.
95	Collecting arms, etc., with the intention of waging war against the Government or the Khedive.	Ditto.	Ditto.	Imprisonment for 14 years, and forfeiture of property.	Ditto.
96	Sedition.	Ditto.	Ditto.	Imprisonment for 3 years and fine, or fine.	Minor District Court, or Magistrate of the first class.
97	Public servant voluntarily allowing prisoner of State or war in his custody to escape.	Ditto.	Ditto.	Imprisonment for 14 years, and fine.	Mudir's Court.
98	Public servant negligently suffering prisoner of State or war in his custody to escape.	Ditto.	Ditto.	Imprisonment for 3 years, and fine.	Minor District Court, or Magistrate of the first class.
99	Aiding escape of, rescuing or harbouring, such prisoner, or offering any resistance to the recapture of such prisoner.	Ditto.	Ditto.	Imprisonment for 14 years, and fine.	Mudir's Court.

No.	Offence		Warrant or summons	Punishment	Court
101	Breach of official trust—				
	(i) if communication is made or attempted to agent of foreign Government;	Ditto.	Ditto.	Imprisonment for 14 years and fine.	Mudir's Court.
	(ii) in any other case.	Ditto.	Summons	Imprisonment for 1 year and fine, or fine.	Minor District Court, or Magistrate of the first class.
102	Disclosure of military information—				
	(i) to agent of foreign Government;	Ditto.	Warrant.	Imprisonment for 14 years and fine.	Mudir's Court.
	(ii) in any other case.	Ditto.	Summons	Imprisonment for 1 year and fine, or fine.	Minor District Court, or Magistrate of the first class.

CHAPTER IX.—OFFENCES RELATING TO THE ARMY AND NAVY.

No.	Offence		Warrant or summons	Punishment	Court
103	Abetting mutiny, or attempting to seduce an officer, soldier or sailor from his allegiance or duty.	May arrest without warrant.	Warrant.	Imprisonment for 14 years and fine.	Mudir's Court.
104	Abetment of mutiny, if mutiny is committed in consequence thereof.	Ditto.	Ditto.	Death or imprisonment for 14 years, and fine.	Ditto.
105	Abetment of an assault by an officer, soldier or sailor on his superior officer, when in the execution of his office, if the assault is committed.	Ditto.	Ditto.	Imprisonment for 7 years and fine.	Mudir's Court or Minor District Court.
105	Abetment of such assault, if the assault is not committed.	Ditto.	Ditto.	Imprisonment for 3 years and fine.	Minor District Court, or Magistrate of the first class.
106	Abetment of the desertion of an officer, soldier or sailor.	Ditto.	Ditto.	Imprisonment for 2 years, or fine, or both.	Minor District Court, or Magistrate of the first or second class.

SCHEDULE I—*continued.*

CHAPTER IX.—OFFENCES RELATING TO THE ARMY AND NAVY—*concluded.*

1	2	3	4	5	6
Section.	Offence.	Whether the police may arrest without warrant or not.	Whether a warrant or a summons shall ordinarily issue in the first instance.	Punishment under the Sudan Penal Code.	By what Court triable.
107	Harbouring such an officer, soldier or sailor who has deserted.	May arrest without warrant.	Warrant. . .	Imprisonment for 2 years, or fine, or both.	Minor District Court, or Magistrate of the first or second class.
108	Abetment of act of insubordination by an officer, soldier or sailor, if the offence be committed in consequence.	Ditto. . .	Ditto. . .	Imprisonment for 6 months, or fine, or both.	Magistrate of the first or second class.
109	Wearing the dress or carrying any token used by a soldier, with intent that it may be believed that he is such a soldier.	Ditto. . .	Summons . .	Imprisonment for 3 months, or fine of L.E. 5, or both.	Ditto.

CHAPTER X.—OFFENCES AGAINST THE PUBLIC TRANQUILITY.

1	2	3	4	5	6
112	Being member of an unlawful assembly.	May arrest without warrant.	Summons . .	Imprisonment for 6 months, or fine, or both.	Magistrate of the first or second class.
113	Joining an unlawful assembly armed with any deadly weapon.	Ditto . .	Warrant. . .	Imprisonment for 2 years, or fine, or both.	Minor District Court, or Magistrate of the first or second class.
114	Joining or continuing in an unlawful assembly, knowing that it has been commanded to disperse.	Ditto. . .	Ditto. . .	Ditto	Ditto.
116	Rioting	Ditto. . .	Ditto. . .	Ditto	Ditto.

	Offence	Whether arrest without warrant	Summons or warrant	Punishment	Court
117	Rioting, armed with a deadly weapon.	Ditto. . . .	Ditto. . . .	Imprisonment for 3 years, or fine, or both.	Minor District Court, or Magistrate of the first class.
118	If an offence be committed by any member of an unlawful assembly, every other member of such assembly shall be guilty of the offence.	According as arrest may be made without warrant for the offence or not.	According as a warrant or summons may issue for the offence.	The same as for the offence.	The Court by which the offence is triable.
119	Promoting or doing anything to assist the promotion of an unlawful assembly.	May arrest without warrant.	Summons, or as for any offence committed by any member of the assembly.	The same as for a member of such assembly, and for any offence committed by any member of such assembly.	According to the offence to the punishment for which the offender is liable.
120	Knowingly joining or continuing in any assembly of five or more persons after it has been commanded to disperse.	Ditto. . . .	Summons . .	Imprisonment for 6 months, or fine, or both.	Magistrate of the first or second class.
121	Assaulting or obstructing public servant when suppressing riots, etc.	Ditto. . . .	Warrant. . .	Imprisonment for 3 years, or fine, or both.	Minor District Court, or Magistrate of the first class.
122	Committing affray. . . .	Shall not arrest without warrant.	Summons . .	Imprisonment for 1 month, or fine of L.E. 2, or both.	Magistrate of the first or second class.

CHAPTER XL.—OFFENCES BY OR RELATING TO PUBLIC SERVANTS.

	Offence	Whether arrest without warrant	Summons or warrant	Punishment	Court
123	Being or expecting to be a public servant, and taking a gratification other than legal remuneration in respect of an official act.	Shall not arrest without warrant.	Summons . .	Imprisonment for 3 years, or fine, or both.	Minor District Court, or Magistrate of the first class.
124	Taking a gratification in order to influence a public servant.	Ditto. . . .	Ditto. . . .	Ditto. . . .	Ditto.
125	Abetment by public servant of an offence under section 124 with reference to himself.	Ditto. . . .	Ditto. . . .	Ditto. . . .	Ditto.

87

SCHEDULE I—*continued.*

CHAPTER XI.—OFFENCES BY OR RELATING TO PUBLIC SERVANTS—*concluded.*

1	2	3	4	5	6
Section.	Offence.	Whether the police may arrest without warrant or not.	Whether a warrant or a summons shall ordinarily issue in the first instance.	Punishment under the Sudan Penal Code.	By what Court triable.
126	Public servant obtaining any valuable thing, without consideration, from a person concerned in any proceeding or business transacted by such public servant.	Shall not arrest without warrant.	Summons	Imprisonment for 2 years, or fine, or both.	Minor District Court, or Magistrate of the first or second class.
127	Public servant disobeying a direction of law with intent to cause injury, or to save person from punishment, or property from forfeiture.	Ditto.	Ditto.	Ditto.	Ditto.
128	Public servant framing an incorrect record or writing or mis-translating document, with intent to cause injury, or to save person from punishment, or property from forfeiture.	Ditto.	Warrant.	Imprisonment for 3 years, or fine, or both.	Minor District Court, or Magistrate of the first class.
129	Public servant in a judicial proceeding corruptly making and pronouncing an order, report, verdict or decision which he knows to be contrary to law.	Ditto.	Ditto.	Imprisonment for 7 years, or fine, or both.	Minor District Court.
130	Commitment for trial or confinement by a person having authority, who known that he is acting contrary to law.	Ditto.	Ditto.	Ditto.	Ditto.

No.	Offence		Warrant or Summons	Punishment	Court
131	Intentional omission to apprehend or intentional sufferance or aiding of escape, on part of public servant bound by law to apprehend an offender or to keep an offender in confinement or custody;				
	if offender is under sentence of death;	Shall not arrest without warrant.	Warrant	Imprisonment for 14 years and fine.	Mudir's Court.
	if offender is under sentence of imprisonment for 10 years or upwards, or is charged with a capital offence;	Ditto.	Ditto.	Imprisonment for 7 years and fine.	Mudir's Court, or Minor District Court.
	if offender is under sentence of imprisonment for less than 10 years, or is charged with offence punishable with imprisonment for 10 years or upwards;	Ditto.	Ditto. . . . . :	Imprisonment for 3 years, or fine, or both.	Minor District Court, or Magistrate of the first class.
	in any other case.	Ditto.	Ditto.	Imprisonment for 2 years, or fine, or both.	Minor District Court, or Magistrate of the first or second class.
132	Negligent omission to apprehend, or negligent sufferance of escape, on part of public servant bound by law to apprehend or to keep in confinement or custody.	Ditto.	Summons . . .	Ditto.	Ditto.
133	Public servant unlawfully engaging in trade.	Ditto.	Ditto.	Imprisonment for 1 year, or fine, or both.	Magistrate of the first or second class.
134	Public servant unlawfully buying or bidding for property.	Ditto.	Ditto.	Imprisonment for 2 years, or both, and confiscation of property, if purchased.	Minor District Court, or Magistrate of the first class.
135	Personating a public servant. . . .	May arrest without warrant.	Warrant . . .	Imprisonment for 2 years, or fine, or both.	Minor District Court, or Magistrate of the first or second class.
136	Wearing garb or carrying token used by public servant with fraudulent intent.	Ditto. . .	Summons . . .	Imprisonment for 3 months, or fine of L.E. 5, or both.	Magistrate of the first or second class.

SCHEDULE I—*continued.*

CHAPTER XII.—CONTEMPTS OF THE LAWFUL AUTHORITY OF PUBLIC SERVANTS.

1	2	3	4	5	6
Section.	Offence.	Whether the police may arrest without warrant or not.	Whether a warrant or a summons shall ordinarily issue in the first instance.	Punishment under the Sudan Penal Code.	By what Court triable.
137	Absconding to avoid service of summons or other proceeding from a public servant.	Shall not arrest without warrant.	Summons	Imprisonment for 1 month, or fine of L.E. 10, or both.	Magistrate of the first or second class.
	If summons or notice require attendance in person, etc., in a Court of Justice.	Ditto.	Ditto.	Imprisonment for 6 months, or fine of L.E. 20, or both.	Ditto.
138	Preventing the service or the affixing of any summons or notice, or the removal of it when it has been affixed, or preventing a proclamation.	Ditto.	Ditto.	Imprisonment for 1 month, or fine of L.E. 10, or both.	Ditto.
	If summons, etc., require attendance in person, etc., in a Court of Justice.	Ditto.	Ditto.	Imprisonment for 6 months, or fine of L.E. 20, or both.	Ditto.
139	Not obeying a legal order to attend at a certain place in person or by agent, or departing therefrom without authority.	Ditto.	Ditto.	Imprisonment for 1 month, or fine of L.E. 10, or both.	Ditto.
	If the order require personal attendance, etc., in a Court of Justice.	Ditto.	Ditto.	Imprisonment for 6 months, or fine of L.E. 20, or both.	Ditto.
140	Intentionally omitting to produce a document to a public servant by a person legally bound to produce or deliver such document.	Ditto.	Ditto.	Imprisonment for 1 month, or fine of L.E. 10, or both.	The Court in which the offence is committed, subject to the provisions of Chapter XII; or, if not committed in a Court, a Magistrate of the first or second class.

No.	Offence			Punishment	Court
141	If the document is required to be produced in or delivered to a Court of Justice.	Ditto.	.	Imprisonment for 6 months, or fine of I.E. 20, or both.	Ditto.
141	Intentionally omitting to give notice or information to a public servant by a person legally bound to give such notice or information.	Ditto.	.	Imprisonment for 1 month, or fine of I.E. 10, or both.	Magistrate of the first or second class.
	If the notice or information required respects the commission of an offence, etc.	Ditto.	.	Imprisonment for 6 months, or fine of I.E. 20, or both.	Ditto.
142	Knowingly furnishing false information to a public servant.	Ditto.	.	Ditto.	Ditto.
143	If the information required respects the commission of an offence, etc.	Ditto.	.	Imprisonment for 2 years, or fine, or both.	Minor District Court, or Magistrate of the first or second class.
143	Giving false information to a public servant in order to cause him to use his lawful power to the injury or annoyance of any person.	Ditto.	.	Imprisonment for 6 months, or fine of I.E. 20, or both.	Magistrate of the first or second class.
144	Refusing oath when duly required to take oath by a public servant.	Ditto.	.	Imprisonment for 6 months, or fine of I.E. 20, or both.	The Court in which the offence is committed, subject to the provisions of Chapter XXII.; or, if not committed in a Court, a Magistrate of the first or second class.
145	Being legally bound to state truth, and refusing to answer questions.	Ditto.	.	Ditto.	Ditto.
146	Refusing to sign a statement made to a public servant when legally required to do so.	Ditto.	.	Imprisonment for 3 months, or fine of I.E. 10, or both.	Ditto.
147	Resistance to the taking of property by the lawful authority of a public servant.	Ditto.	.	Imprisonment for 6 months, or fine of I.E. 20, or both.	Magistrate of the first or second class.
148	Obstructing sale of property offered for sale by authority of a public servant.	Ditto.	.	Imprisonment for 1 month, or fine of I.E. 10, or both.	Ditto.

91

SCHEDULE I—*continued.*

CHAPTER XII.—CONTEMPTS OF THE LAWFUL AUTHORITY OF PUBLIC SERVANTS—*concluded.*

1	2	3	4	5	6
Section.	Offence.	Whether the police may arrest without warrant or not.	Whether a warrant or a summons shall ordinarily issue in the first instance.	Punishment under the Sudan Penal Code.	By what Court triable.
149	Bidding, by a person under a legal incapacity to purchase it, for property at a lawfully authorized sale, or bidding without intending to perform the obligations incurred thereby.	Shall not arrest without warrant.	Summons	Imprisonment for 1 month, or fine of L.E. 10, or both.	Magistrate of the first or second class.
150	Obstructing public servant in discharge of his public functions.	Ditto.	Ditto.	Imprisonment for 3 months, or fine of L.E. 10, or both.	Ditto.
151	Omission to assist public servant when bound by law to give such assistance.	Ditto.	Ditto.	Imprisonment for 6 months, or fine of L.E. 10, or both.	Ditto.
152	Disobedience to an order lawfully promulgated by a public servant, if such disobedience causes obstruction, annoyance or injury to persons lawfully employed.	Ditto.	Ditto.	Imprisonment for 1 month, or fine of L.E. 5, or both.	Ditto.
	If such disobedience causes danger to human life, health or safety, etc.	Ditto.	Ditto.	Imprisonment for 6 months, or fine of L.E. 20, or both.	Ditto.
153	Threatening a public servant with injury to him, or one in whom he is interested, to induce him to do or forbear to do any official act.	Ditto.	Ditto.	Imprisonment for 2 years, or fine, or both.	Minor District Court, or Magistrate of the first or second class.
154	Threatening any person to induce him to refrain from making a legal application for protection from injury.	Ditto.	Ditto.	Imprisonment for 1 year, or fine, or both.	Magistrate of the first or second class.

CHAPTER XIII.—FALSE EVIDENCE AND OFFENCES AGAINST PUBLIC JUSTICE.

Of False Evidence.

No.	Offence	Shall not arrest without warrant	Warrant	Punishment	Court
157	Giving or fabricating false evidence in a judicial proceeding.		Warrant.	Imprisonment for 7 years and fine.	Minor District Court, or Magistrate of the first class.
	Giving or fabricating false evidence in any other case.	Ditto.	Ditto.	Imprisonment for 3 years and fine.	Ditto.
158	Giving or fabricating false evidence with intent to cause any person to be convicted of a capital offence.	Ditto.	Ditto.	Imprisonment for 14 years and fine.	Mudir's Court.
	If innocent person be thereby convicted and executed.	Ditto.	Ditto.	Death or imprisonment for life, and fine.	Ditto.
159	Giving or fabricating false evidence with intent to procure conviction of an offence punishable with imprisonment for 7 years or upwards.	Ditto.	Ditto.	The same as for the offence.	Mudir's Court, or (if the offence is so triable) Minor District Court.
160	Using in a judicial proceeding evidence known to be false or fabricated.	Ditto.	Ditto.	The same as for giving or fabricating false evidence.	Minor District Court, or Magistrate of the first class.
161	Knowingly issuing or signing a false certificate relating to any fact of which such certificate is by law admissible in evidence.	Ditto.	Ditto.	The same as for giving false evidence.	Ditto.
162	Using as a true certificate one known to be false in a material point.	Ditto.	Ditto.	Ditto.	Ditto.
163	False statement made in any declaration which is by law receivable as evidence.	Ditto.	Ditto.	Ditto.	Ditto.
164	Using as true any such declaration known to be false.	Ditto.	Ditto.	Ditto.	Ditto.

SCHEDULE I—*continued.*

CHAPTER XIII.—FALSE EVIDENCE AND OFFENCES AGAINST PUBLIC JUSTICE—*continued.*

Of the Screening of Offenders, &c.

1	2	3	4	5	6
Section.	Offence.	Whether the police may arrest without warrant or not.	Whether a warrant or a summons shall ordinarily issue in the first instance.	Punishment under the Sudan Penal Code.	By what Court triable.
165	Causing disappearance of evidence of an offence committed to screen offender, or giving false information touching it to screen the offender or prevent his apprehension, or harbouring an offender:—				
	if a capital offence;	Shall not arrest without warrant.	Warrant. . .	Imprisonment for 5 years and fine.	Minor District Court.
	if punishable with imprisonment for 10 years or upwards;	Ditto.	Ditto. . . .	Imprisonment for 3 years and fine.	Minor District Court, or Magistrate of the first class.
	if punishable with less than 10 years' imprisonment.	Ditto.	Ditto. . . .	Imprisonment for a quarter of the longest term provided for the offence, or fine, or both.	Minor District Court, or Magistrate of the first class, or Court by which the offence is triable.
166	Taking gift, etc., to screen an offender from punishment, or offering gift or restoration of property in consideration of screening offender:—				
	if the offence be capital;	Ditto.	Ditto. . . .	Imprisonment for 5 years and fine.	Minor District Court.
	if punishable with imprisonment for 10 years or upwards;	Ditto.	Ditto. . . .	Imprisonment for 3 years and fine.	Minor District Court, or Magistrate of the first class.
	if punishable with less than 10 years' imprisonment.	Ditto.	Ditto. . . .	Imprisonment for a quarter of the longest term provided for the offence, or fine, or both.	Minor District Court, Magistrate of the first class, or Court by which the offence is triable.

167	Harbouring robbers or brigands.	May arrest without warrant	Imprisonment for 7 years and fine.	Mudir's Court, or Minor District Court.
168	Resistance or obstruction to the lawful apprehension of another person, or rescuing him from lawful confinement or custody;	Ditto.	Imprisonment for 2 years, or fine, or both.	Minor District Court, or Magistrate of the first or second class.
	if charged with offence punishable with imprisonment for 10 years or upwards:	Ditto.	Imprisonment for 3 years and fine.	Minor District Court, or Magistrate of the first class.
	if charged with a capital offence, or under sentence of imprisonment for 10 years or upwards;	Ditto.	Imprisonment for 7 years and fine.	Mudir's Court, or Minor District Court.
	if under sentence of death	Ditto.	Imprisonment for 10 years and fine.	Mudir's Court.

Of Resistance to Apprehension.

169	Resistance or obstruction by a person to his lawful apprehension for an offence with which he is charged or of which he has been convicted, or escape from custody in respect of such offence.	Ditto.	Imprisonment for 2 years, or fine, or both.	Minor District Court, or Magistrate of the first or second class.
170	Resistance or obstruction to apprehension or escape in other cases.	Ditto.	Imprisonment for 6 months, or fine, or both.	Magistrate of the first or second class.

Of Fraudulent Dealings with Property.

171	Fraudulent or dishonest dealing with property to prevent its seizure or its application according to law.	Shall not arrest without warrant.	Imprisonment for 2 years, or fine, or both.	Minor District Court, or Magistrate of the first or second class.
172	Fraudulently suffering a decree to pass for a sum not due, or suffering decree to be executed after it has been satisfied.	Ditto.	Ditto.	Minor District Court, or Magistrate of the first class.
173	Fraudulently obtaining a decree for a sum not due, or causing a decree to be executed after it has been satisfied.	Ditto.	Ditto.	Ditto.

SCHEDULE I—*continued.*

CHAPTER XIII.—FALSE EVIDENCE AND OFFENCES AGAINST PUBLIC JUSTICE—*concluded.*

Of Fraudulent Dealings with Property—concluded.

Section.	Offence.	Whether the police may arrest without warrant or not.	Whether a warrant or a summons shall ordinarily issue in the first instance.	Punishment under the Sudan Penal Code.	By what Court triable.
174	Fraudulent execution of deed of transfer for containing a false statement of consideration.	Shall not arrest without warrant.	Warrant.	Imprisonment for 2 years, or fine, or both.	Minor District Court, or Magistrate of the first or second class.
	Miscellaneous.				
175	Giving false information respecting an offence committed.	Ditto.	Ditto.	Ditto.	Ditto.
176	Secreting or destroying any document to prevent its production as evidence.	Ditto.	Ditto.	Ditto.	Minor District Court, or Magistrate of the first class.
177	Personation for the purpose of any act, or proceeding in a suit or criminal prosecution, or for becoming bail or security.	Ditto.	Ditto.	Imprisonment for 3 years, fine, or both.	Ditto.
178	False charge of offence made with intent to injure.	Ditto.	Ditto.	Imprisonment for 2 years, fine, or both.	Ditto.
	If offence charged be punishable with imprisonment for 7 years or upwards.	Ditto.	Ditto.	Imprisonment for 7 years and fine.	Ditto.
179	Taking gift to help to recover movable property of which a person has been deprived by an offence, without endeavouring to cause apprehension of offender.	Ditto.	Ditto.	Imprisonment for 2 years, or fine, or both.	Ditto.

	Offence		Summons	Punishment	Court
180	Intentional insult or interruption to a public servant sitting in any stage of a judicial proceeding.	Ditto. . .	Summons . .	Imprisonment for 6 months, or fine of L.E. 20, or both.	Ditto. . .

CHAPTER XIV.—OFFENCES RELATING TO COIN.

	Offence		Summons	Punishment	Court
182	Counterfeiting or performing any part of the process of counterfeiting coin.	May arrest without warrant	Warrant . .	Imprisonment for 7 years and fine.	Minor District Court.
183	Making, buying or selling instrument for the purpose of counterfeiting coin.	Ditto.	Ditto.	Imprisonment for 5 years and fine.	Minor District Court, or Magistrate of the first class.
184	Possession of instrument or material for the purpose of using the same for counterfeiting coin.	Ditto.	Ditto.	Ditto.	Ditto.
185	Import or export of counterfeit coin, knowing the same to be counterfeit.	Ditto.	Ditto.	Imprisonment for 7 years and fine.	Ditto.
186	Altering appearance of any coin with intent that it shall pass as a coin of a different description, or fraudulently diminishing the weight or altering the composition of any coin.	Ditto.	Ditto.	Imprisonment for 5 years and fine.	Ditto.
187	Delivery to another of coin possessed with the knowledge that it is altered.	Ditto.	Ditto.	Imprisonment for 7 years and fine.	Ditto.
188	Possession of counterfeit or altered coin by a person who knew it to be counterfeit or altered when he became possessed thereof.	Ditto.	Ditto.	Imprisonment for 5 years and fine.	Ditto.
189	Knowingly delivering to another any counterfeit coin as genuine which, when first possessed, the deliverer did not know to be counterfeit.	Ditto.	Ditto.	Imprisonment for 2 years, or fine of ten times the value of the coin counterfeited, or both.	Minor District Court, or Magistrate of the second class.
190	Delivery to another of coin as genuine which, when first possessed, the deliverer did not know to be altered.	Ditto.	Ditto.	Imprisonment for 2 years, or fine of ten times the value of the coin, or both.	Ditto.

G

97

SCHEDULE I—*continued.*

CHAPTER XV.—OFFENCES RELATING TO REVENUE STAMPS.

1	2	3	4	5	6
Section.	Offence.	Whether the police may arrest without warrant or not.	Whether a warrant or a summons shall ordinarily issue in the first instance.	Punishment under the Sudan Penal Code.	By what Court triable.
192	Counterfeiting a revenue stamp.	May arrest without warrant.	Warrant.	Imprisonment for 10 years and fine.	Mudir's Court, or Minor District Court.
193	Having possession of an instrument or material for the purpose of counterfeiting a revenue stamp.	Ditto.	Ditto.	Imprisonment for 7 years and fine.	Minor District Court.
194	Making, buying or selling instrument for the purpose of counterfeiting a revenue stamp.	Ditto.	Ditto.	Ditto.	Ditto.
195	Using as genuine or selling a revenue stamp known to be counterfeit.	Ditto.	Ditto.	Ditto.	Ditto.
196	Having possession of a counterfeit revenue stamp.	Ditto.	Ditto.	Ditto.	Ditto.
197	Effacing any writing from a substance bearing a revenue stamp, or removing from a document a stamp used for it with intent to cause loss to any Government.	Ditto.	Ditto.	Imprisonment for 3 years, or fine, or both.	Minor District Court, or Magistrate of the first class.
198	Using a revenue stamp known to have been used before.	Ditto.	Ditto.	Imprisonment for 2 years, or fine, or both.	Minor District Court, or Magistrate of the first or second class.
199	Erasure of mark denoting that stamp has been used.	Ditto.	Ditto.	Imprisonment for 3 years, or fine, or both.	Minor District Court, or Magistrate of the first class.

CHAPTER XVI.—OFFENCES RELATING TO WEIGHTS AND MEASURES.

No.	Offence				Magistrate of the first or second class.
200	Fraudulent use of false instrument for weighing.	Shall not arrest without warrant	Summons	Imprisonment for 1 year, or fine, or both.	Magistrate of the first or second class.
201	Fraudulent use of false weight or measure.	Ditto.	Ditto.	Ditto.	Ditto.
202	Being in possession of false weights or measures for fraudulent use.	Ditto.	Ditto.	Ditto.	Ditto.
203	Making or selling false weights or measures for fraudulent use.	Ditto.	Ditto.	Ditto.	Ditto.

CHAPTER XVII.—OFFENCES AFFECTING THE PUBLIC HEALTH, SAFETY, CONVENIENCE, DECENCY AND MORALS.

No.	Offence				Magistrate of the first or second class.
205	Adulterating food or drink intended for sale, so as to make the same noxious.	Shall not arrest without warrant	Summons	Imprisonment for 6 months, or fine of L.E. 20, or both.	Magistrate of the first or second class.
206	Selling any food or drink as food and drink, knowing the same to be noxious.	Ditto.	Ditto.	Ditto.	Ditto.
207	Adulterating any drug or medical preparation intended for sale so as to lessen its efficacy, or to change its operation, or to make it noxious.	Ditto.	Ditto.	Ditto.	Ditto.
208	Offering for sale or issuing from a dispensary any drug or medical preparation known to have been adulterated.	Ditto.	Ditto.	Ditto.	Ditto.
209	Knowingly selling or issuing from a dispensary any drug or medical preparation as a different drug or medical preparation.	Ditto.	Ditto.	Ditto.	Ditto.
210	Defiling the water of a public spring or reservoir.	Ditto.	Ditto.	Imprisonment for 3 months, or fine of L.E. 10, or both.	Ditto.

SCHEDULE I—*continued.*

CHAPTER XVII.—OFFENCES AFFECTING THE PUBLIC HEALTH, SAFETY, CONVENIENCE, DECENCY AND MORALS—*concluded.*

1	2	3	4	5	6
Section.	Offence.	Whether the police may arrest without warrant or not.	Whether a warrant or a summons shall ordinarily issue in the first instance.	Punishment under the Sudan Penal Code.	By what Court triable.
211	Making atmosphere noxious to health.	Shall not arrest without warrant.	Summons	Fine of L.E. 10.	Magistrate of the first or second class.
212	Exhibition of a false light, mark or buoy.	May arrest without warrant.	Warrant.	Imprisonment for 7 years, or fine, or both.	Mudir's Court, or Minor District Court.
213	Causing obstruction in any public way or line of navigation.	Ditto.	Summons	Fine of L.E. 5.	Magistrate of the first or second class.
214	Rash or negligent act or conduct endangering human life, etc.	Ditto.	Ditto.	Imprisonment for 6 months, or fine of L.E. 20, or both.	Ditto.
215	A person omitting to take order with any animal in his possession, so as to guard against danger to human life, or of grievous hurt, from such animal.	Ditto.	Ditto.	Ditto.	Ditto.
216	Committing a public nuisance	Shall not arrest without warrant.	Ditto.	Fine of L.E. 5.	Ditto.
217	Continuance of nuisance after injunction to discontinue.	May arrest without warrant.	Ditto.	Imprisonment for 6 months, or fine, or both.	Ditto.
218	Obscene or indecent acts.	Ditto.	Warrant.	Imprisonment for 1 year, or fine, or both.	Ditto.
219	Sale, etc., of obscene books, etc., or having such books in possession for sale or exhibition.	Ditto.	Ditto.	Imprisonment for 3 months, or fine, or both.	Ditto.

100

No.	Offence			Punishment	Court
220	Obscene songs, etc.		Ditto.	Ditto.	Ditto.
221	Keeping a lottery office.	Shall not arrest without warrant.	Summons	Imprisonment for 6 months, or fine, or both.	Ditto.
	Publishing proposals relating to lotteries.	Ditto.	Ditto.	Fine of L.E. 20.	Ditto.
222	Keeping a gaming-house.	Ditto.	Ditto.	Imprisonment for 6 months, or fine, or both.	Ditto.
	Being found in a gaming-house.	Ditto.	Ditto.	Imprisonment for 1 month, or fine, or both.	Ditto.

CHAPTER XVIII.—OFFENCES RELATING TO RELIGION.

No.	Offence			Punishment	Court
223	Destroying, damaging or defiling a place of worship or sacred object with intent to insult the religion of any class of persons.	May arrest without warrant.	Summons	Imprisonment for 2 years, or fine, or both.	Minor District Court, or Magistrate of the first or second class.
224	Causing a disturbance to an assembly engaged in religious worship.	Ditto.	Ditto.	Imprisonment for 1 year, or fine, or both.	Magistrate of the first or second class.
225	Trespassing in place of worship or sepulture or disturbing funeral, with intention to wound the feelings or to insult the religion of any person, or offering indignity to a human corpse.	Ditto.	Ditto.	Ditto.	Ditto.

CHAPTER XIX.—OFFENCES AFFECTING THE HUMAN BODY.

Of Offences affecting Life.

No.	Offence			Punishment	Court
230	Murder	May arrest without warrant.	Warrant.	Death, or imprisonment for life, and fine.	Mudir's Court.
231	Murder by a person under sentence of imprisonment for life.	Ditto.	Ditto.	Death.	Ditto.
232	Culpable homicide not amounting to murder.	Ditto.	Ditto.	Imprisonment for life and fine, or fine.	Ditto.

101

SCHEDULE I—*continued.*

CHAPTER XIX.—OFFENCES AFFECTING THE HUMAN BODY—*continued.*

Of *Offences affecting Life*—concluded.

Section.	Offence.	Whether the police may arrest without warrant or not.	Whether a warrant or a summons shall ordinarily issue in the first instance.	Punishment under the Sudan Penal Code.	By what Court triable.
233	Causing death by rash or negligent act.	May arrest without warrant.	Warrant.	Imprisonment for 2 years, or fine, or both.	Minor District Court, or Magistrate of the first class.
234	Abetment of suicide committed by a child, or insane or delirious person, or an idiot, or a person intoxicated.	Ditto.	Ditto.	Death, or imprisonment for life, and fine.	Mudir's Court.
235	Abetting the commission of suicide.	Ditto.	Ditto.	Imprisonment for 10 years and fine.	Ditto.
236	Attempt to murder.	Ditto.	Ditto.	Ditto.	Ditto.
	If such act cause hurt to any person.	Ditto.	Ditto.	Imprisonment for 14 years and fine.	Ditto.
	Attempt by life-convict to murder, if hurt is caused.	Ditto.	Ditto.	Death, or as above.	Ditto.
237	Attempt to commit culpable homicide.	Ditto.	Ditto.	Imprisonment for 3 years, or fine, or both.	Mudir's Court or Minor District Court.
	If such act cause hurt to any person.	Ditto.	Ditto.	Imprisonment for 7 years, or fine, or both.	Ditto.
238	Attempt to commit suicide.	Ditto.	Ditto.	Imprisonment for 1 year, or fine, or both.	Magistrate of the first or second class.

Of the Causing of Miscarriage; of Injuries to Unborn Children; of the Exposure of Infants; and of the Concealment of Births.

No.	Offence		Punishment	Court
239	Causing miscarriage	Shall not arrest without warrant.	Imprisonment for 3 years, or fine, or both.	Mudir's Court.
	If the woman be quick with child .	Ditto.	Imprisonment for 7 years and fine.	Ditto.
240	Causing miscarriage without woman's consent.	Ditto.	Imprisonment for 10 years and fine.	Ditto.
241	Death caused by an act done with intent to cause miscarriage.	Ditto.	Imprisonment for 10 years and fine.	Ditto.
	If act done without woman's consent.	Ditto.	Imprisonment for life and fine.	Ditto.
242	Act done with intent to prevent a child being born alive, or to cause it to die after its birth.	Ditto.	Imprisonment for 10 years, or fine, or both.	Ditto.
243	Causing death of a quick unborn child by an act amounting to culpable homicide.	Ditto.	Imprisonment for 10 years and fine.	Ditto.
244	Exposure of a child under 12 years of age by parent or person having care of it with intention of wholly abandoning it.	May arrest without warrant	Imprisonment for 7 years, or fine, or both.	Mudir's Court or Minor District Court.
245	Concealment of birth by secret disposal of dead body.	Ditto.	Imprisonment for 2 years, or fine, or both.	Minor District Court, or Magistrate of the first or second class.

Of Hurt.

No.	Offence		Punishment	Court
250	Voluntarily causing hurt on grave and sudden provocation, not intending to hurt any other than the person who gave the provocation.	Shall not arrest without warrant. Summons	Imprisonment for 1 month, or fine of L.E. 10, or both.	Magistrate of the first or second class.
251	Causing grievous hurt on grave and sudden provocation, not intending to hurt any other than the person who gave the provocation.	May arrest without warrant	Imprisonment for 4 years, or fine of L.E. 50, or both.	Minor District Court, or Magistrate of the first or second class.

SCHEDULE I—*continued.*

CHAPTER XIX.—OFFENCES AFFECTING THE HUMAN BODY—*continued.*
Of Hurt—concluded.

1	2	3	4	5	6
Section.	Offence.	Whether the police may arrest without warrant or not.	Whether a warrant or a summons shall ordinarily issue in the first instance.	Punishment under the Sudan Penal Code.	By what Court triable.
252	Voluntarily causing hurt.	Shall not arrest without warrant.	Summons	Imprisonment for 1 year, or fine of L.E. 20, or both.	Magistrate of the first or second class.
253	Voluntarily causing grievous hurt.	May arrest without warrant.	Ditto.	Imprisonment for 7 years and fine.	Minor District Court, or Magistrate of the first or second class.
254	(i) Voluntarily causing hurt by dangerous weapon or means.	Ditto.	Ditto.	Imprisonment for 3 years, or fine, or both.	Ditto.
	(ii) If the hurt be grievous	Ditto.	Warrant.	Imprisonment for 14 years and fine.	Mudir's Court.
255	Administering stupefying drug with intent to cause hurt, etc.	Ditto.	Ditto.	Imprisonment for 10 years and fine.	Mudir's Court, or Minor District Court.
256	(i) Voluntarily causing hurt to extort property or a valuable security, or to constrain to do anything which is illegal or which may facilitate the commission of an offence.	Ditto.	Ditto.	Ditto.	Ditto.
	(ii) If the hurt be grievous	Ditto.	Ditto.	Imprisonment for 14 years and fine.	Mudir's Court.
257	(i) Voluntarily causing hurt to extort confession or information, or to compel restoration of property, etc.	Ditto.	Ditto.	Imprisonment for 7 years and fine.	Minor District Court.
	(ii) If the hurt be grievous	Ditto.	Ditto.	Imprisonment for 10 years and fine.	Mudir's Court.

258	(i) Voluntarily causing hurt to deter public servant from his duty.	Ditto.	Ditto.	Imprisonment for 3 years, or fine, or both.	Minor District Court, or Magistrate of the first class.
	(ii) If the hurt be grievous.	Ditto.	Ditto.	Imprisonment for 10 years and fine.	Mudir's Court, or Minor District Court.
259	(i) Causing hurt by an act which endangers human life, etc.	Ditto.	Summons	Imprisonment for 6 months, or fine of L.E. 10, or both.	Magistrate of the first or second class.
	(ii) If the hurt be grievous.	Ditto.	Ditto.	Imprisonment for 2 years, or fine of L.E. 20, or both.	Minor District Court, or Magistrate of the first or second class.

Of Wrongful Restraint and Wrongful Confinement.

262	Wrongfully restraining any person.	Ditto.	Ditto.	Imprisonment for 1 month, or fine of L.E. 10, or both.	Magistrate of the first or second class.
263	Wrongfully confining any person.	Ditto.	Ditto.	Imprisonment for 1 year, or fine of L.E. 20, or both.	Ditto.
264	Wrongfully confining for three or more days.	Ditto.	Ditto.	Imprisonment for 2 years, or fine, or both.	Minor District Court, or Magistrate of the first or second class.
265	Wrongfully confining for ten or more days.	Ditto.	Ditto.	Imprisonment for 3 years and fine.	Ditto.
266	Keeping any person in wrongful confinement, knowing that a writ has been issued for his liberation.	Ditto.	Ditto.	Imprisonment for 2 years in addition to imprisonment under any other section.	Minor District Court.
267	Wrongful confinement in secret.	Ditto.	Ditto.	Ditto.	Ditto.
268	Wrongful confinement for the purpose of extorting property, or constraining to an illegal act, etc.	Ditto.	Ditto.	Imprisonment for 3 years and fine.	Minor District Court, or Magistrate of the first class.
269	Wrongful confinement for the purpose of extorting confession or information, or of compelling restoration of property, etc.	Ditto.	Ditto.	Ditto.	Ditto.

SCHEDULE I—continued.

CHAPTER XIX.—OFFENCES AFFECTING THE HUMAN BODY—concluded.

Of Criminal Force and Assault.

Section.	Offence.	Whether the police may arrest without warrant or not.	Whether a warrant or a summons shall ordinarily issue in the first instance.	Punishment under the Sudan Penal Code.	By what Court triable.
273	Assault or use of criminal force otherwise than on grave provocation.	Shall not arrest without warrant.	Summons	Imprisonment for 3 months, or fine of L.E. 10, or both.	Magistrate of the first or second class.
274	Assault or use of criminal force on grave provocation.	Ditto.	Ditto.	Imprisonment for 1 month, or fine of L.E. 5, or both.	Ditto.
275	Assault or use of criminal force to deter a public servant from discharge of his duty.	May arrest without warrant.	Warrant.	Imprisonment for 2 years, or fine, or both.	Minor District Court, or Magistrate of the first or second class.
276	Assault or use of criminal force to a woman with intent to outrage her modesty.	Ditto.	Ditto.	Ditto.	Ditto.
277	Assault or criminal force in attempt to commit theft of property worn or carried by a person.	Ditto.	Ditto.	Ditto.	Ditto.
278	Assault or use of criminal force in attempt wrongfully to confine a person.	Ditto.	Ditto.	Imprisonment for 1 year, or fine of I.E. 20, or both.	Magistrate of the first or second class.

Of Kidnapping, Abduction and Forced Labour.

Section.	Offence.	Whether the police may arrest without warrant or not.	Whether a warrant or a summons shall ordinarily issue in the first instance.	Punishment under the Sudan Penal Code.	By what Court triable.
281	Kidnapping.	Ditto.	Ditto.	Imprisonment for 7 years and fine.	Minor District Court, or Magistrate of the first class.
282	Kidnapping or abducting in order to murder.	Ditto.	Ditto.	Imprisonment for 14 years and fine.	Mudir's Court.

No.	Offence	Whether may arrest without warrant	Summons or warrant	Punishment	Court
283	Kidnapping or abducting with intent secretly and wrongfully to confine a person.	Ditto.	. . .	Imprisonment for 7 years and fine.	Minor District Court, or Magistrate of the first class.
284	Kidnapping or abducting a woman to compel her marriage or to cause her defilement, etc.	Ditto.	. . .	Imprisonment for 10 years and fine.	Mudir's Court.
285	Kidnapping or abducting in order to subject a person to grievous hurt, etc.	Ditto.	. . .	Ditto.	Ditto.
286	Concealing or keeping in confinement a kidnapped or abducted person.	Ditto.	. . .	Punishment for kidnapping or abduction.	Court by which offence of kidnapping, or abduction could be tried.
287	Buying, selling, hiring, or letting to hire a minor for purposes of prostitution, etc.	Ditto.	. . .	Imprisonment for 10 years and fine.	Mudir's Court or Minor District Court.
288	Unlawful compulsory labour	Ditto.	. . .	Imprisonment for 1 year, or fine, or both.	Magistrate of the first or second class.
289	Kidnapping or abducting in order to subject to unlawful compulsory labour.	Ditto.	. . .	Imprisonment for 7 years and fine.	Mudir's Court, or Minor District Court.
290	Transferring control of person of any man or woman, for money or money's worth, with intent to enable him or her to be subjected to unlawful confinement or unlawful compulsory labour.	Ditto.	. . .	Ditto.	Ditto.

Of Rape.

No.	Offence	Whether may arrest without warrant	Summons or warrant	Punishment	Court
292	Rape— if the sexual intercourse was by a man with his own wife;	Shall not arrest without warrant.	Summons	Imprisonment for 14 years and fine.	Mudir's Court.
	In any other case	May arrest without warrant	Warrant	Ditto.	Ditto.

Of Unnatural Offences.

No.	Offence	Whether may arrest without warrant	Summons or warrant	Punishment	Court
293	Unnatural offence.	Ditto.	Ditto.	Imprisonment for 14 years and fine.	Mudir's Court or Minor District Court.

SCHEDULE I—*continued.*
CHAPTER XX.—OFFENCES AGAINST PROPERTY.
Of Theft.

Section.	Offence.	Whether the police may arrest without warrant or not.	Whether a warrant or a summons shall ordinarily issue in the first instance.	Punishment under the Sudan Penal Code.	By what Court triable.
1	2	3	4	5	6
295	Theft.	May arrest without warrant.	Warrant.	Imprisonment for 3 years, or fine, or both.	Minor District Court, or Magistrate of the first or second class.
296	Theft in a building, tent or vessel	Ditto.	Ditto.	Imprisonment for 7 years and fine, or fine.	Ditto.
297	Theft by clerk or servant of property in possession of master or employer.	Ditto.	Ditto.	Ditto.	Ditto.
298	Theft, preparation having been made for causing death, or hurt, or restraint, or fear of death, or of hurt or of restraint, in order to the committing of such theft, or to retiring after committing it, or to retaining property taken by it.	Ditto.	Ditto.	Imprisonment for 10 years and fine.	Mudir's Court or Minor District Court.

Of Extortion.

Section.	Offence.	Whether the police may arrest without warrant or not.	Whether a warrant or a summons shall ordinarily issue in the first instance.	Punishment under the Sudan Penal Code.	By what Court triable.
300	Extortion	Shall not arrest without warrant.	Ditto.	Imprisonment for 3 years, or fine, or both.	Minor District Court, or, Magistrate of the first or second class.
301	Putting or attempting to put in fear of injury, in order to commit extortion.	Ditto.	Ditto.	Imprisonment for 2 years, or fine, or both.	Ditto.
302	Extortion by putting a person in fear of death or grievous hurt.	Ditto.	Ditto.	Imprisonment for 10 years and fine.	Mudir's Court.

No.	Offence	May arrest without warrant	Punishment	Mudir's Court, Minor District Court, or Magistrate of the first class.
303	Putting or attempting to put a person in fear of death or grievous hurt in order to commit extortion.	Ditto.	Imprisonment for 7 years and fine.	Ditto.
304	Extortion by threat of accusation of an offence punishable with death, or imprisonment for 10 years.	Ditto.	Imprisonment for 10 years and fine.	Ditto.
305	Putting a person in fear of accusation of offence punishable with death, or with imprisonment for 10 years, in order to commit extortion.	Ditto.	Imprisonment for 10 years and fine.	Ditto.

Of Robbery and Brigandage.

No.	Offence	May arrest without warrant	Punishment	Court
308	Robbery.	May arrest without warrant	Imprisonment for 10 years and fine.	Mudir's Court, Minor District Court, or Magistrate of the first class.
	If committed on the highway or from a person sleeping in the open air, between sunset and sunrise.	Ditto.	Imprisonment for 14 years and fine.	Ditto.
309	Attempt to commit robbery.	Ditto.	Imprisonment for 7 years and fine.	Ditto.
10	Person voluntarily causing hurt in committing or attempting to commit robbery or any other person jointly concerned in such robbery.	Ditto.	Imprisonment for 14 years and fine.	Ditto.
311	Brigandage.	Ditto.	Imprisonment for 7 years and fine.	Mudir's Court.
312	Murder in brigandage.	Ditto.	Death, or imprisonment for life, and fine.	Ditto.
313	Robbery or brigandage, with attempt to cause death or grievous hurt.	Ditto.	Imprisonment for not less than 7 years.	Ditto.
314	Making preparation to commit brigandage.	Ditto.	Imprisonment for 10 years and fine.	Mudir's Court, or Minor District Court.
315	Belonging to a gang of persons associated for the purpose of habitually committing brigandage.	Ditto.	Imprisonment for 14 years and fine.	Mudir's Court.

SCHEDULE I—*continued.*

CHAPTER XX.—OFFENCES AGAINST PROPERTY—*continued.*

Of Robbery and Brigandage—*concluded.*

1 Section.	2 Offence.	3 Whether the police may arrest without warrant or not.	4 Whether a warrant or a summons shall ordinarily issue in the first instance.	5 Punishment under the Sudan Penal Code.	6 By what Court triable.
316	Belonging to a wandering gang of persons associated for the purpose of habitually committing thefts.	May arrest without warrant.	Warrant.	Imprisonment for 7 years and fine.	Minor District Court, or Magistrate of the first class.
317	Being one of five or more persons assembled for the purpose of committing brigandage.	Ditto.	Ditto.	Ditto.	Minor District Court.

Of Criminal Misappropriation of Property.

318	Dishonest misappropriation of movable property or converting it to one's own use.	Shall not arrest without warrant.	Ditto.	Imprisonment for 2 years, or fine, or both.	Minor District Court, or Magistrate of the first or second class.
319	Dishonest misappropriation of property, knowing that it was in possession of a deceased person at his death, and that it has not since been in the possession of any person legally entitled to it.	Ditto.	Ditto.	Imprisonment for 3 years and fine.	Ditto.
	If by clerk or person employed by deceased.	Ditto.	Ditto.	Imprisonment for 7 years and fine.	Ditto.

Of Criminal Breach of Trust.

321	Criminal breach of trust.	May arrest without warrant.	Ditto.	Imprisonment for 3 years, or fine, or both.	Ditto.

No.	Offence	Arrest	Punishment	Court
322	Criminal breach of trust by a carrier, wharfinger, etc.	Ditto.	Imprisonment for 7 years and fine.	Minor District Court, or Magistrate of the first class.
323	Criminal breach of trust by a clerk or servant.	Ditto.	Ditto.	Minor District Court, or Magistrate of the first or second class.
324	Criminal breach of trust by public servant or by banker, merchant or agent, etc.	Ditto.	Imprisonment for 10 years and fine.	Mudir's Court, Minor District Court, or Magistrate of the first class.

Of the Receiving of Stolen Property.

No.	Offence	Arrest	Punishment	Court
326	Dishonestly receiving stolen property, knowing it to be stolen.	Ditto.	Imprisonment for 3 years, or fine, or both.	Minor District Court, or Magistrate of the first or second class.
327	Dishonestly receiving stolen property, knowing that it was obtained by brigandage.	Ditto.	Imprisonment for 14 years and fine.	Mudir's Court.
328	Habitually dealing in stolen property.	Ditto.	Ditto.	Ditto.
329	Assisting in concealment or disposal of stolen property, knowing it to be stolen.	Ditto.	Imprisonment for 3 years, or fine, or both.	Minor District Court, or Magistrate of the first or second class.

Of Cheating.

No.	Offence	Arrest	Punishment	Court
332	Cheating.	Shall not arrest without warrant.	Imprisonment for 1 year, or fine, or both.	Magistrate of the first or second class.
333	Cheating a person whose interest the offender was bound, either by law or by legal contract, to protect.	Ditto.	Imprisonment for 3 years, or fine, or both.	Minor District Court, or Magistrate of the first class.
334	Cheating by personation.	May arrest without warrant.	Ditto.	Minor District Court, or Magistrate of the first or second class.
335	Cheating and thereby dishonestly inducing delivery of property, or the making, alteration or destruction of a valuable security.	Ditto.	Imprisonment for 7 years and fine.	Minor District Court, or Magistrate of the first class.

SCHEDULE I—*continued.*

CHAPTER XX.—OFFENCES AGAINST PROPERTY—*continued.*

Of Mischief.

Section.	Offence.	Whether the police may arrest without warrant or not.	Whether a warrant or a summons shall ordinarily issue in the first instance.	Punishment under the Sudan Penal Code.	By what Court triable.
337	Mischief.	Shall not arrest without warrant.	Summons	Imprisonment for 3 months, or fine, or both.	Magistrate of the first or second class.
338	Mischief, and thereby causing damage to the amount of P.T. 200 or upwards.	Ditto.	Warrant.	Imprisonment for 2 years, or fine, or both.	Minor District Court, or Magistrate of the first or second class.
339	Mischief by killing, poisoning, maiming or rendering useless any animal of the value of P.T. 75 or upwards.	May arrest without warrant.	Ditto.	Ditto.	Ditto.
340	Mischief by killing, poisoning, maiming or rendering useless any camel, horse, etc., whatever may be its value, or any other animal of the value of P.T. 300 or upwards.	Ditto.	Ditto.	Imprisonment for 5 years, or fine, or both.	Ditto.
341	Mischief by causing diminution of supply of water for agricultural purposes, etc.	Ditto.	Ditto.	Ditto.	Ditto.
342	Mischief by injury to public road, railway, bridge, navigable river, or navigable channel, and rendering it impassable or less safe for travelling or conveying property.	Ditto.	Ditto.	Ditto.	Ditto.
343	Mischief by causing inundation or obstruction to public drainage, attended with damage.	Ditto.	Ditto.	Ditto.	Ditto.

No.	Offence		Arrest	Summons/Warrant	Punishment	Court
344	Mischief by destroying or moving or rendering less useful a light-house or sea-mark, or by exhibiting false lights.	.	Ditto.	Ditto.	Imprisonment for 7 years, or fine, or both.	Mudir's Court or Minor District Court.
345	Mischief by destroying or moving, etc., a land-mark fixed by public authority.	.	Shall not arrest without warrant.	Ditto.	Imprisonment for 1 year, or fine, or both.	Magistrate of the first or second class.
346	Mischief by fire or explosive substance with intent to cause damage to amount of L.E. 5 or upwards, or, in case of agricultural produce, L.E. 1 or upwards.	.	May arrest without warrant	Ditto.	Imprisonment for 7 years and fine.	Minor District Court, or Magistrate of the first class.
347	Mischief by fire or explosive substance with intent to destroy a house, etc.	.	Ditto.	Ditto.	Imprisonment for 14 years and fine.	Mudir's Court.
348	Mischief with intent to destroy or make unsafe a decked vessel or a vessel of 100 tons burden.	.	Ditto.	Ditto.	Imprisonment for 10 years and fine.	Ditto.
349	The mischief described in the last section when committed by fire or any explosive substance.	.	Ditto.	Ditto.	Imprisonment for 14 years and fine.	Ditto.
350	Running vessel ashore with intent to commit theft, etc.	.	Ditto.	Ditto.	Imprisonment for 10 years and fine.	Ditto.
351	Mischief committed after preparation made for causing death, or hurt, etc.	.	Ditto.	Ditto.	Imprisonment for 5 years and fine.	Minor District Court, or Magistrate of the first class.

Of Criminal Trespass.

No.	Offence		Arrest	Summons/Warrant	Punishment	Court
358	Criminal trespass	.	Ditto.	Summons	Imprisonment for 3 months, or fine of L.E. 10, or both.	Magistrate of the first or second class.
359	House-trespass	.	Ditto.	Warrant.	Imprisonment for 1 year, or fine of L.E. 20, or both.	Ditto.
360	House-trespass in order to the commission of an offence punishable with death.	.	Ditto.	Ditto.	Imprisonment for 14 years and fine.	Mudir's Court.

H

SCHEDULE I—*continued.*

CHAPTER XX.—OFFENCES AGAINST PROPERTY—*concluded.*

Of Criminal Trespass—concluded.

1	2	3	4	5	6
Section.	Offence.	Whether the police may arrest without warrant or not.	Whether a warrant or a summons shall ordinarily issue in the first instance.	Punishment under the Sudan Penal Code.	By what Court triable.
361	House-trespass in order to the commission of an offence punishable with 14 years imprisonment.	May arrest without warrant.	Warrant.	Imprisonment for 10 years and fine.	Mudir's Court.
362	House-trespass in order to the commission of an offence punishable with imprisonment.	Ditto.	Ditto.	Imprisonment for 2 years and fine.	Minor District Court, or Magistrate of the first or second class.
	If the offence is theft.	Ditto.	Ditto.	Imprisonment for 7 years and fine.	Ditto.
363	House-trespass having made preparation for causing hurt, assault, etc.	Ditto.	Ditto.	Ditto.	Ditto.
364	Lurking house-trespass or house-breaking.	Ditto.	Ditto.	Imprisonment for 2 years and fine.	Ditto.
365	Lurking house-trespass or house-breaking in order to the commission of an offence punishable with imprisonment.	Ditto.	Ditto.	Imprisonment for 3 years and fine.	Ditto.
	If the offence is theft.	Ditto.	Ditto.	Imprisonment for 10 years and fine.	Mudir's Court, or as above.
366	Lurking house-trespass or house-breaking after preparation made for causing, hurt, assault, etc.	Ditto.	Ditto.	Ditto.	Mudir's Court, Minor District Court, or Magistrate of the first class.
367	Lurking house-trespass or house-breaking by night.	Ditto.	Ditto.	Imprisonment for 3 years and fine.	Minor District Court, or Magistrate of the first or second class.

No.					Court
368	Lurking house-trespass or house-breaking by night in order to the commission of an offence punishable with imprisonment.	Ditto.	Ditto.	Imprisonment for 5 years and fine.	Ditto.
	If the offence is theft.	Ditto.	Ditto.	Imprisonment for 14 years and fine.	Mudir's Court, Minor District Court, or Magistrate of the first class.
369	Lurking house-trespass or house-breaking by night, after preparation made for causing hurt, etc.	Ditto.	Ditto.	Ditto.	Ditto.
370	Grievous hurt caused whilst committing lurking house-trespass or house-breaking.	Ditto.	Ditto.	Ditto.	Mudir's Court.
371	Death or grievous hurt caused by one of several persons jointly concerned in house-breaking by night, etc.	Ditto.	Ditto.	Ditto.	Ditto.
372	Dishonestly breaking open or unfastening any closed receptacle containing or supposed to contain property.	Ditto.	Ditto.	Imprisonment for 2 years, or fine, or both.	Minor District Court, or Magistrate of the first or second class.
373	Being entrusted with any closed receptacle containing or supposed to contain any property, and fraudulently opening the same.	Ditto.	Ditto.	Imprisonment for 3 years, or fine, or both.	Ditto.

CHAPTER XXI.—OFFENCES RELATING TO DOCUMENTS AND TO PROPERTY OR OTHER MARKS.

No.					Court
376	Forgery.	Shall not arrest without warrant.	Ditto.	Imprisonment for 2 years, or fine, or both.	Minor District Court, or Magistrate of the first class.
377	Forgery of a record of a Court of Justice or of a Register of births, etc., kept by a public servant.	Ditto.	Ditto.	Imprisonment for 7 years and fine.	Minor District Court.
378	Forgery of a valuable security, will, or authority to make or transfer any valuable security, or to receive any money, etc.	Ditto.	Ditto.	Imprisonment for 10 years and fine.	Mudir's Court, or Minor District Court.

115

SCHEDULE I—*continued.*

CHAPTER XXI.—OFFENCES RELATING TO DOCUMENTS AND TO PROPERTY OR OTHER MARKS—*concluded.*

1	2	3	4	5	6
Section.	Offence.	Whether the police may arrest without warrant or not.	Whether a warrant or a summons shall ordinarily issue in the first instance.	Punishment under the Sudan Penal Code.	By what Court triable.
379	Forgery for the purpose of cheating.	Shall not arrest without warrant.	Warrant.	Imprisonment for 7 years and fine.	Minor District Court, or Magistrate of the first class.
380	Forgery for the purpose of harming the reputation of any person, or knowing that it is likely to be used for that purpose.	Ditto.	Ditto.	Imprisonment for 3 years and fine.	Ditto.
382	Using as genuine a forged document which is known to be forged.	Ditto.	Ditto.	Punishment for forgery of such document.	Same Court as that by which the forgery is triable.
383	Making or counterfeiting a seal, plate, etc., with intent to commit forgery, or possessing with like intent any such seal, plate, etc., knowing the same to be counterfeit.	Ditto.	Ditto.	Imprisonment for 7 years and fine.	Minor District Court, or Magistrate of the first class.
384	Having possession of a document of the description mentioned in sections 377 or 378 of the Sudan Penal Code. knowing it to be forged, with intent to use it as genuine.	Ditto.	Ditto.	Ditto.	Minor District Court.
385	Counterfeiting a device or mark used for authenticating documents, or possessing counterfeit marked material.	Ditto.	Ditto.	Ditto.	Ditto.

No.	Offence				Punishment	By what Court triable
386	Fraudulently destroying or defacing, or attempting to destroy or deface, or secreting, a will, etc.	Ditto.	Ditto.	Ditto.	· · · · ·	Ditto.
387	Falsification of accounts.	Ditto.	Ditto.	Ditto.	Imprisonment for 7 years, or fine, or both.	Ditto.

Of Property and other Marks.

No.	Offence				Punishment	By what Court triable
390	Using a false property-mark with intent to deceive or injure any person.	Ditto.	Ditto.	Ditto.	Imprisonment for 1 year, or fine, or both.	Magistrate of the first or second class.
391	Counterfeiting a property-mark used by another, with intent to cause damage or injury.	Ditto.	Ditto.	Ditto.	Imprisonment for 2 years, or fine, or both.	Minor District Court, or Magistrate of the first or second class.
392	Counterfeiting a property-mark used by a public servant, or any mark used by him to denote the manufacture, quality, etc., of any property.	Ditto.	Ditto.	Summons	Imprisonment for 3 years and fine.	Minor District Court, or Magistrate of the first class.
393	Fraudulently making or having possession of any die, plate or other instrument for counterfeiting any public or private property-mark.	Ditto.	Ditto.	Ditto.	Imprisonment for 3 years, or fine, or both.	Ditto.
394	Knowingly selling goods marked with a counterfeit property-mark.	Ditto.	Ditto.	Ditto.	Imprisonment for 1 year, or fine, or both.	Magistrate of the first or second class.
395	Fraudulently making a false mark upon any package or receptacle containing goods, with intent to cause it to be believed that it contains goods which it does not contain, etc.	Ditto.	Ditto.	Ditto.	Imprisonment for 3 years, or fine, or both.	Minor District Court, or Magistrate of the first or second class.
396	Making use of any such false mark.	Ditto.	Ditto.	Ditto.	· · · · ·	Ditto.
397	Removing, destroying or defacing any property-mark with intent to cause injury.	Ditto.	Ditto.	Ditto.	Imprisonment for 1 year, or fine, or both.	Magistrate of the first or second class.

117

SCHEDULE I—*continued.*

Chapter XXII.—Criminal Breach of Contracts of Service.

1	2	3	4	5	6
Section.	Offence.	Whether the police may arrest without warrant or not.	Whether a warrant or a summons shall ordinarily issue in the first instance.	Punishment under the Sudan Penal Code.	By what Court triable.
398	Being bound by contract to render personal service during a voyage or journey or to convey or guard any property or person and voluntarily omitting to do so.	Shall not arrest without warrant.	Summons	Imprisonment for 1 month, or fine of L.E. 5, or both.	Magistrate of the first or second class.
399	Being bound to attend on or supply the wants of a person who is helpless from youth, unsoundness of mind or disease, and voluntarily omitting to do so.	Ditto.	Ditto.	Imprisonment for 3 months, or fine of L.E. 10, or both.	Ditto.
400	Being bound by contract to render personal service for a certain period at a distant place to which the employé is conveyed at the expense of the employer, and voluntarily deserting the service or refusing to perform the duty.	Ditto.	Ditto.	Imprisonment for 1 month, or fine of double the expense incurred, or both.	Ditto.

Chapter XXIII.—Offences relating to Marriage.

1	2	3	4	5	6
401	A man by deceit causing a woman not lawfully married to him to believe that she is lawfully married to him and to cohabit with him in that belief.	Shall not arrest without warrant.	Warrant.	Imprisonment for 10 years and fine.	Mudir's Court.

No.	Offence				Court
402	Marrying again during the lifetime of a husband or wife.	Ditto.	Ditto,	Imprisonment for 7 years and fine.	Ditto.
403	Same offence with concealment of the former marriage from the person with whom subsequent marriage is contracted.	Ditto.	Ditto.	Imprisonment for 10 years and fine.	Ditto.
404	A person with fraudulent intention going through the ceremony of being married, knowing that he is not thereby lawfully married.	Ditto.	Ditto.	Imprisonment for 7 years and fine.	Ditto.
405	Adultery with married woman.	Ditto.	Summons.	Imprisonment for 2 years, fine, or both.	Minor District Court, or Magistrate of the first class.
406	Adultery by married woman.	Ditto.	Ditto.	Ditto.	Ditto.
407	Enticing or taking away or detaining with a criminal intent a married woman.	Ditto.	Warrant.	Imprisonment for 2 years, fine, or both.	Minor District Court, or Magistrate of the second class.

CHAPTER XXIV.—DEFAMATION.

No.	Offence				Court
409	Defamation.	Shall not arrest without warrant.	Warrant.	Imprisonment for 2 years, fine, or both.	Minor District Court, or Magistrate of the first class.
410	Printing or engraving matter knowing it to be defamatory.	Ditto.	Ditto.	Ditto.	Ditto.
411	Sale of printed or engraved substance containing defamatory matter, knowing it to contain such matter.	Ditto.	Ditto.	Ditto.	Ditto.

119

SCHEDULE I—*concluded.*

CHAPTER XXV.—CRIMINAL INTIMIDATION, INSULT AND ANNOYANCE.

1	2	3	4	5	6
Section.	Offence.	Whether the police may arrest without warrant or not.	Whether a warrant or a summons shall ordinarily issue in the first instance.	Punishment under the Sudan Penal Code.	By what Court triable.
413	Insult intended to provoke a breach of the peace.	Shall not arrest without warrant.	Warrant.	Imprisonment for 2 years, or fine, or both.	Minor District Court, or Magistrate of the first or second class.
414	False statement, rumour, etc., circulated with intent to cause mutiny or offence against the public peace.	Ditto.	Ditto.	Ditto.	Minor District Court, or Magistrate of the first class.
415	Criminal intimidation.	Ditto.	Ditto.	Ditto.	Ditto.
	If threat be to cause death or grievous hurt, etc.	Ditto.	Ditto.	Imprisonment for 7 years, or fine, or both.	Ditto.
416	Criminal intimidation by anonymous communication or having taken precaution to conceal whence the threat comes.	Ditto.	Ditto.	Imprisonment for 2 years in addition to the punishment under above section.	Ditto.
417	Uttering any word or making any gesture intended to insult the modesty of a woman, etc.	Ditto.	Ditto.	Imprisonment for 1 year, or fine, or both.	Magistrate of the first class.
418	Appearing in a public place, etc., in a state of intoxication, and causing annoyance to any person.	Ditto.	Summons	Imprisonment for 24 hours, or fine of P.T. 100, or both.	Magistrate of the first or second class.

120

OFFENCES AGAINST OTHER LAWS.

If punishable with death, imprisonment for a term which may exceed 7 years, or fine which may exceed L.E. 100.	May arrest without warrant.	Warrant.	......	Mudir's Court.
If punishable with imprisonment for a term which may exceed 3 years, or fine which may exceed L.E. 50.	Ditto.	Ditto.	......	Mudir's Court, or Minor District Court.
If punishable with imprisonment for a term which may exceed 2 years, or fine which may exceed L.E. 25.	Shall not arrest without warrant.	Summons.	......	Mudir's Court, Minor District Court, or Magistrate of the first class.
If not punishable as above	Ditto.	Ditto.	......	Mudir's Court, Minor District Court, or Magistrate of the first or second class.

SCHEDULE II.

(See section 22.)

ORDINARY POWERS OF MAGISTRATES.

I.—Ordinary Powers of a Magistrate of the Third Class.

(1) Power to arrest or direct the arrest of, and to commit to custody, a person committing an offence in his presence, section 28.
(2) Power to arrest, or direct the arrest in his presence of, an offender, section 29.
(3) Power to endorse a warrant, or to order the removal of an accused person arrested under a warrant, sections 57, 58 and 59.
(4) Power to issue search-warrant, section 68.
(5) Power to direct execution of search-warrant, section 75.
(6) Power to direct search in his presence, section 77.
(7) Power to conduct preliminary inquiry when police report is presented, or to give directions as to police-investigation, section 81.
(8) Power to authorise detention of a person during a police-investigation, section 85.
(9) Power to take cognizance of offence which he is competent to try, section 97.
(10) Power to postpone issue of process, section 101.
(11) Power to transfer case to superior Magistrate, section 168.
(12) Power to recover forfeited bond for appearance before Magistrate's Court, section 229.
(13) Power to make order as to disposal of property, section 232.
(14) Power to sell perishable property of a suspected character, section 239.
(15) Power to command unlawful assembly to disperse, section 240.
(16) Power to use civil force to disperse unlawful assembly, section 241.
(17) Power to require military force to be used to disperse unlawful assembly, section 243.

II.—Ordinary Powers of a Magistrate of the Second Class.

(1) The ordinary powers of a Magistrate of the third class.
(2) Power to issue search-warrant otherwise then in the course of an inquiry, section 70.
(3) Power to issue search-warrant for discovery of persons wrongfully confined, section 71.
(4) Power to issue process in respect of an offence committed outside jurisdiction, section 95.
(5) Power to take cognizance of offence, section 97.
(6) Power to transfer case, section 100.
(7) Power to commit for trial, section 110.
(8) Power to discharge accused when complainant is absent, section 154.
(9) Power, with Mudir's sanction, to tender pardon, section 159.
(10) Power to discharge sureties, section 227.
(11) Power to recover forfeited bond, section 229.
(12) Power to destroy libellous matter, etc., section 235.
(13) Power to award compensation in respect of arrest, section 263.

III.—Powers of a Magistrate of the First Class.

(1) The ordinary powers of a Magistrate of the second class.
(2) Power to compel restoration of abducted female, section, 262.

IV.—Powers of a Mudir.

(1) The powers of a Magistrate of the first class.
(2) Power to issue proclamations, section 60.
(3) Power to attach and sell property, section 61.
(4) Power to restore attached property, section 62.

122

SCHEDULE II—*concluded.*

(5) Power to direct by what Court offence shall be inquired into or tried section 93.
(6) Power to direct transfer of case, section 94.
(7) Power to sanction certain proceedings, sections 105, 106.
(8) Power to sanction tender of pardon, section 159.
(9) Power to advise on point of law, section 170.
(10) Power of a confirming authority, sections 181, 184, 187, and 189.
(11) Power of revision, section 188.
(12) Power to fill up vacancy in Court to which judgment is sent back by confirming authority, section 191.
(13) Power to issue death-warrant on confirmation of sentence, section 193.
(14) Power to direct examination, and provide for custody, of person of unsound mind, sections 218 and 219.
(15) Power to direct admission to bail or reduction of bail, section 223.
(16) Power to sell property alleged or suspected to have been stolen, section 238.
(17) Power to cause prisoner in jail to be brought up for examination, section 253.

SCHEDULE III.

OFFENCES TRIABLE SUMMARILY.

I.—Offences triable Summarily by a Magistrate of the Third Class.

		Section of Sudan Penal Code.
(1)	Wearing the dress or carrying any token used by a soldier	103
(2)	Being member of an unlawful assembly	112
(3)	Knowingly joining or continuing in any assembly of five or more persons after it has been commanded to disperse	120
(4)	Committing affray	122
(5)	Wearing garb or carrying token used by public servant	136
(6)	Not attending before the Magistrate when ordered	139
(7)	Not producing document to the Magistrate when ordered	140
(8)	Defiling the water of a public spring or reservoir	210
(9)	Making atmosphere noxious to health	211
(10)	Committing a public nuisance	216
(11)	Hurt	250, 252
(12)	Wrongful restraint	262
(13)	Assault or criminal force	273, 274
(14)	Theft, where value of property stolen does not exceed P.T. 50	295
(15)	Misappropriation of property, where value does not exceed P.T. 50	318
(16)	Mischief	337
(17)	Criminal trespass	358
(18)	Insult intended to provoke a breach of the peace	413
(19)	Appearing in public place in state of intoxication, &c.	418
(20)	Attempt to commit any offence above-mentioned.	
(21)	Abetment of any offence above-mentioned.	
(22)	The offences mentioned in sections 212 & 216 of this Code, if committed before the Court of the Magistrate. (See sections 140, 144, 145, 146 and 180 of the Sudan Penal Code.	

II.—Offences triable Summarily by a Magistrate of the First or Second Class.

		Section of Sudan Penal Code.
(1)	Offences not punishable with death or imprisonment for a term exceeding six months.	
(2)	Offences relating to false measures	200, 201, 202
(3)	Hurt	352
(4)	Theft, where value of the property stolen does not exceed L.E. 3.	295, 296, 297

SCHEDULE III—*concluded.*

Section of Sudan
Penal Code.

(5) Misappropriation of property, where value does not exceed L.E. 3.   318
(6) Receiving, or assisting in concealment or disposal of, stolen property where value does not exceed L.E. 3 . . . . . . 326, 329
(7) Mischief 338
(8) House trespass 359, 362, 364
(9) Insult intended to provoke a breach of the peace 413
(10) Criminal intimidation. 415
(11) Attempt to commit any offence above-mentioned.
(12) Abetment of any offence above-mentioned.

SCHEDULE IV.

(See section 204.)

FORMS.

I.—SUMMONS TO AN ACCUSED PERSON.

(See section 43.)

To   of   -   .

WHEREAS your attendance is necessary to answer to a charge of *(state shortly the offence charged)*, you are hereby required to appear in person *(or by pleader, as the case may be)* before the *(Magistrate)* of   , on the   day of   .

Dated this   day of   , 19 . .

(Seal.)   *(Signature.)*

II.—WARRANT OF ARREST.

(See section 50.)

To *(name and designation of the person or persons who is or are to execute the warrant.)*

WHEREAS   of   stands charged with the offence of *(state the offence)*, you are hereby directed to arrest the said   , and to produce him before me.

Dated this   day of   , 19 .

(Seal.)   *(Signature.)*

III.—BOND AND BAIL-BOND AFTER ARREST UNDER A WARRANT.

(See section 59.)

I, *(name)* of   , being brought before the Mudir of   . *(or as the case may be)* under a warrant issued to compel my appearance to answer to the charge of   , do hereby bind myself to attend in the Court of   on the   day of   next, to answer to the said charge, and to continue so to attend until otherwise directed by the Court ; and, in case of my making default herein, I bind myself to forfeit to the Government of the Sudan the sum of P.T.   .

Dated this   day of   , 19 .

(Signature.)

SCHEDULE IV—*continued.*

I do hereby declare myself surety for the above-named   of
    , that he shall attend in the Court of
on the   day of   next to answer to the charge on which he
has been arrested, and shall continue so to attend until otherwise directed by
by the Court ; and in case of his making default therein, I bind myself to forfeit
to the Government of the Sudan the sum of P.T.   .

Dated this   day of   , 19 .

           (Signature.)

IV.—MUDIR'S PROCLAMATION REQUIRING THE APPEARANCE OF A PERSON ACCUSED.

(See section 60.)

WHEREAS complaint has been made before *(name of Magistrate before whom complaint was made)* that *(name, description and address)* has committed *(or is suspected to have committed)* the offence of   , punishable under section
    of the Sudan Penal Code, and, the said *(name of Magistrate)*
having thereupon issued a warrant for the arrest of the said *(name)*, it has been
returned to such warrant that the said *(name)* cannot be found : and whereas it
has been shewn to my satisfaction that the said *(name)* has absconded *(or is
concealing himself to avoid the service of the said warrant)* ;

Proclamation is hereby made that the said   of   is
required to appear at *(place)* before *(the Magistrate or Court)* to answer the said
complaint within   days from this date.

Dated this   day of   , 19 .

(Seal.)   *(Signature.)*
           Mudir.

V.—PROCLAMATION BY MUDIR REQUIRING THE ATTENDANCE OF A WITNESS.

(See section 60.)

WHEREAS complaint has been made before *(name of Magistrate before whom complaint was made)* that *(name, description and address)* has committed *(or is suspected to have committed)* the offence of *(mention the offence concisely)* and a warrant has been issued to compel the attendance of *(name, description and address of the witness)* before *(the Court of the Magistrate before whom the witness was required to appear)* to be examined touching the matter of the said complaint; and whereas it has been returned to the said warrant that the said *(name of witness)* cannot be served, and it has been shown to my satisfaction that he has absconded *(or is concealing himself to avoid the service of the said warrant)*;

Proclamation is hereby made that the said *(name)* is required to appear at *(place)* before the Court of   on the   day of
    next at   o'clock to be examined touching the matter
of the said complaint.

Dated this   day of   , 19 .

(Seal.)   *(Signature.)*
           Mudir.

VI.—ORDER OF ATTACHMENT BY MUDIR TO COMPEL THE ATTENDANCE OF A WITNESS.

(See section 61.)

To the Police-officer in charge of the Police-station at   .

WHEREAS a warrant has been duly issued to compel the attendance of
(name, description and address) to testify concerning a complaint pending before
(mention the Court or Magistrate), and it has been returned to the said warrant

SCHEDULE IV—*continued.*

that it cannot be served ; and whereas it was shown to my satisfaction that the
said ·had absconded (*or* was concealing himself to avoid the service of
the said warrant : and thereupon a Proclamation was duly issued and published
requiring him to appear and give evidence at the time and place mentioned
therein, and he has failed to appear;

This is to authorise and require you to attach by seizure movable property belonging to the said   to the value of P.T.   , which
you may find within the Province of   and to hold the said property
under attachment pending my further order and to return this warrant with an
endorsement certifying the manner of its execution.

Dated this   day of   , 19   .

(Seal.)   *(Signature.)*
                                                          Mudir.

VII.—ORDER OF ATTACHMENT BY MUDIR TO COMPEL THE APPEARANCE OF
A PERSON ACCUSED.

(See section 61.)

To (*Name and designation of the person or persons who is or are to execute the
warrant*).

WHEREAS complaint has been made before (*mention the Magistrate to whom
complaint was made*) that (*name, description and address*) has committed (*or* is
suspected to have committed) the offence of   punishable under
section   of the Sudan Penal Code, and it has been returned to a
warrant of arrest thereupon issued that the said (*name*) cannot be found ; and
whereas it was shown to my satisfaction that the said (*name*) had absconded
(*or* was concealing himself to avoid the service of the said warrant), and thereupon a Proclamation was duly issued and published requiring the said
to appear to answer the said charge within   days ; and whereas the
said   is possessed of the following property other than land paying
revenue to Government in the village (*or* town) of   , in the Province
of   , viz.,   , and an order has been made for the
attachment thereof;

You are hereby required to attach the said property by seizure, and to hold
the same under attachment pending my further order and to return this
warrant with an endorsement certifying the manner of its execution.

Dated this   day of   , 19   .

(Seal.)

                                                          (Signature.)
                                                          Mudir.

VIII.—ORDER BY MUDIR AUTHORISING AN ATTACHMENT BY THE MUDIR OF
ANOTHER PROVINCE.

(See section 61.)

To the Mudir of the Province of   .

WHEREAS complaint has been made before (*mention the Magistrate to whom
complaint was made*) that (*name, description and address*) has committed (*or* is
suspected to have committed) the offence of   , punishable under
section   of the Sudan Penal Code ; and it has been returned to a
warrant of arrest thereupon issued that the said (*name*) cannot be found; and
whereas it has been shown to my satisfaction that the said (*name*) has absconded
)*or* is concealing himself to avoid the service of the said warrant) and thereupon a Proclamation was duly issued and published requiring the said
                                    to appear to answer the said charge within

SCHED. IV.]   *Criminal Procedure.*

SCHEDULE IV—*continued.*

days, but he has not appeared ; and whereas the said   is possessed of certain land paying revenue to Government in the village (*or* town) of
            in the Province of   :
    You are hereby authorised and requested to cause the said land to be attached,
and to be held under attachment pending my further order, and to certify
without delay what you may have done in pursuance of this order.

Dated this   day of   , 19   .

(*Seal.*)

(*Signature.*)

[*Note.*—This order will be endorsed by the Mudir to whom it is directed (S. 61 (2)).]

IX.—WARRANT IN THE FIRST INSTANCE TO BRING UP A WITNESS.

(*See section* 63.)

To (*name and designation of the Police-officer or other person or persons
who is or are to execute the warrant.*)

WHEREAS complaint has been made before me that   of
has (*or* is suspected to have) committed the offence of (*mention the offence
concisely*), and it appears likely that (*name and description of witness*) can give
evidence concerning the said complaint: and whereas I have good and sufficient
reason to believe that he will not attend as a witness on the hearing of the said
complaint unless compelled to do so;

    This is to authorise and require you to arrest the said (*name*), and on
the   day of   to bring him before this Court, to be examined
touching the offence complained of.

Give under my hand and the seal of the Court, this   day of   19

(*Seal.*)

(*Signature.*)

X.—WARRANT TO SEARCH AFTER INFORMATION OF A PARTICULAR OFFENCE.

(*See section* 68.)

To (*name and designation of the Police-officer or other person or persons who is
or are to execute the warrant.*)

WHEREAS information has been laid (*or* complaint has been made) before
me of the commission (*or* suspected commission) of the offence of (*mention the
offence concisely*), and it has been made to appear to me that the production of
(*specify the thing clearly*) is essential to the inquiry now being made (*or* about
to be made) into the said offence (*or* suspected offence) ;

    This is to authorise and require you to search for the said (*the thing speci-
fied*) in the (*describe the house or place or part thereof to which the search is to
be confined*), and if found, to produce the same forthwith before this Court,
returning this warrant with an endorsement certifying what you have done
under it, immediately upon its execution.

Give under my hand and the seal of the Court, this   day of   , 19   .

(*Seal.*)

(*Signature.*)

XI.—WARRANT TO SEARCH SUSPECTED PLACE OF DEPOSIT.

(*See section* 70.)

To (*name and designation of a Police-officer above the rank of a Constable.*)

WHEREAS information has been laid before me, and on due inquiry thereupon I have been led to believe that the (*describe the house or other place*)
is used as a place for the deposit (*or* sale) of stolen property (*or if for either of*

127

SCHEDULE IV—*continued.*

the other purposes expressed in the section, state the purpose in the words of the section) ;

This is to authorise and require you to enter the said house *(or other place)* with such assistance as shall be required, and to use, if necessary, reasonable force for that purpose, and to search every part of the said house *(or other place, or if the search is to be confined to a part, specify the part clearly)*, and to seize and take possession of any property *(describe clearly the nature of the property for which search is to be made)*, and forthwith to bring before this Court such of the said things as may be taken possession of, returning this warrant, with an endorsement certifying what you have done under it, immediately upon its execution.

Given under my hand and the seal of the Court, this   day of   , 19   .

(Seal.)

(Signature.)

XII.—BOND AND BAIL-BOND ON A PRELIMINARY INQUIRY BEFORE A POLICE-OFFICER.

(See section 86.)

I, *(name)* of   being charged with the offence of   , and being after investigation called upon to enter into my own recognizance to appear when required, do hereby bind myself to appear at   , in the Court of   , on such day as I may hereafter be required to attend to answer further to the said charge, and, in case of my making default herein, I bind myself to forfeit to the Government of the Sudan the sum of P.T.   .

Dated this   day of   , 19   .

(Signature.)

I hereby declare myself *(or* we jointly and severally declare ourselves and each of us)* surety *(or* sureties)* for the above-said   that he shall attend at   , in the Court of   , on such day as he may hereafter be required to attend, further to answer to the charge pending against him, and, in case of his making default therein, I hereby bind myself *(or* we hereby bind ourselves)* to forfeit to the Government of the Sudan the sum of P.T.   .

Dated this   day of   , 19   .

(Signature.)

XIII.—BOND TO PROSECUTE OR GIVE EVIDENCE.

(See section 87.)

I, *(name)* of *(place)*, do hereby bind myself to attend at   in the Court of   , at   o'clock on the   day of   next, and then and there to prosecute *(or* to prosecute and give evidence)* *(or* to give evidence)* in the matter of a charge of   against one A. B., and, in case of making default herein, I bind myself to forfeit to the Government of the Sudan the sum of P.T.   .

Dated this   day of   , 19   .

(Signature.)

SCHEDULE IV—*continued.*

XIV.—CHARGES.

(See sections 124, 125, 126.)

(I)—CHARGES WITH ONE HEAD.

(*a*) I, [*name and office of Magistrate, &c.*], hereby charge you [*name of accused person*] as follows :—

(*b*) that you, on or about the _____ day of _____ , at
On Penal Code, section 93. _____ , waged war against the Government of the Sudan and thereby committed an offence punishable under section 93 of the Sudan Penal Code, and within the cognizance of the Mudir's Court.

(*c*) And I hereby direct that you be tried by such Court on the said charge.

[*Signature and seal of the Magistrate.*]

[*To be substituted for (b)*]:—

(2) That you, being a public servant in the _____ Department,
On section 123. directly accepted from [*state the name*], for another party [*state the name*], a gratification other than legal remuneration, as a motive for forbearing to do an official act, and thereby committed an offence punishable under section 123 of the Sudan Penal Code, and within the cognizance of a Minor District Court.

(3) That you, on or about the _____ day of _____ , at
On section 127. _____ , did [*or* omitted to do, *as the case may be*] _____ , such conduct being contrary to the provisions of the
Ordinance _____ , section _____ , and known by you to be prejudical to _____ , and thereby committed an offence punishable under section 127 of the Sudan Penal Code, and within the cognizance of a Minor District Court.

(4) That you, on or about the _____ day of _____ , at
On section 157. _____ , in the course of the trial of _____ , before _____ stated in evidence that " _____ ", which statement you either knew or believed to be false, or did not believe to be true, and thereby committed an offence punishable under section 157 of the Sudan Penal Code, and within the cognizance of a Minor District Court.

(5) That you, on or about the _____ day of _____ , at
On section 232. _____ , committed culpable homicide not amounting to murder. causing the death of _____ , and thereby committed an offence punishable under section 232 of the Sudan Penal Code, and within the cognizance of the Mudir's Court.

(6) That you, on or about the _____ day of _____ , at
On section 235. _____ abetted the commission of suicide by *A. B.*, a person in a state of intoxication, and thereby committed an offence punishable under section 235 of the Sudan Penal Code, and within the cognizance of the Mudir's Court.

(7) That you, on or about the _____ day of _____ , at
On section 253. _____ voluntarily caused grievous hurt to _____ , and thereby committed an offence punishable under section 253 of the Sudan Penal Code, and within the cognizance of a Minor District Court.

(8) That you, on or about the _____ day of _____ , at
On section 308. _____ , robbed [*state the name*], and thereby committed an offence punishable under section 308 of the Sudan Penal Code, and within the cognizance of the Mudir's Court [*or* a Minor District Court.].

I

129

SCHEDULE IV—*continued.*

(9) That you, on or about the   day of   , at
<small>On section 311.</small>   , committed brigandage, an offence punishable
under section 311 of the Sudan Penal Code, and within
the cognizance of the Mudir's Court.

[*In cases tried by Magistrates substitute* "within my cognizance" *for*
"within the cognizance of the Mudir's Court (*or* of a Minor District Court),"
and in (*c*) *omit* "by such Court."]

(II)—CHARGES WITH TWO OR MORE HEADS.

(*a*) I, [*name and office of Magistrate, etc.*], hereby charge you [*name of
accused person*] as follows :—

(*b*) *First.*—That you, on or about the   day of   , at
<small>On section 189.</small>   knowing a coin to be counterfeit, delivered
the same to another person, by name *A. B.*, as genuine,
and thereby committed an offence punishable under section 189 of the Sudan
Penal Code, and within the cognizance of a Minor District Court.

Secondly.—That you, on or about the   day of   , at
, knowing a coin to be counterfeit, attempted to induce another person,
by name *A. B.*, to receive it as genuine, and thereby committed an offence
punishable under section 189 of the Sudan Penal Code, and within the cognizance of a Minor District Court.

(*c*) And I hereby direct that you be tried by such Court on the said charge.

[*Signature and seal of the Magistrate.*]

[*To be substituted for (b)*] :—

(2) *First.*—That you, on or about the   day of   , at
<small>On sections 230 and 232.</small>   , committed murder by causing the
death of   , and thereby committed an
offence punishable under section 230 of the Sudan Penal Code, and within the
cognizance of the Mudir's Court.

Secondly.—That you, on or about the   day of   , at
, by causing the death of   , committed culpable homicide
not amounting to murder, and thereby committed an offence punishable under
section 232 of the Sudan Penal Code, and within the cognizance of the Mudir's
Court.

(3) *First.*—That you, on or about the   day of   , at
<small>On sections 295 and 298.</small>   , committed theft, and thereby committed
an offence punishable under section 295 of the
Sudan Penal Code, and within the cognizance of a Minor District Court [*or*
the Mudir's Court.].

Secondly.—That you, on or about the   day of   , at
, committed theft, having made preparation for causing death to a person
in order to the committing of such theft, and thereby committed an offence
punishable under section 298 of the Sudan Penal Code, and within the cognizance of a Minor District Court [*or* the Mudir's Court.].

Thirdly.—That you, on or about the   day of   , at
, committed theft, having made preparation for causing restraint to
a person in order to the effecting of your escape after the committing of such
theft, and thereby committed an offence punishable under section 298 of the
Sudan Penal Code, and within the cognizance of a Minor District Court [*or* the
Mudir's Court.].

Fourthly.—That you, on or about the   day of   , at
committed theft, having made preparation for causing fear of hurt
to a person in order to the retaining of property taken by such theft, and

SCHEDULE IV—*continued.*

thereby committed an offence punishable under section 298 of the Sudan Penal Code, and within the cognizance of a Minor District Court [*or* the Mudir's Court.].

(4) That you, on or about the   day of   , at
Alternative charges   , in the course of the inquiry into
on section 157.   , before   , stated in evidence that
"   ", and that you, on or about the   day of   ,
at   , in the course of the trial of   , before   ,
stated in evidence that "   ", one of which statements you either knew or believed to be false, or did not believe to be true, and thereby committed an offence punishable under section 157 of the Sudan Penal Code, and within the cognizance of a Minor District Court.

[*In cases tried by Magistrates substitute* "within my cognizance" *for* "within the cognizance of the Mudir's Court (*or* of a Minor District Court)" *and in (c) omit* "by such Court".].

XV.—WARRANT OF COMMITMENT ON A SENTENCE OF IMPRISONMENT OR FINE IF PASSED BY A MAGISTRATE.

(*See sections 145 and 153.*)

To the Keeper of the Jail at   .

WHEREAS on the   day of   , 19   , (*name of prisoner*), the (1st, 2nd, 3rd, *as the case may be*) prisoner in case No.   of the Calendar for 19   , was convicted before me (*name and official designation*) of the offence of (*mention the offence or offences concisely*) under section (*or sections*) of the Sudan Penal Code (*or of the   Ordinance   *), and was sentenced to (*state the punishment fully and distinctly*) ;

This is to authorise and require you, the said Keeper, to receive the said (*prisoner's name*) into your custody in the said Jail, together with this warrant, and there carry the aforesaid sentence into execution according to law.

Give under my hand and the seal of the Court, this   day of   , 19   .

(*Seal.*)

(*Signature.*)

XVI.—SUMMONS TO WITNESS.

(*See sections 43 and 147.*)

To   of   .

WHEREAS complaint has been made before me that   of   has (*or* is suspected to have) committed the offence of (*state the offence concisely with time and place*), and it appears to me that you are likely to give material evidence for the prosecution ;

You are hereby summoned to appear before this Court on the   day of   next at ten o'clock in the forenoon, to testify what you know concerning the matter of the said complaint, and not to depart thence without leave of the Court : and you are hereby warned that, if you shall without just excuse neglect or refuse to appear on the said date, a warrant will be issued to compel your attendance.

Give under my hand and the seal of the Court, this   day of   , 19   .

(*Seal.*)

(*Signature.*)

131

SCHEDULE IV—*continued.*

XVII.—WARRANT OF COMMITMENT UNDER SENTENCE OF DEATH.

(See section 193.)

To the Keeper of the Jail at

WHEREAS at the Mudir's Court held on the day of 19 , (*name of prisoner*), the (1st, 2nd, 3rd, *as the case may be*) prisoner in case No. of the Calendar for 19 , was duly convicted of the offence of culpable homicide amounting to murder under section of the Sudan Penal Code, and sentenced to suffer death, subject to the confirmation of the said sentence by the Governor-General;

This is to authorise and require you, the said Keeper, to receive the said (*prisoner's name*) into your custody in the said Jail together with this warrant, and him there safely to keep until you shall receive the further warrant or order of this Court, carrying into effect the order of the Governor-General.

Given under my hand and the seal of the Court, this day of , 19 .

(*Seal.*)

(*Signature*).
President of the Court.

XVIII.—MUDIR'S WARRANT OF EXECUTION ON A SENTENCE OF DEATH.

(See section 193.)

To the Keeper of the Jail at

WHEREAS (*name of prisoner*), the (1st, 2nd, 3rd, *as the case may be*) prisoner in case No. of the Calendar at the Session of the Mudir's Court held on the day , 19 , has been by a warrant of that Court, dated the day of , committed to your custody under sentence of death; and whereas the order of the Governor-General confirming the said sentence has been received by me;

This is to authorise and require you, the said Keeper, to carry the said sentence into execution by causing the said to be hanged by the neck until he be dead, at (*time and place of execution*), and to return this warrant to me with an endorsement certifying that the sentence has been executed.

Given under my hand and seal, this day of , 19

(*Seal.*)

(*Signature.*)
Mudir.

XIX.—WARRANT OF COMMITMENT ON A SENTENCE OF IMPRISONMENT AFTER THE CASE HAS BEEN SENT BACK FOR RECONSIDERATION BY THE CONFIRMING AUTHORITY.

(See section 187.)

To the Keeper of the Jail at

WHEREAS at the Mudir's Court held on the day of , 19 , (*name of prisoner*), the (1st, 2nd, 3rd, *as the case may be*) prisoner in case No. of the Calendar at such Session of the Court was convicted of the offence of culpable homicide amounting to murder, and was sentenced to suffer death, subject to the confirmation of the said sentence by the Governor-General, and was thereupon, by warrant dated the said day

SCHEDULE IV—*continued.*

of   , 19   , committed to your custody ; and whereas the Governor-
General did not confirm the said sentence. but returned the case to the said
Court for reconsideration ; and whereas. the case coming for reconsideration
before the said Court under my presidency on the   day of
          , 19   , the said (*prisoner's name*) was convicted of the offence of
(*mention the offence concisely*) under section   of the Sudan Penal Code, and
was sentenced to imprisonment for the term of   years from the   day of
          19   ; and whereas the said sentence of imprisonment
has been confirmed by the order of the Governor-General (a duplicate of which
is hereunto annexed) ;

This is to authorise and require you, the said Keeper, safely to keep (*prisoner's name*) in the said jail, and there to carry into execution the aforesaid sentence
of imprisonment according to law.

Give under my hand and the seal of the Court, this   day
of   . 19   .

(*Seal.*)

(*Signature.*)

XX.—Warrant after a Remission of a portion of a Sentence.

(*See section 207.*)

To the Keeper of the Jail at

Whereas at a Minor District Court held on the   day of
          , 19   , under the presidency of   , (*name of prisoner*)
the (1st, 2nd, 3rd, *as the case may be*) prisoner in case No.   of the Calendar
at such Session of the Court, was convicted of the offence of   ,
punishable under section   of the Sudan Penal Code, and was sentenced to
imprisonment for the term of   years from the   day of   , 19   ,
and was thereupon, by warrant dated the said day of   , 19   , committed to
your custody ; and whereas by order of the Governor-General (a duplicate of
which is hereunto annexed) the said term of imprisonment has been reduced to
the term of   years ;

This is to authorise and require you, the said Keeper, safely to keep the said
(*prisoner's name*) in your custody in the said jail, and there to carry into execution according to law the punishment of imprisonment for such reduced term of
     years from the   day of   , 19   , in place of the term
named in the said warrant.

Give under my hand and seal, the   day of   , 19   .
(*Seal.*)

(*Signature.*)
Mudir.

XXI.—Warrant to levy a Fine by Distress and Sale.

(*See section 198.*)

To (*name and designation of the Police-officer or other person or persons who is
or are to execute the warrant*).

Whereas (*name and description of the offender*) was on the   day
of   19   , convicted before me of the offence of (*mention the
offence concisely*), and sentenced to pay a fine of P.T.   , and whereas the said
(*name*), although required to pay the said fine. has not paid the same or any
part thereof ;

This is to authorise and require you to make distress by seizure of any
movable property belonging to the said (*name*) which may be found within the
Province of   ; and, if within (*state the number of days or hours
allowed*) next after such distress the said sum shall not be paid (*or forthwith*),

133

SCHEDULE IV—*continued.*

to sell the movable property distrained, or so much thereof as shall be sufficient to satisfy the said fine, returning this warrant, with an endorsement certifying what you have done under it, immediately upon its execution.

Given under my hand and the seal of the Court, this   day of   , 19 .

    (*Seal.*)   .

                                              (*Signature.*)

XXII.—WARRANT OF COMMITMENT IN CERTAIN CASES OF CONTEMPT WHEN A FINE IS IMPOSED.

(*See section 212.*)

To the Keeper of the Jail at

  - WHEREAS at a Court holden before me on this day (*name and description of the offender*) in the presence (*or* view) of the Court committed wilful contempt;

And whereas for such contempt the said (*name of offender*) has been adjudged by the Court to pay a fine of P.T.   , or in default to suffer imprisonment for the space of (*state the number of months or days*);

This is to authorise and require you, the Keeper of the said Jail, to receive the said (*name of offender*) into your custody, together with this warrant, and him safely to keep in the said jail for the said period of (*term of imprisonment*), unless the said fine be sooner paid; and, on the receipt thereof, forthwith to set him at liberty, returning this warrant with an endorsement certifying the manner of its execution.

Given under my hand and the seal of the Court, this   day of   , 19 .

    (*Seal.*)   (*Signature.*)

XXIII.—PRESIDING MAGISTRATE'S WARRANT OF COMMITMENT OF WITNESS REFUSING TO ANSWER.

(*See section 216.*)

To (*name and designation of officer of Court*).

WHEREAS (*name and description*), being summoned (*or* brought) before this Court as a witness and this day required to give evidence on an inquiry into an alleged offence, refused to answer a certain question (*or* certain questions) put to him touching the said alleged offence, and duly recorded, without alleging any just excuse for such refusal, and for his contempt has been adjudged detention in custody for (*term of detention adjudged*);

This is to authorise and require you to take the said (*name*) into custody, and him safely to keep in your custody for the space of   days, unless in the meantime he shall consent to be examined and to answer the questions asked of him, and on the last of the said days, or forthwith on such consent being known, to bring him before this Court to be dealt with according to law, returning this warrant with an endorsement certifying the manner of its execution.

Given under my hand and the seal of the Court, this   day of   , 19 .

    (*Seal.*)   (*Signature.*)

XXIV.—BOND AND BAIL-BOND ON A PRELIMINARY INQUIRY BEFORE A MAGISTRATE.

(*See sections 221 and 224.*)

  I, (*name*), of (*place*), being brought before the Magistrate of (*as the case may be*), charged with the offence of   , and required to give security for my attendance in this Court and at a Minor District Court or the Mudir's

SCHEDULE IV—*continued.*

Court, if required. do bind myself to attend at the Court of the said Magistrate on every day of the preliminary inquiry into the said charge, and. should the case be sent for trial by a Minor District Court or by the Mudir's Court, to be, and appear, before such Court when called upon to answer the charge against me; and. in case of my making default herein, I bind myself to forfeit to the Government of the Sudan. the sum of P.T.

Dated this   day of   19   .
.
                                                    (*Signature.*)

I hereby declare myself (*or* We jointly and severally declare ourselves and each of us) surety (*or* sureties) for the said (*name*) that he shall attend at the Court of   on every day of the preliminary inquiry into the offence charged against him, and, should the case be sent for trial by a Minor District Court or the Mudir's Court, that he shall be. and appear, before such Court to answer the charge against him, and. in case of his making default therein, I bind myself (*or* we bind ourselves) to forfeit to the Government of the Sudan, the sum of P.T.   .

Dated this   day of   , 19
                                                    (*Signature.*)

XXV.—Warrant to discharge a Person imprisoned on Failure to give Security.

(*See section 225.*)

To the Keeper of the Jail at   (*or other officer in whose custody the person is*).

Whereas (*name and description of prisoner*) was committed to your custody under warrant of this Court, dated the   day of   . and has since with his surety (*or* sureties) duly executed a bond under section 221 of the Code of Criminal Procedure;

This is to authorise and require you forthwith to discharge the said (*name*) from your custody. unless he is liable to be detained for some other matter.

Given under my hand and the seal of the Court, this   day of   , 19   .
     (*Seal.*)
                                                    (*Signature.*)

XXVI.—Warrant of Attachment to enforce a Bond.

(*See section 229.*)

To the Police-officer in charge of the Police-station at   .

Whereas (*name, description and address of person*) has failed to appear on (*mention the occasion*) pursuant to his recognizance, and has by such default forfeited to the Government of the Sudan the sum of P.T. (*the penalty in the bond*); and whereas the said (*name of person*) has, on due notice to him, failed to pay the said sum or show any sufficient cause why payment should not be enforced against him;

This is to authorise and require you to attach any movable property of the said (*name*) that you may find within the Province of   , by seizure and detention, and, if the said amount be not paid within three days, to sell the property so attached or so much of it as may be sufficient to realise the amount aforesaid, and to make return of what you have done under this warrant immediately upon its execution.

Given under my hand and the seal of the Court, this   day of   , 19   .
     (*Seal.*)
                                                    (*Signature.*)

SCHEDULE IV—*concluded.*

XXVII.—NOTICE TO SURETY ON BREACH OF A BOND.

(*See section 229.*)

To of .

WHEREAS on the day of , 19 , you became surety for (*name*) of (*place*) that he should appear before this Court on the day of , and bound yourself in default thereof to forfeit the sum of P.T. to the Government of the Sudan; and whereas the said (*name*) has failed to appear before this Court, and by reason of such default you have forfeited the aforesaid sum of P.T. ;

You are hereby required to pay the said penalty or show cause, within days from this date, why payment of the said sum should not be enforced against you.

Given under my hand and the seal of the Court, this day of , 19 .

(*Seal.*) (*Signature.*)

XXVIII.—WARRANT OF ATTACHMENT AGAINST A SURETY.

(*See section 229.*)

To of .

WHEREAS (*name, description and address*) has bound himself as surety for the appearance of (*mention the condition of the bond*), and the said (*name*) has made default, and thereby forfeited to the Government of the Sudan, the sum of P.T. (*the penalty in the bond*).

This is to authorise and require you to attach any movable property of the said (*name*) which you may find within the Province of , by seizure and detention; and, if the said amount be not paid within three days, to sell the property so attached, or so much of it as may be sufficient to realize the amount aforesaid, and make return of what you have done under this warrant immediately upon its execution.

Given under my hand and the seal of the Court, this day of , 19 .

(*Seal.*) (*Signature.*)

XXIX.—WARRANT OF COMMITMENT OF THE SURETY OF AN ACCUSED PERSON ADMITTED TO BAIL.

(*See section 229.*)

To the Keeper of the Jail at .

WHEREAS (*name and description of surety*) has bound himself as a surety for the appearance of (*state the condition of the bond*) and the said (*name*) has therein made default whereby the penalty mentioned in the said bond has been forfeited to the Government of the Sudan; and whereas the said (*name of surety*) has, on due notice to him, failed to pay the said sum or show any sufficient cause why payment should not be enforced against him, and the same cannot be recovered by attachment and sale of movable property of his, and an order has been made for his imprisonment in the jail for (*specify the period*);

This is to authorise and require you, the said Keeper, to receive the said (*name*) into your custody with this warrant and him safely to keep in the said jail for the said (*term of imprisonment*), and to return this warrant with an endorsement certifying the manner of its execution.

Given under my hand and the seal of the Court, this day of , 19 .

(*Seal.*) (*Signature.*)

(Signed) KITCHENER OF KHARTOUM,

GOVERNOR GENERAL.